Mightier than the Sword

Mightier than the Sword

How the News Media Have Shaped American History

Rodger Streitmatter

WestviewPress
A Division of HarperCollins*Publishers*

Published in 1997 in the United States of America by Westview Press, 5500 Central Avenue, Boulder, Colorado 80301-2877, and in the United Kingdom by Westview Press, 12 Hid's Copse Road, Cumnor Hill, Oxford OX2 9JJ

A CIP catalog record for this book is available from the Library of Congress.
ISBN 0-8133-3210-9

The paper used in this publication meets the requirements of the American National Standard for Permanence of Paper for Printed Library Materials Z39.48-1984.

10 9 8 7 6 5 4 3 2

To my sister, Doris Boehle,
a good and selfless nurturer
who makes the world a better place

Contents

Illustrations

Acknowledgments

Because of the breadth of this book, it would be impossible for any one researcher to be a true expert on every topic covered in these pages, and I certainly will not claim that distinction. Instead, I want to acknowledge that I am deeply indebted to a host of talented and dedicated scholars who have previously examined many of the events that are the subjects of this book. Although I have listed those individuals in the bibliography, I also would like to describe their contributions here.

Rather than trying to discuss how each of these individuals contributed to my work, I wish to highlight one particular scholar and her research. In the bibliographical listing for Chapter 3, "Slowing the Momentum for Women's Rights," readers will find an entry for Karen K. List, "The Post-Revolutionary Woman Idealized: Philadelphia Media's 'Republican Mother.'" Professor List, a member of the journalism department at the University of Massachusetts, deserves far more credit than that brief citation, for it was Karen who pored over hundreds of late eighteenth- and early nineteenth-century women's magazines to identify and analyze the messages that those publications communicated to their readers, as well as to suggest the impact they had on American women *writ large*. In other words, Karen provided the road map that led me to the magazines that I quote from in my chapter. I went to those magazines and read the articles myself, but I readily acknowledge that without Karen's trailblazing efforts my work would have been enormously more difficult. I gratefully acknowledge her help—as well as that of numerous other scholars who preceded and guided me in researching many of the topics covered in this book.

With regard to the overall content and direction of this work, I want to thank the woman who has served as my mentor beginning with the first manuscript I ever submitted to a scholarly journal: Susan Henry. Not only is this the third book I have written but it also is the third book that has been profoundly shaped by Susan's personal commitment to the highest standards of scholarly research. I thank her.

I also want to thank the American University Senate Research Committee and Dean of Academic Affairs Ivy Broder for supporting both me and my work through a university research grant. That support was invaluable both in encouraging me and in providing me with the time to proceed with this project.

On my own faculty in American University's School of Communication, I thank Dean Sanford J. Ungar for his confidence, trust, and friendship. Without Sandy's unwavering support, I would neither have begun teaching the course How the News Media Shape History nor have committed that course to paper through this book.

Because much of the material contained in this book has evolved from my classroom lectures and from the materials I have written for my course, I am indebted to the hundreds of students who have provided me with feedback on the material. In particular, I thank Deborah Acomb, Jim Montalto, Maureen Rich, and Kyle Rose for their substantive comments in the final stages of the writing. I still marvel at the fact that even though I wear the mantle of *teacher*, I learn so much from my magnificently creative students.

Some of the material in this book originated as conference papers and articles in scholarly journals. Among those persons whose contributions I want to acknowledge, therefore, are dozens of individuals I cannot name because their identities are masked behind the blind review process of the American Journalism Historians Association, International Communications Association, and Association for Education in Journalism and Mass Communication. I especially want to thank those members of the AEJMC History Division who honored me in 1996 for my work on the 1920s newspaper crusade against the Ku Klux Klan.

Finally, I thank my children, Matt and Kate, and my life partner, Tom Grooms, for continuing to enrich my life and make its activities worthwhile—whether writing a book or walking the dog.

Rodger Streitmatter

Introduction

In 1990, I created a course titled How the News Media Shape History. The interdisciplinary course, which combined journalism and history, became part of the General Education Program at American University. After receiving positive responses from the students who had taken the course, the director of the program was soon urging me to teach the course not just once a year, but twice—or even more often, if I was willing. I still remember the vivid image that the director, Ann Ferren, used to persuade me: "Rodger, students are clamoring to get into this course. If you teach it only once a year, it's like putting one tiny little jelly bean in the middle of the quad and telling all 12,000 of our students to fight over who gets it."

Why have students been so eager to grab my little jelly bean of a course? They have been strongly attracted, hundreds of students have since told me, to the concept of the news media *shaping* this country.

Today's college students, as well as the public in general, recognize that the American news media are one of this country's most powerful institutions. They see journalism as so powerful, in fact, that newspaper publishers and television anchors are perceived as more influential than members of the United States Congress or Supreme Court. Many students and other observers criticize the news media as being *too* powerful; others praise the news media's power, arguing that a free press is fundamental to democracy. But the detractors and defenders both agree on one point: The news media have impact.

It is those perceptions that have made my course popular, and it is that continued popularity that has impelled me to commit the material I use in the course to paper. *Mightier than the Sword* describes fourteen discrete episodes in American history during which the news media have played a critical role in shaping landmark events.

I have chosen the word *shaping* with considerable care. For as I try to impress upon my students at the beginning of each semester, I do not mean to imply that the Fourth Estate single-handedly *causes* events to occur. To suggest such a causal relationship between the news media and American history would be simplistic, as it would ignore the interdependence among governmental, legal, social, and economic institutions driving this nation. I am convinced, however, that journalistic coverage can *shape*—and profoundly so—an issue. More specifically, the news media can place an issue on the public agenda . . . can move it to the front burner . . . can get people talking about the issue. And once an issue has been moved into the spotlight, other institutions can cause real change to occur.

Each chapter in this book focuses on such a milestone in the evolution of the United States that was significantly influenced by journalism paying attention to it. Ultimately, these fourteen separate stories coalesce to relate a single phenomenon of singular importance to understanding the past as well as the future of this country: As the American news media report and comment on the events of the day, they wield enormous *influence* on those events.

I have selected the particular episodes in this book for several reasons. They span more than two centuries—from Thomas Paine's influence on the coming of the American Revolution to Rush Limbaugh's curiously similar role in the Republican Revolution of the 1990s. They represent a variety of print and electronic media, ranging from newspapers and news magazines to radio, television, and electronic mail. At the same time, these particular vignettes illustrate how the news media have interacted with a broad range of other forces—from foreign policy strategists to captains of industry to rabble-rousing demagogues—to have far-reaching effects on the political, economic, and social fabric of this nation.

Many of the topics are familiar to anyone with a rudimentary knowledge of journalism history, such as how William Randolph Hearst helped build public pressure for the Spanish-American War and how, a century later, television news played a major role in ending the war in Southeast Asia; other topics take communication scholarship in new directions, such as how 1920s newspapers helped defeat the Ku Klux Klan and how news organizations helped propel millions of American women into the World War II work force. The topics consciously expand the definition of landmark *events* far beyond wars and politics, as those milestones also include social movements, describing how the news media have treated—or *mis*treated—women, Jews, and African Americans.

Although each nexus between the news media and American history described in the following pages is important, by no means does this book provide a comprehensive history of the evolution of American journalism. Looking at such a limited number of episodes cannot document the myriad incidents and trends that have marked the development of this country's news media. Indeed, I have assiduously *avoided* compiling the mind-numbing lists of names, dates, and newspaper titles that bog down the standard journalism history tomes. I also have attempted to keep this book focused and concise—seeking to create a work that is not only illuminating but also engaging and perhaps even, at times, vivid.

The examples I have selected include negative as well as positive assessments. As a former newspaper reporter and now a journalism professor, I firmly believe that journalism is a noble pursuit that can, at its best, shine the bright beacon of truth into the darkest corners of life—and then move the human spirit to clean up those dark corners. At the same time, however, I know the news media sometimes squander the rights guaranteed to them in the First Amendment. Several chapters of *Mightier than the Sword* focus on such regrettable instances when this powerful institution behaved to the detriment of the people it purported to serve.

This book concludes with a final chapter that focuses on *how* the news media have shaped history. More specifically, by drawing examples from the material described in the previous chapters, I identify some of the common characteristics displayed by the news media involved in shaping this nation. I am hopeful that contemporary newsmen and newswomen—as well as the news organizations they work for—may be inspired to adopt some of these characteristics while pursuing their work today and in the future.

Mightier than the Sword: How the News Media Have Shaped American History, like my two previous books—*Raising Her Voice: African-American Women Journalists Who Changed History* and *Unspeakable: The Rise of the Gay and Lesbian Press in America*—builds on both my professional background in daily journalism and my Ph.D. in United States history in an effort to increase our understanding of both American journalism and American history.

In writing this particular book, I had two specific audiences in mind. The first is journalism students. For young men and women entering the field, *Mightier than the Sword* provides a sense of the history, power, and responsibility inherent in a journalism career. The second and much larger audience is the broad one of men and women who want to learn more about the intertwining of the American news media and American history—as well as what that phenomenon means in the context of the 1990s. These readers are legion.

Indeed, it is difficult to name a more white-hot topic than the power of the news media. The contentious debate includes such thorny questions as: Is the media's job to *report* the news objectively or should they also *lead society*? Do the news media represent a public trust that is responsible for serving the people, or are the news media merely a business that is responsible only for serving its stockholders?

What are—or should be—the limits of news media influence? *Mightier than the Sword* speaks to each of these questions.

Some historians will criticize my tight focus on the news media, saying it does not provide sufficient context. Those critics will be on solid ground. I readily acknowledge, for example, that my chapter about the news media's role in Watergate could be expanded into a 200-page discussion of the various forces that brought about and helped expose the men responsible for that shocking episode of political corruption. Indeed, dozens of books *have* been written on that subject. What has not been written—until now—is a single book that synthesizes a sampling of major events, such as Watergate, that have been *shaped by* the news media. This is the unique perspective *Mightier than the Sword* offers.

Some critics also will find fault with several of the works I classify as *news* media. They will argue that Paine's essays are partisan rhetoric, not journalism, and that Limbaugh's and Father Charles Coughlin's jeremiads are social and political commentary, not journalism. I disagree. Paine's essays were news in the 1770s because they introduced new *ideas* into the most vital conversation of the day. The essays functioned as journalism, even though they sought not only to inform readers but also to persuade them to support a particular point of view. All colonial publications were partisan, as the concept of journalistic objectivity did not emerge until the nineteenth century. If 1700s partisan publications are not news media, eighteenth century American journalism did not exist. As for Limbaugh's and Coughlin's tirades, I see no difference between them and the opinions published on the *New York Times* editorial page. Indeed, if the words of these two radio commentators are not part of the news media, neither are *Times* editorials.

Before beginning the story of how the news media have shaped American history, I want to acknowledge the man who inspired the title for this book: Thomas Jefferson. In a letter to Tom Paine in 1792, Jefferson lauded Paine's critical role in propelling the American colonists toward independence from Great Britain and then wrote encouragingly: "Go on then in doing with your pen what in other times was done with the sword: show that reformation is more practicable by operating on the mind of man than on the body."[1]

1

Sowing the Seeds of Revolution

IN THE SUMMER OF 1776, a band of political rebels turned the world upside down. They showed, for the first time in the history of the world, that the discontent of a few colonists could swell into open rebellion so strong and so potent that it could create a world power all its own. Such impudence evolving into pure might was unheard of in the eighteenth century or in any of the centuries that had preceded it. The same process would occur again and again—in France, Russia, Cuba, the Philippines—but the events of 1776 stand alone. For they were the first.

Such redefinition of human history does not erupt overnight, as forces had been working long before the fifty-six rebels signed their names to the Declaration of Independence. Among those forces were the powerful words of determined men who possessed both the talent and the intellectual insight to craft graceful and passionate prose that demanded freedom from an oppressive government. Those words helped change the course of human events, transforming lukewarm patriots into fiery revolutionaries.

The transformation unfolded through a series of publications produced by several political dissidents. It was very much a continuum. Individuals expressing their outrage in those early publications laid the psychological groundwork for the fight that was to come. These journalists created the consciousness and mind-set that allowed for political and social revolution—as well as armed conflict. Important milestones in the journalistic march toward independence included publication of the "Journal of Occurrences" in 1768 and 1769, followed by the extended verbal response to the Boston Massacre of 1770. Those two publishing phenomena set the stage for Thomas Paine's clarion call for independence in early 1776. Paine's *Common Sense* impelled thousands of mildly discontented subjects of the British crown to become political insurgents fully committed both to revolution and, ultimately, to shaping American history.

Dissension Takes Root

One place to begin the political background of the American Revolution is with the 1763 British victory in the decade-long conflict with the French. With that military triumph, the British defeated the French in North America as well as in India. The hard-fought victory meant the French finally were expelled from America, leaving the fur trade solely to the British. But the high cost of victory also left the British treasury near bankruptcy.

In search of ways to pay the cost of defending the wide frontiers that had been won in the war, officials in London decided the American colonists had gained so much in the victory over the French that they should pay the bulk of the war debts and defense costs. The colonists were willing to help—up to a point. Colonial legislatures were prepared to increase levies, but they did not raise enough revenue to satisfy the British.

Economics was not the only factor in the coming revolution, as ideas were stirring people, too. This is where the press played a pivotal role. The literature of the colonial era appeared in newspapers, magazines, pamphlets, and broadsides that expressed the arguments—as well as the passions—of the rebels. Revolutions seldom, if ever, occur because of logic. They require passion, and this emotional element was brought to the movement by a group of radical visionaries fully aware of the power of the press.

The earliest wave of rebels insisted that the people deserved a larger voice in their governance. Specifically, they believed the colonies needed to be granted home rule. They argued that citizens themselves, not the higher level of government, should make the laws governing the colonists—although all but the most radical of them continued to accept that the British crown should remain the final authority in their lives.

Sam Adams: Firebrand of the Revolution

The best known of the early radical writers was Sam Adams, the cousin of John Adams and the man who would, in 1773, organize the Boston Tea Party. In the 1760s, the firebrand of the Revolution became a prominent voice in the *Boston Gazette,* writing hundreds of political essays and news articles. Because other newspapers reprinted his pieces, Adams's radical message spread throughout the colonies.

Adams's words were worthy of note. As early as 1764 he argued that the British Parliament was overstepping its authority by imposing too many taxes on the colonists. If the House of Commons could compel New England to pay ruinous taxes on a staple such as molasses, Adams insisted, the colonists' liberty was held on uncertain tenure. Parliament would continue to increase taxes, he said, asking rhetorically, "If our Trade may be taxed why not our Lands? Why not the Produce of our Lands & every thing we possess or make use of? This we apprehend annihilates our Charter Right to govern & tax ourselves." Adams's protests, in short, represented one of the earliest cries against taxation without representation.[1]

Sam Adams and the other radicals who gathered around him in the *Boston Gazette* office firmly believed the only way the colonies could resolve their disputes with Britain was to secure home rule. That meant they had come to the position—considered extreme by the vast majority of British citizens in the 1760s—that it was imperative for the colonies, not the Mother Country, to establish the laws of governance for the colonies, although the crown would continue to hold veto power. This idea was highly controversial. To develop their own laws would be tantamount to a child determining his or her own limits of behavior.

Although Adams was Harvard educated and from one of the most prosperous families in the colonies, he was also a backstairs politician who understood, as well as any man of the age, the need to arouse public opinion as a step toward gaining grassroots support for the revolutionary ideas that he and his associates espoused. He wrote, "Where there is a Spark of patriotick fire, *we* will enkindle it."[2]

"Journal of Occurrences" as News Service

To this end, Adams conceived of what became America's first systematic gathering and distributing of news—a precursor of such modern-day operations as the Associated Press and United Press International.

Adams named his intercolonial news service the "Journal of Occurrences," and it quickly evolved into an important communication network that spread his particular anti-British rhetoric to every corner of the colonies.

Items for the journal were written by Adams and other Boston agents and then were reprinted in the thirty-five weekly newspapers being published in the colonies at the time. The process began with Adams and other Boston radicals writing accounts of events and sending them to John Holt, who published the *New York Journal*. Upon receiving an item from Boston, Holt published it in the next edition of his weekly newspaper. Holt then sent copies of his newspaper to the publishers of newspapers throughout the colonies, who reprinted the items in their future issues.

Adams's impetus for establishing the "Journal" was Britain's decision to station troops in Boston. Officials of the crown were concerned that they were losing control of the colonies, particularly because of an increasing number of riots and protests over tax initiatives. So the British sent four regiments of British soldiers to Boston to maintain order and remind the restless colonists that they were, in fact, British subjects.

The "Journal of Occurrences" began operating in September 1768, the same month the troops arrived. It became immediately apparent that the purpose of Adams's innovative journalistic venture was to build opposition to the troops—and, therefore, to the British—by creating and disseminating a record of the loathsome acts the British soldiers were committing against the colonists.

The journal was organized like a personal diary. Each installment listed the dates for a particular week, and under each date were descriptions of the individual bits of news that had occurred on that particular day. A typical weekly installment covered about three columns on the front page of each newspaper. The first ended with a note to publishers: *"The above Journal you are desired to publish for the general satisfaction, it being strictly fact."*[3]

Names of the correspondents were not published, but historians who have studied the style of the material have identified the authors who helped Adams maintain a continuing daily flow of news. They included Benjamin Eades, publisher of the *Boston Evening Post*, and Isaiah Thomas, a young printer who soon would found the *Massachusetts Spy* as the most radical of the patriot papers.[4]

The "Journal" created a shocking record of misdeeds. Many news items spoke generally of the soldiers' uncouth behavior and low morals. Some reported that the soldiers uttered "the most profane & abusive language," and others said that the British troops were constantly involved in "drunkenness, debaucheries, and other extravagancies" and exhibited "licentious and outrageous behaviour." Still other items accused the men of committing crimes at the expense of the American colonists, such as extorting money from people walking on the street and stealing merchandise from colonial shopkeepers.[5]

The most frequent single subject covered in the "Journal" was soldiers insulting and mistreating law-abiding citizens—with most of the victims not identified by name. Accounts told of physicians and merchants being "jostled," having bayonets thrust at them, and being knocked to the ground while merely walking down the street or having a drink in a coffeehouse. Typical of the items was one relating how three soldiers surrounded a man walking on the street, "damning him, and asking why he did not answer when hail'd; immediately upon which, one of them without any provocation gave him a blow, which was seconded by another, whereby he was brought to the ground; they then stamped upon him, using means to prevent his calling out; then they robbed him of all the money in his pocket."[6]

The most disturbing items were those chronicling brutalities against Boston women. One item began, "A girl at New-Boston, was lately knock'd down and abused by soldiers for not consenting to their beastly proposal." Another read, "A young woman lately passing thro' Long-Lane, was stopt and very ill treated by some soldiers, the cry of the person assaulted, brought out another woman into the street, who for daring to expostulate with the ruffians, received a stroke from one of them."[7]

Several incidents involved what today would be classified as capital offenses. One item reported that a woman had filed a complaint with a local magistrate "against a soldier, and some others for a violent attempt upon her, but a rape was prevented, by the timely appearance of a number of persons." Another described a soldier who entered the home of an "aged woman" on the pretense of seeking medical advice but then "seized her, by the shoulders, threw her upon the floor, and not withstanding her years, attempted a rape upon her." The item reported that the "brutal behaviour" ended only because the woman's persistent screams brought help from her neighbors. Another entry told of a woman dying after being "ravished by soldiers unknown," with the attending physicians attributing her death to "the over exertion of her strength" at resisting their attacks.[8]

Regardless of the circumstances, the items came wrapped in a tone of outrage as Adams and the other correspondents made liberal use of biased phrasing. Affronts against the colonists were described as "gross" and "shocking to humanity." The soldiers were labeled "villains," "wretches," and "bloody-backed rascals." A woman's call for assistance became a "cry of murder."[9]

In addition, the authors also attached editorial comments to many of the items, with the additions printed in italic type. The editorial comments clearly exposed that the creative minds behind the news items were adamantly opposed to the British troops being stationed in Boston. One early comment came at the end of a long list of insults and abuses: *"Here Americans you may behold some of the first fruits springing up from that root of bitterness a standing army."* Later remarks reinforced the writers' agenda: *"These are times in which no inhabitant knows what ground he stands upon, or can call his own"* and *"The peace and good order of the town is not like to be preserved or promoted by our military inmates."*[10]

Adams was an impassioned writer who crafted a broad array of spicy news items that readers found far more delectable than the diet of sermons and outdated weather reports that readers of the era had become accustomed to. The descriptions of improper behavior by the British troops became popular reading fare—as the blood pressure of the colonists continued to rise.

In their private correspondence, British officials indignantly denied that the troops were the monsters Adams painted them to be. Massachusetts Colonial Governor Francis Bernard wrote of the news items, "If the Devil himself were of the Party, there would not have been got together a greater collection of impudent virulent & Seditious Lies, Perversions of Truth & Misrepresentations than are to be found in this Publication." Thomas Hutchinson, soon to replace Bernard, wrote, "Nine tenths of what you read in the Journal of Occurrences in Boston is either absolutely false or grossly misrepresented."[11]

And yet the British officials also had to acknowledge that the accounts were having the impact Adams had hoped. As early as January 1769, Hutchinson wrote British officials that the "Infamous falsehoods" were turning large numbers of American colonists against both the British troops and the crown. Six months later, feelings toward the troops had grown so rancorous that British officials admitted that the presence of the troops was fomenting hostility rather than quelling it. Officials therefore decided to withdraw the militiamen, who left Boston in August 1769. In short, Adams and his journalistic strategy had triumphed magnificently.[12]

The "Journal of Occurrences" then ceased operation. It had produced some 300 individual entries—essentially, one for each day during the ten months that British troops were stationed in Boston. The incidents chronicled in the "Journal"—occurring with complete regularity day after day, week after week, month after month—were effective in ridding Boston of the unwanted British soldiers and in gaining support for Adams and his radical notions. According to today's standards of news professionalism, however, there was a fundamental problem with most—if not all—of the accounts: They were not true.

Evidence that a large number of the items were either fabrications or extreme exaggerations evolves from the exact dates they were printed in the newspapers. The attempted rape on the elderly woman, for example, allegedly took place on April 30, but it was not reported in Boston newspapers until June 26. If such a violent physical attack actually had occurred, surely the Boston newsmen would have warned their fellow townspeople as quickly as possible. Surely they would not have followed the drawn-out procedures of first publishing the item in the *New York Journal* and only later publishing it in the Boston papers—resulting in a two-month delay between the attack and its being reported to local residents. If such an attack against a local woman had, in fact, occurred and the story about it was news rather than propaganda, certainly the Boston correspondents would have reported the event in their local papers *immediately* so their fellow townspeople could have taken precautions to protect themselves from the danger in their midst.[13]

The colonial editors apparently felt justified in publishing the descriptions of imaginary incidents because they believed fanning the flames of hatred against the British served the patriot cause. At the same time, the pioneering journalists recognized the need to suggest as strongly as possible that the items were, indeed, based on fact. The sense of authenticity was enhanced by the initial note stating that the journal items were *"strictly fact,"* and by each incident being listed under the specific date on which it was alleged to have occurred.

Those apocryphal accounts were by no means the last examples of sensationalistic material published during the colonial era. In fact, the picture painted by these incidents of British soldiers abusing colonial citizens laid the groundwork for the next chapter in the journalistic trail toward revolution. For that new phase began where the "Journal of Occurrences" left off, raising the decibel level of emotional rhetoric even higher.

Boston Massacre: Not to Be Forgotten

When the Boston Massacre erupted on the commons on March 5, 1770, the accounts seethed with an anger rarely seen in the news reports disseminated today. One *Boston Gazette* article said of the British troops, "A mercenary, licentious rabble of banditti are encouraged to riot uncontrol'd, and tear the bowels and vitals of their brave but peaceable fellow subjects, and *to wash the ground with a profusion of innocent blood.*" To ensure the message was fully communicated to illiterate colonists who might see the paper but not be able to read it, the *Gazette* accompanied the account with woodcuts of coffins representing the five men killed by the British soldiers.[14]

Adams shrieked with outrage when the trial of the British officer and six of his men involved in the incident led only to light punishments. Adams wrote angrily in the *Gazette* under the pen name "Vindex the Avenger" when five of the men were released and the two others were ordered merely to have their hands branded. Adams labeled the British soldiers "barbarous & cruel, infamously mean & base" and peppered his lengthy accounts of the trial testimony with statements such as, "The Soldiers again loaded their guns and were then, ready to repeat the bloody 'action', and fire upon the people as they were taking care of the dead!"[15]

The most incendiary material about the massacre did not follow immediately after the incident or trial, however, but in the years after it. That rhetoric appeared primarily in the form of broadsides. These one-page communiqués were particularly well suited to radical voices because they could be produced more quickly than multipage pamphlets. Tacked at night on trees, posts, and the doors of neighborhood taverns or passed secretly from hand to hand, broadsides were read aloud to the groups who gathered around them the next day, and thus their influence spread far beyond the confines of the literate.

Typical were the histrionic words distributed widely on the second anniversary of the infamous event. One broadside began: "AMERICANS! Bear in Remembrance the HORRID MASSACRE!" It went on to describe the five victims as "Being basely and most INHUMANLY MURDERED! And SIX others badly wounded!" and continued to shriek:

> May AMERICA be preserved,
> From weak and wicked monarchs,
> Tyrannical Ministers,
> Abandoned Governors,
> Their Underlings and Hirelings!
> And may the
> Machinations of Artful, DESIGNING wretches,
> Who would ENSLAVE this People,
> Come to an end,
> Let their NAMES and MEMORIES
> Be buried in eternal oblivion.

Such exclamations of rage not only kept the fight for liberty fresh in the consciousness of the citizenry but also fueled a public desire for revenge—challenging the colonists to avenge the murders.[16]

The publications recounting the murders on the Boston Commons were, in fact, forerunners of the atrocity stories published during later eras. Just as stories of Iraqi soldiers ripping Kuwaiti babies from their incubators helped Americans justify the Persian Gulf War, the telling and retelling of the taking of lives in the Boston Massacre prepared the colonists for the armed conflict that was to come.

In the words of David Ramsay, a soldier who fought in the American Revolution, the broadsides written in response to the Boston Massacre "administered fuel to the fire of liberty, and kept it burning with an incessant flame."[17]

Tom Paine: Voice of Inspiration

The final and most decisive phase of the pro-revolution media campaign began after armed hostilities had broken out in Lexington and Concord in April 1775 and was led by the most important writer of the colonial era, a penniless and somewhat disreputable newcomer to American shores: Thomas Paine.

After initial failure in the corset-making business in London, young Paine was hired to collect taxes on liquor and other items. When Paine began to agitate for higher pay for himself and his fellow workers, however, the British government discharged him. By happenstance, Paine met Benjamin Franklin, then at the height of his career as American spokesman in Europe. Franklin saw so much merit in Paine that he encouraged the fiery young agitator to go to America, providing a letter of introduction for him.

When Paine arrived in Philadelphia in November 1774, the thirty-seven-year-old Quaker came with the intent of founding an academy to educate young women. He veered from his course, however, when his connection to Franklin led to an offer to edit *Pennsylvania Magazine*. Although the magazine survived only eight months, Paine's writing in it was sufficient to gain him a reputation as an insightful commentator on the issues of the day.

Colonists came to know Paine as an independent thinker who wrote inspiring discourse on behalf of the masses. In the first issue of *Pennsylvania Magazine*, for example, he lambasted the "profligacy" in Britain while praising the "virtue" of the American colonies. His words published in another Philadelphia newspaper, *Pennsylvania Journal and the Weekly Advertiser*, demonstrated his willingness to support unpopular positions such as the abolition of slavery, an institution widely embraced by the colonists. He urged readers to consider the contradiction being displayed by colonial slaveholders: "They complain so loudly of attempts to enslave *them,* while they hold so many hundred thousands of Africans in slavery."[18]

Common Sense *Ignites a Nation*

In January 1776, Paine wrote the material that secured him monumental fame as a revolutionary writer. *Common Sense* evolved after the youthful Benjamin Rush urged Paine to write an essay on the future of the American colonies "beyond the ordinary short and cold address of newspaper publication." That he did.[19]

Others had offered political and economic arguments, but Tom Paine advocated nothing short of social revolution. His pamphlet served as important a purpose as any piece of journalism in the history of this country: Its message has been credited with transforming thousands of mildly disillusioned colonists into defiant rebels fully prepared to fight for a utopian new world.

Before Paine published his pamphlet, most colonists aspired only for what they saw as their rights as English subjects. *Common Sense* argued that those men and women not only deserved, but were obligated as citizens of the human race, to demand much more. Paine's profound message was that the issues facing the colonists were neither transitory nor parochial, but timeless and universal. He wrote, "The cause of America is in a great measure the cause of all mankind . . . the concern of every man to whom nature hath given the power of feeling." He returned to the theme repeatedly in later passages, appealing to his readers' sense of destiny: "The sun never shined on a cause of greater worth. 'Tis not the affair of a City, a County, a Province, or a Kingdom. 'Tis not the concern of a day, a year, or an age; posterity are virtually involved in the contest, and will be affected even to the end of time."[20]

Paine assaulted the contemporary embodiment of hereditary rule, dubbing King George III "the Royal Brute of Great Britain" and the English constitution "the base remains of ancient tyrannies." He further struck out at the monarchy by boldly declaring, "Of more worth is one honest man to society, and in the sight of God, than all the crowned ruffians that ever lived." Paine was the first writer in America to denounce the British monarchy and constitution so utterly.[21]

Only after dispensing with these institutions did Paine begin to discuss colonial independence—a concept so controversial that Rush had counseled Paine to avoid using the word "independence" in his pamphlet. Radicals such as Sam Adams had mentioned the concept occasionally, but most colonists still refused to consider such an extreme

COMMON SENSE;

ADDRESSED TO THE

INHABITANTS

OF

A M E R I C A,

On the following intereſting

S U B J E C T S.

I. Of the Origin and Deſign of Government in general, with conciſe Remarks on the Engliſh Conſtitution.

II. Of Monarchy and Hereditary Succeſſion.

III. Thoughts on the preſent State of American Affairs.

IV. Of the preſent Ability of America, with ſome miſcellaneous Reflections.

Man knows no Maſter ſave creating HEAVEN,
Or thoſe whom choice and common good ordain.

THOMSON.

PHILADELPHIA;
Printed, and Sold, by R. BELL, in Third-Street.

MDCCLXXVI.

After the pamphlet Common Sense *appeared in January 1776, the concept of independence spread like wildfire through the American colonies. Reprinted by permission of the Library of Congress.*

step. Paine, in contrast, presented separation from Britain as the only viable option for the colonies and then went on to sketch a breathtaking vision of what American independence could mean for all of humankind: "We have it in our power to begin the world over again. The birthday of a new world is at hand."[22]

Paine managed to turn the struggle over the rights of the American colonists into a contest with ramifications of unparalleled dimension for all the world: "O! ye that love mankind! Ye that dare oppose not only the tyranny but the tyrant, stand forth! Every spot of the old world is overrun with oppression. Freedom hath been hunted round the Globe. Asia and Africa have long expelled her. Europe regards her like a stranger, and England hath given her warning to depart. O! receive the fugitive, and prepare in time an asylum for mankind."[23]

Common Sense was not remarkable for its substance alone. Rather, much of the genius of Paine's pamphlet was the masterful way he packaged ideas—royal corruption, rights of the governed, vision of an American empire—into a comprehensive argument that related each of these ideas to the common experiences of the colonists.

With *Common Sense,* Paine pioneered a new style of political writing aimed at extending political discussion to all classes. Most writers of the eighteenth century believed that to write for a mass audience meant to sacrifice refinement for coarseness, to reject a lofty literary style in favor of a vulgar one. The American pamphleteers before Paine had come largely from the high social strata of lawyers, merchants, planters, and ministers; Paine, however, had sprung from that same mass audience that he was so successful at reaching.

Paine later wrote, "As it is my design to make those that can scarcely read understand, I shall therefore avoid every literary ornament and put it in language as plain as the alphabet." He eliminated the flowery language that might have impressed highly educated readers, and he provided translations for the few Latin phrases he used. The hallmarks of his writing were the same as those of journalism today—clarity, directness, force. His vocabulary and grammar were straightforward, and he carried his readers along with great care from one argument to the next. Paine's message, stated explicitly and reiterated by his tone and style, was that everyone could grasp the nature of—and play a role in—their own governance.[24]

The response to *Common Sense* was astonishing. At a time when colonial newspapers were fortunate if they sold 2,000 copies and pamphlets were printed in one or two editions of a few thousand, more than 150,000 copies of *Common Sense* were sold within three months. And by year's end the pamphlet had gone through twenty-five separate editions.

Impact was not measured in numbers alone, for people were instantly affected by Paine's remarkable words, reading their simple message and overnight becoming committed to independence. In a matter of weeks, his passion had infected virtually every American colonist who was either literate or was in earshot of one of the hundreds of voices who read the inspirational words aloud in coffeehouses, taverns, and town squares from New England to Georgia.

In the most famous comment on the impact of Paine's words, General George Washington observed, "By private letters, which I have lately received from Virginia, I find 'Common Sense' is working a powerful change there in the minds of many men." Others agreed. Abigail Adams thanked her husband, John, for sending her a copy and gushed about its impact in Massachusetts: "Tis highly prized here and carries conviction wherever it is read. I have spread it as much as it lay in my power, every one assents to the weighty truths it contains." Thomas Jefferson observed, "No writer has exceeded Paine in ease and familiarity of style, in perspicuity of expression, happiness of elucidation, and in simple and unassuming language."[25]

Perhaps even more important evidence of the pamphlet's impact came from comments by common citizens. In a letter to the *Connecticut Gazette*, a man spoke directly to Paine: "You have declared the sentiments of Millions. Your production may justly be compared to a land-flood that sweeps all before it. We were blind, but on reading these enlightening works the scales have fallen from our eyes. The doctrine of Independence hath been in times past, greatly disgustful; we abhorred the principle—it is now become our delightful theme, and commands our purest affection." A Philadelphia man attributed "the progress of the idea of Colonial independence in three weeks or a month" solely to *Common Sense*, adding that "tens of thousands of common farmers and tradesmen" were suddenly prepared "to part with the abominable chain."[26]

The soldier David Ramsay lauded *Common Sense* as a publishing phenomenon that "produced surprising effects." Ramsay continued: "Many thousands were convinced, and were led to approve and long for a separation from the Mother Country. Though that measure, a few months before, was not only foreign from their wishes, but the object of their abhorrence, the current suddenly became so strong in its favour, that it bore down all opposition. The multitude was hurried down the stream."[27]

Common Sense did not single-handedly *cause* the American Revolution or propel the authors of the Declaration of Independence to craft their historic document less than six months after Tom Paine wrote his extraordinary pamphlet. But there is no question that

Paine's words had significant impact. He articulated the larger meaning of the struggle with Britain to readers focused on attaining their rights as subjects of the British crown—and suddenly those same citizens embraced the concept of independence that previously had been anathema to them. Paine biographer Eric Foner wrote, "The success of *Common Sense* reflected the perfect conjunction of a man and his time, a writer and his audience, and it announced the emergence of Paine as the outstanding political pamphleteer of the Age of Revolution."[28]

Crisis *Essays Inspire an Army*

Despite Paine's singular contribution to the revolutionary cause, his work as an inspirational writer had not yet ended. He joined the Continental army in August 1776 and, like his fellow soldiers, felt the might of a well-armed and well-trained British army. As the summer wore into winter, companies began breaking up. The British cut the Americans to pieces in numerous battles, and Paine saw hundreds of his adopted countrymen die.

Making his way to Washington's headquarters, Paine saw the defeated Americans preparing to retreat across the Delaware River. Legend has it that Paine wrote his *Crisis* essays at Washington's request. The general could see that the winter cold, combined with poor food and inadequate uniforms, was taking a severe toll on his soldiers; he called on Paine to write words that would inspire the men to continue fighting. Legend also has it that Paine wrote his moving words by candlelight on a drum head. Although these stories can be disputed, there is no doubt that Paine wrote under pressure and from the soul.

In December 1776, the first installment of the *Crisis* papers went into print in the *Pennsylvania Journal* and was immediately reprinted in pamphlet form. Washington had the essay read to his suffering and dispirited troops, and a week later they won a crucial victory at Trenton.

That first essay began with the line that was to be remembered by future generations as Paine's most famous: "These are the times that try men's souls." For more than two centuries, literature classes have struggled to understand the power of that alliterative phrasing. Paine continued, "The summer soldier and the sunshine patriot will, in this crisis, shrink from the service of their country; but he that stands it *now*, deserves the love and thanks of man and woman. Tyranny, like hell, is not easily conquered; yet we have this consolation with us, that the harder the conflict, the more glorious the triumph."[29]

Historians credit essay writer Tom Paine with helping to transform lukewarm patriots into fiery revolutionaries. Reprinted by permission of the Library of Congress.

Other *Crisis* papers appeared as the need demanded, with twelve being published by December 1783. Each burst with a new flurry of inspiration: "The heart that feels not now, is dead: the blood of his children will curse his cowardice, who shrinks back at a time a little might have saved the whole" and "Let it be told to the future world, that in the depth of winter, when nothing but hope and virtue could survive, that the city and the country, alarmed at one common danger, came forth to meet it and to repulse it."[30]

Despite Tom Paine's seminal contribution to both American journalism and American history, his adopted countrymen rejected him for his radicalism. After inspiring the colonists to seek independence and later fighting in both the American and French Revolutions, Paine died ignored in 1809. His tombstone listed his most important contribution as creating *Common Sense.*

Stunning Impact

Just as the American Revolution stands as a unique event in the history of the United States, colonial American journalism provides a stunning example of the impact the news media have had on shaping American history. For the series of publications produced in the colonies during the 1760s and 1770s helped lead the colonists toward political and social revolution. "That rebellion," one historian wrote, "would have been impossible without the spur of the press."[31]

The early phase of the apocalyptic campaign began in 1768 and was orchestrated by political firebrand Sam Adams. Through the "Journal of Occurrences," he and his radical associates artfully mobilized colonial public opinion against the British troops stationed in Boston and, therefore, against the crown. Their sensationalistic reports of British soldiers mistreating the good people of Boston spawned strong negative reaction that, in turn, helped persuade British officials to withdraw the troops—providing the colonists with a victory that propelled them toward further action.

Colonial resentment toward the British grew even stronger during the 1770s. Radical patriots not only reported the brutality of the Boston Massacre immediately after the episode but again employed sensationalism through an incessant flow of commemorative broadsides. Those hysterical retellings of the events on Boston Commons kept the massacre fresh in the minds and hearts of the colonists, helping to push those men and women closer and closer to their breaking point.

Despite their importance, these early publications were mere prelude to Tom Paine's remarkable work. In the early months of 1776,

Common Sense became the *magnum opus* that not only helped arouse the colonists to the revolutionary concept of independence but also thrust them toward open rebellion. *Common Sense* played a singular role in transforming mildly discontented subjects of the British crown into political insurgents fully committed to social mutiny, to fighting for their freedom, and, ultimately, to changing the course of human history in the second millennium.

2

Abolition: Turning America's Conscience Against the Sins of Slavery

In the fall of 1837, Rev. Elijah P. Lovejoy made the supreme sacrifice. While waging a two-pronged journalistic campaign in opposition to slavery and in support of press freedom, he gave his very life to the two causes. As the editor of an abolitionist weekly, Rev. Lovejoy had endured pro-slavery forces destroying his first printing press, then his second, then his third. Because he continued to speak out against the sale of African Americans, an angry mob attempted to destroy his fourth press as well. When Rev. Lovejoy attempted to prevent the destruction of his property, he was shot dead.

Rev. Lovejoy did not, however, die in vain. His martyrdom propelled thousands of converts into the Abolition Movement, as his murder clearly demonstrated that an anti-slavery stand endangered not only the rights of African Americans but the civil liberties of all Americans—white as well as black.

Though Rev. Lovejoy's sacrifice was dramatic and its impact far reaching, his was only one of many losses that advocacy journalists suffered from the 1820s to the 1860s as they successfully turned the American conscience against the sins of slavery. Mainstream journalists took up the cause by the 1850s, but it was the abolitionist editors who first built the national momentum against slavery in the 1830s and 1840s. The most famous of the crusading editors was William Lloyd Garrison, whose *Liberator* became synonymous with the abolitionist press. Although only one of several dozen anti-slavery papers, the *Liberator* remained the focal point of the crusade because of Garrison's strident rhetoric, ongoing hand-to-hand combat with pro-slavery editors, and repeated public demonstrations—including burning the United States Constitution—that kept abolition a white-hot topic. Less well known than Garrison but also important were the men and women of African descent who, as early as the 1820s, began to plead their own case through the early black press.

The "Peculiar Institution" Divides a Nation

Slavery had been a controversial issue throughout the history of the United States, but economic developments created a geographic fault line that in the early 1800s split the country into two distinct sections. In the 1820s, the North began to industrialize, with a burgeoning of urban-based factories. The South, on the other hand, remained an agrarian society with an economy dominated by the production of cotton and tobacco—both relying on slave labor for their profitability.

But the enslavement of human beings was more than an economic issue. Slavery was the rallying cry for northern progressives who wanted massive social change, a salient issue that crystallized complex social and economic differences between the two regions. And just as Sam Adams and Tom Paine had appealed to the emotions to translate colonial opposition to the British into terms the average man and woman could understand, abolitionist editors used highly charged rhetoric to place the slavery debate on a plane the average citizen could understand.

In the 1830s, the Abolition Movement focused on convincing all Americans that slavery was a sin that should not be allowed to exist. Many Southerners saw slavery from a different perspective. They argued that it introduced a backward people to Christian civilization. In addition, apologists said slaves received food, clothing, shelter, and security during sickness and old age. For abolitionists, however, one fundamental consideration canceled out every defense: Slaves were not free. Slaves could not benefit from the fruits of their own labor, were not guaranteed the right to participate in the domestic relations of marriage and parenthood, and could not regulate their conduct to prepare the immortal soul for eternity. Slaves were, in short, denied their rights as children of God.

To spread this message, abolitionists created their own newspapers—from the *Instigator* in Providence to the *Liberalist* in New Orleans. The common motivation behind all these publications was a determination to disseminate the anti-slavery ideology to a larger audience throughout the North while intensifying the negative feelings against the "peculiar institution" in the South—and, in fact, against the South as a whole. The abolitionist press set out to unite the North not only against slavery but against the social and economic way of life that perpetuated slavery.

The Rev. Elijah P. Lovejoy: Journalistic Martyr

Elijah Parish Lovejoy was born in Maine in 1802, the son of a Congregational minister. After graduating first in his class from Waterville College in his home state, Lovejoy taught school and then earned a divinity degree from Princeton Theological Seminary. Powered by a Puritan conscience and a burning desire to reform the wrongs of society, Rev. Lovejoy established a Presbyterian newspaper in the far western state of Missouri in 1834.

Slavery soon emerged as the *St. Louis Observer*'s most controversial topic, particularly because the state of Missouri continued to condone slavery. Rev. Lovejoy wrote, "The groans, and sighs, and tears, and blood of the poor slave have gone up as a memorial before the throne of Heaven. As surely as there is a thunderbolt in Heaven and strength in God's right arm to launch it, so surely will it strike the authors of such cruel oppression."[1]

Rev. Lovejoy initially spoke with a degree of moderation. He did not insist that emancipation be granted immediately but advocated slavery being phased out over time. In 1835 he wrote, "On the general subject of Slavery we are decidedly gradual." When reform did not progress at the pace Rev. Lovejoy had hoped, however, he became increasingly impatient. After he had published his weekly newspaper for two years and Missouri had yet to establish an anti-slavery society, Rev. Lovejoy's rhetoric became more strident. In early 1836 he sternly announced: "Slavery is a *sin*—now, heretofore, hereafter, and forever, a sin. Consequently it follows that whoever has participated, or does now participate, in that sin, ought to repent without a moment's delay."[2]

As the *Observer* became more defiant, the establishment press in St. Louis mobilized community opposition to it. Lovejoy's paper should be silenced, the *Missouri Republican* argued, because its anti-slavery stance encouraged blacks to commit violent acts against whites. The *Republican* also attacked Lovejoy on economic grounds, warning that southern states would refuse to do business with Missouri if the state allowed Lovejoy to continue preaching against slavery. The paper further argued that Lovejoy "merited the full measure of the community's indignation" and "forfeited all claims to the protection of that or any other community." Virtually demanding violence against Lovejoy, the *Republican* said of Missouri citizens, "Every consideration for their own and their neighbor's prosperity requires them to stop the course of the *Observer*."[3]

Fearing for the safety of his wife and toddler son, Rev. Lovejoy relocated across the Mississippi River in Illinois, a free state. But during the move, slavery advocates pushed his printing press into the river. He then purchased a second press and proceeded to publish his paper in Illinois. In the first issue of the *Alton Observer*, he reiterated, "American negro Slavery is an awful evil and sin, and it is the duty of us all to effect the speedy and entire emancipation of our fellow-men in bondage." In response to the destruction of his press, Rev. Lovejoy also began a second crusade: for freedom of expression. Never, he insisted, would he be intimidated by mob pressure against "the rights of conscience, the freedom of opinion, and of the press."[4]

Rev. Lovejoy soon learned that Illinois was not as accepting of his abolition stance as he had hoped. While the editor was at home, a mob entered the *Observer* office and destroyed his second press. At this point, the determined editor called on fellow abolitionists for support. Anti-slavery leaders throughout the North sent him money to purchase a third press, which pro-slavery forces promptly destroyed. Despite the continuing setbacks, Rev. Lovejoy remained steadfast. In October 1837, he stated that he had no intention of leaving Alton: "Should I attempt it, I should feel that the angel of the Lord, with his flaming sword, was pursuing me wherever I went. The contest has commenced here; and here it must be finished."[5]

Even some die-hard abolitionists, however, questioned whether it was judicious to continue to support the cleric's effort that increasingly seemed to be driven by his own obstinacy. Despite the deteriorating support, Lovejoy borrowed the money to purchase a fourth press. When it arrived on November 7, 1837, he stored it in a warehouse near the river. That fateful night, a crowd of 200 men gathered outside the warehouse and directed Lovejoy to abandon the building. When he refused, events escalated into a riot. Several men placed a ladder against an exterior wall of the building, and one carried a torch to the top and set the roof on fire. As the building began to blaze, Lovejoy ran outside and aimed his pistol at the man on the ladder. Shots rang out from the crowd, and Lovejoy fell to the ground. Five bullets were found in his corpse.

The death of a well-educated, Eastern-born clergyman—compounded with the failure of law enforcement officials to arrest anyone for his murder—sent shock waves through the nation. It also transformed the

Abolition Movement. Because Rev. Lovejoy was killed by a mob while defending freedom of the press, the issue mushroomed from the relatively narrow one of denying rights to a disenfranchised minority to the much broader one of threatening the civil liberties of all Americans.

In an editorial outlined in a heavy black border, William Lloyd Garrison used the murder of "a representative of Justice, Liberty and Christianity" to condemn the United States as a nation "diseased beyond the power of recovery" but swore Rev. Lovejoy's death would serve both his crusade against slavery and his defense of a free press. Garrison wrote, "In destroying his press, the enemies of freedom have compelled a thousand to speak out in its stead. In murdering a loyal and patriotic citizen, they have stirred up a national commotion which causes the foundations of the republic to tremble. O most insane and wicked of mankind!"[6]

Denunciations came from others as well. Former President John Quincy Adams praised Lovejoy: "He was a man of strong religious, conscientious feeling, deeply indignant at what he deemed the vices and crimes of the age. He has fallen a martyr to the cause of human freedom." Edward Beecher, president of Illinois College, said of the slain editor, "His enemies have failed in their purpose, and he has triumphed in his fall." Rev. William Ellery Channing, the international man of letters and founder of American Unitarianism, condemned the murder as an assault on freedom of expression and a violent attack on public order and the law.[7]

Such statements ignited a tide of indignation, resentment, and rage that spread like wildfire. Hundreds of ministers preached sermons eulogizing Lovejoy, and thousands of activists organized public protests supporting free expression and civil liberties. The American Anti-Slavery Society capitalized on the groundswell of protest, arranging a commemorative service to Lovejoy in the Broadway Tabernacle in New York, complete with funeral dirge and inspirational sermons. In a well-orchestrated campaign to keep the murder fresh in the memories of the American people, the society adopted the slain editor as a martyr, printed 40,000 copies of a publication that described the Alton riot, and issued stationery embossed with the slogan: "LOVEJOY the first MARTYR to American LIBERTY. MURDERED for asserting the FREEDOM of the PRESS."[8]

As thousands of men and women previously indifferent to the issue of slavery realized for the first time that their own civil liberties might be imperiled, local anti-slavery societies burst into existence and new members flocked into the national network that was infused with unparalleled life and energy.

In addition to swelling the anti-slavery ranks, Rev. Lovejoy's martyrdom also propelled the Abolition Movement into a new phase. Before this time, abolitionists had perceived all Americans as fundamentally reasonable people who could be swayed by arguments addressed to their higher natures. They sincerely believed that when slave owners were informed of the sins of slavery, they would voluntarily free their slaves. Rev. Lovejoy's murder demonstrated, however, that this strategy—known as moral suasion—would fail to end slavery. The Alton riot showed anti-slavery forces that their crusade would not triumph unless they took direct action. If men and women committed to the cause intended to rouse public opinion, they would have to enter the rough-and-tumble of politics.

William Lloyd Garrison: Fanatic Abolitionist Editor

The most influential abolitionist editor, William Lloyd Garrison, founded and emerged as chief prophet of the American abolitionist crusade during the early and mid–nineteenth century. The primary vehicle Garrison used to spread his gospel was the *Liberator*, the Boston weekly he edited for thirty-five years.

Garrison was born in Newburyport, Massachusetts, in 1805. Poverty forced him to leave school at the age of ten, when he became an apprentice printer. While helping abolitionist Benjamin Lundy edit his *Genius of Universal Emancipation* in Baltimore during the 1820s, Garrison grew increasingly vehement in his attacks on American slave traders.

In 1829, Garrison set his sights on Francis Todd, who took slaves to Louisiana sugar plantations on his ship, the *Francis*. In an item labeled "Black List," Garrison accused Todd of mistreating his slaves, stating: "Any man can gather up riches, if he does not care by what means they are obtained. The *Francis* carried off *seventy-five* slaves, chained in a narrow place between decks."[9]

Todd filed a libel suit, saying that the slaves had not been chained but had been free to move below deck and that Garrison had relied on hearsay for his article. The jury agreed with Todd, finding Garrison guilty. Garrison probably could have avoided a jail sentence if he had been contrite, but the self-righteous editor refused. Because of his lack of remorse, he was forced to spend the next forty-nine days behind bars.

Garrison then moved to Boston and began publishing, in 1831, what emerged as the epitome of advocacy journalism in American history. Although he founded both a local abolition group and the American

Anti-Slavery Society, his primary tool for arousing apathetic Northerners to the sins of slavery was the *Liberator*.

The strident editor was a man of courage and conviction, imbued with the righteous indignation of a fanatic. Most abolitionists were willing to compromise by supporting a gradual reduction in slavery over a period of years, but Garrison demanded immediate emancipation of all slaves. He wrote: "I *will be* as harsh as truth, and as uncompromising as justice. On this subject, I do not wish to think, or speak, or write, with moderation. No! No! Urge me not to use moderation in a cause like the present. I am in earnest—I will not equivocate—I will not excuse—I will not retreat a single inch—AND I WILL BE HEARD."[10]

Although the *Liberator* achieved a circulation of only 1,000 during its early years, Garrison was soon known throughout the country because of his success as a provocateur. His ingenious system began with the simple act of exchanging his newspaper for the newspapers of some 100 other editors, most of them pro-slavery. The editors Garrison sent his paper to were so offended by his invectives that they quoted his words—accompanied by their own words of outrage—to show readers the extreme nature of the abolitionist ideology. When Garrison received his copy of a paper in which an editor had lambasted him, he did not shudder with pain: He celebrated. For Garrison then reprinted the editorial attack, along with his own vehement response—thereby giving his readers far more compelling discourse than his original editorial.

For instance, after the editor of Connecticut's *Middletown Gazette* read Garrison's first editorial salvos against slavery, the Northern editor retorted with contempt: "Mr. Garrison can do no good, either to the cause of humanity or to the slaves, by his violent and intemperate attacks on the slaveholders. That mawkish sentimentality which weeps over imaginary suffering, is proper to be indulged by boarding school misses and antiquated spinsters; but men, grown up men, ought to be ashamed of it." Garrison not only reprinted the *Gazette*'s attack but used typographical flourishes to ridicule the paper's suggestion that slavery did not cause pain, repeating the phrase in disbelief: "*IMAGINARY suffering!!*" Garrison then attacked the *Gazette* for betraying the progressive nature of the region of the country that it and the *Liberator* shared: "Such sentiments, emanating at the south, would excite no surprise; but being those of New-England men, they fill us with disgust."[11]

Criticism published in pro-slavery papers—and eventually reprinted in the *Liberator*—often combined paranoia with its venom. The *Free Press* in Tarboro, North Carolina, reported that Garrison had hired

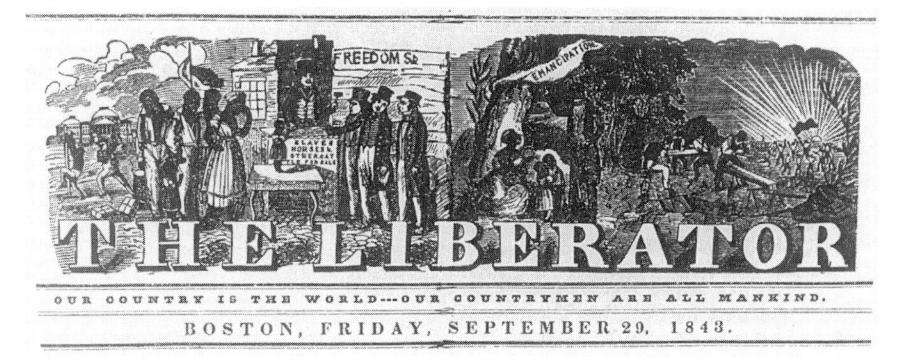

Each week the Liberator's *nameplate provided readers with a graphic reminder that African-American men, women, and children were sold on the auction block just like horses and cattle. Reprinted by permission of the Library of Congress.*

"secret agents" in every county in the state to distribute the *Liberator* and advised readers to "Keep a sharp look out for these villains, and if you catch them, by all that is sacred, you ought to barbacue [sic] them." Garrison reprinted the charge under the heading "Incendiary Publications," describing the *Free Press* accusation as "murderous and abominable."[12]

Although the explosive combination of Garrison's extreme positions and his ability to set off editorial chain reactions raised his national profile, they did not make him popular. One letter to the editor read: "Your paper cannot much longer be tolerated. Shame on the Freemen of Boston for permitting such a vehicle of outrage and rebellion to spring into existence among them!" Another screamed: "O! you pitiful scoundrel! you toad eater! you d—d son of a —! hell is gaping for you! the devil is feasting in anticipation! you are not worth —!"[13]

Much of the anger sprang from the belief among Southerners that Garrison was using the *Liberator* to incite violence, such as the 1831 slave rebellion that Nat Turner led in southern Virginia, killing sixty whites. And, indeed, much of Garrison's rhetoric did seem to promote violence. Typical was the message communicated in a verse titled "The Insurrection":

> *Wo if it come with storm, and blood, and fire,*
> *When midnight darkness veils the earth and sky!*
> *Wo to the innocent babe*—the guilty sire—
> *Mother and daughter*—friends of kindred tie!
> *Stranger and citizen alike shall die!*[14]

Evidence of Garrison's influence on the national conscience came in the form of the numerous governmental bodies that attempted to squelch his words. The Georgia legislature offered a $5,000 bounty for Garrison, and then a group of men in Mississippi upped the ante to $20,000. Columbia, South Carolina, offered a reward to any person who apprehended *Liberator* distributors, and the city of Georgetown in the District of Columbia prohibited blacks from receiving the paper. On the federal level, United States Postmaster General Amos Kendall condoned southern vigilante groups that rifled official mail sacks to destroy copies of the *Liberator*.

Boston took its own action. In 1835, a mob of 100 men assembled outside a hall where Garrison was speaking. Fearing for his safety, the editor slipped out a back window and sought refuge in a carpenter shop, where he climbed into the loft and hid behind a pile of lumber. The mob tracked him down, screaming "Lynch him!" Several men then dragged Garrison to the window of the loft, stripped him, and coiled a rope around his neck. Just before the mob hurled Garrison out the window, supporters rescued him.

Such acts of intimidation did not cause Garrison's radicalism to abate, but to escalate. In 1844, he proclaimed that Americans could no longer pledge their allegiance to a slaveholding and racist government and that all non-slaveholders should secede from the union. Garrison wrote: "The existing national compact should be instantly dissolved. Secession from the government is a religious and political duty. The motto inscribed on the banner of Freedom should be, NO UNION WITH SLAVEHOLDERS."[15]

Despite this revolutionary rhetoric and the *Liberator*'s status as the most widely known voice for abolition, the paper did not build a large circulation. Paid subscribers never exceeded 2,500, most of them African Americans. Garrison paid his printing costs through the fees he charged for speaking engagements, even though his words were almost always accompanied by jeering and heckling—and often stones and rotten eggs—from pro-slavery demonstrators.

The most notorious example of how far Garrison would go to arouse the American people to his cause came during a Fourth of July celebration in 1854. Henry David Thoreau first addressed those gathered in the picnic grove in Framingham, Massachusetts, speaking on behalf of an imprisoned slave. But Garrison was the sensation of the day. An article about the event in the *Liberator* described his dramatic gesture, "Holding up the U.S. Constitution, he branded it as the source and parent of all the other atrocities—'a covenant with death, and an agreement with hell.'" Garrison then set fire to the document. As the Constitution burst into flames, Garrison declared, "So perish all compromises with tyranny! And let all the people say, Amen!" A few hisses and protests were drowned out by a tremendous shout from the crowd: "Amen!"[16]

With regard to rhetoric, Garrison's most dramatic words of the 1850s came in response to John Brown's attack on the United States military arsenal at Harper's Ferry. When the radical abolitionist led seventeen whites and five blacks in the 1859 insurrection, Garrison praised Brown's willingness to kill others of his race for being partisans of chattel slavery. After Brown was captured and hanged, Garrison wrote: "Whenever there is a contest between the oppressed and the oppressor, God knows my heart must be with the oppressed, and always against the oppressor. Therefore, I cannot but wish success to all slave insurrections."[17]

By the 1850s, Garrison was by no means a lone voice against slavery, as mainstream newspapers also had joined the crusade. By 1852, the weekly edition of the *New York Tribune* had a circulation of 200,000 and was widely acknowledged as the leading opponent of slavery among mainstream papers. Publisher Horace Greeley became such an ardent opponent of slavery that he abandoned the Whigs to help organize the Republican Party that brought Abraham Lincoln to the White House in 1860. In the West, Joseph Medill built the *Chicago Tribune* into a strong advocate of abolition.

Between 1861 and 1865, more than 600,000 Americans died in the Civil War. And then, finally, in December 1865 the Thirteenth Amendment to the Constitution abolished slavery.

With Garrison's goal achieved, he ceased publishing the *Liberator*. Other journalistic voices then praised him for transforming public sentiment on the most controversial issue of the era. *Nation* magazine wrote of Garrison's commitment to the Abolition Movement, "It is, perhaps, the most remarkable instance on record of single-hearted devotion to a cause." The magazine went on to say of the *Liberator*, "It has dropped its water upon the nation's marble heart. Its effect on the moral sentiment of the country was exceedingly great. It went straight to the conscience, and it did more than any one thing beside to create that power of moral conviction which was so indomitable."[18]

In recognition of the central role Garrison had played in abolishing slavery, he was invited to Charleston for a great jubilee. The climax of his day came when a throng of liberated slaves hoisted him triumphantly onto their shoulders and carried him to a platform in Zion's Church, surrounded by thousands of African-American men and women who understood what he had done for them. Black orator and activist Frederick Douglass spoke for the multitude, calling Garrison "the man to whom more than any other in this Republic we are indebted for the triumph we are celebrating today."[19]

Men at the highest level of government joined in lionizing Garrison. Secretary of War Edwin Stanton invited him to Washington for a private interview. United States Senators Charles Sumner and Henry Wilson accompanied Garrison onto the Senate floor. And in the ultimate statement of honor, President Abraham Lincoln received Garrison at the White House for an hour-long session in which the men talked privately; it was a historic meeting that brought together the two men who did more to end slavery than any others.

African-American Journalists Find Their Voices

Although African-American journalists had begun, by the late 1820s, to publish their own newspapers, the abolition of slavery did not dominate the early black press to the same degree it did Lovejoy's *Observer* or Garrison's *Liberator*. In a country that remained largely hostile to people of African descent, it was remarkable for newspapers owned and operated by blacks to speak at all. For such voices to speak loudly was impossible.

Besides, the African-American editors had plenty of other material to give their readers. The first black papers were published in the North, the only section of the country where African Americans had any opportunities whatsoever for education or progress. So the editors used their publishing enterprises to help other members of their race improve their status. From the 1820s to 1850s, the importance of education was the single most frequent topic of discussion in the nascent African-American press.

The first black newspaper was *Freedom's Journal*, founded in New York City in 1827. The premier issue contained the eloquent purpose that would continue to sustain the genre for generations to come: "We wish to plead our own cause. Too long have others spoken for us." That "we" referred to Rev. Samuel Cornish, who had founded a Presbyterian church in Manhattan, and John B. Russwurm, who had graduated from Bowdoin College the previous year. The two young men focused their historic four-page weekly on promoting education, convinced it was the key to their race advancing in society. Not until halfway through their inaugural 2,000-word editorial did the editors so much as mention slavery. Even then, the reference was a vague one delivered with none of Garrison's urgency: "We would not be unmindful of our brethren who are still in the iron fetters of bondage. They are our kindred by all the ties of nature; and though but little can be effected by us, still let our sympathies be poured forth, and our prayers in their behalf, ascend to Him who is able to succour them."[20]

Like the African-American publications that have followed it, *Freedom's Journal* faced severe financial difficulties. Advertising was impossible to secure because very few businesses targeted black consumers, whose economic strength was minimal. The first black newspaper ceased publication in late 1829, never having approached the decibel level of the *Liberator*.

It is not surprising, then, that the first defiant African-American journalist spoke not in the black press, but from the pages of the *Liberator*. What *is* surprising is that the voice came from a woman. For during the early nineteenth century, society relegated most women—black or white—to the home, reserving the realms of business, economics, and politics exclusively to men.

Maria Stewart refused to accept that limited definition of a woman's *place*. Born free in Hartford, Connecticut, in 1803, Stewart was orphaned at the age of five and widowed while still in her twenties. Propelled by the sorrow of her own life and the zeal of religious conviction, she began writing for the *Liberator* in 1831. Garrison showcased Stewart's essays by creating a "Ladies' Department," complete with a woodcut of a black woman in chains.

Much of her passion and eloquence was aimed at the abolition of slavery. She admonished her fellow African Americans to look up from their labor and see the reality surrounding them, "Cast your eyes about, look as far as you can see; all, all is owned by the *lordly* white, except here and there a lowly dwelling which the man of color—midst deprivations, fraud, and opposition—has been scarce able to procure." Stewart went on to castigate the United States as a civilization defined by sin, saying, "America has become like the great city of Babylon, for she has boasted in her heart,—'I sit a queen and am no widow, and shall see no sorrow!' She is indeed a seller of slaves and the souls of men; she has made the Africans drunk with the wine of her fornication." Using terms such as "*lordly* white" and "fornication" while accusing white America of practicing "fraud" and repeating the sins of Babylon clearly placed Stewart in the camp of militant abolitionists, far closer to the radicalism of Garrison than the caution of Cornish and Russwurm.[21]

Boston's African-American community denounced Stewart's fiery discourse, saying it was unseemly for a woman to speak so boldly. In a graphic expression of their disapproval, local black men pelted Stewart with rotten tomatoes. Because of this sexual discrimination, in 1833 Stewart moved to New York and shifted her energies from journalism to education, eventually founding her own school for African-American children.

The country's first strident black abolitionist newspapers were the publishing enterprises of Frederick Douglass. Born into slavery about

1817, Douglass ran away from his Maryland plantation in 1838. With the support of abolitionists, Douglass became a riveting speaker who described from firsthand experience the most heinous dimensions of chattel slavery. His gift as a speaker and his intellectual acumen made him the most important African-American leader of the nineteenth century.

Douglass's most influential journalistic work was the *North Star*, a weekly he founded in Rochester, New York, in 1847. Douglass stated forthrightly, "The object of the *North Star* will be to attack Slavery in all its forms and aspects; Advocate Universal Emancipation; and hasten the day of FREEDOM to the Three Millions of our Enslaved Fellow Countrymen."[22]

Douglass modeled his paper after the *Liberator*, with his editorial tone and content mirroring Garrison's—differing only in that the black editor's writing had a grace the white editor's lacked. Douglass's prose was often informed by memories of his early life in bondage. An 1848 article read, "He is no other than a thief who calls *me* or *you* his own property, and if one sinner is such above all others, it is he who would inflict stripes upon a human being, and quote scripture in justification, as did a master of mine, when brutally flogging a female slave—'They who know their master's will and do it not, shall be beaten with many stripes.' The slaveholder is a depraved man."[23]

The *North Star*, widely respected for its intellectual rigor, was read not only in the United States but also in Europe and the West Indies. Its international distribution during an era when two-thirds of northern blacks and virtually all southern blacks were illiterate boosted circulation considerably. With five white subscribers for every African-American one, the *North Star* soon surpassed the *Liberator* with a circulation of 3,000.

Douglass was as uncompromising in his position as Garrison. In an article titled "The Slaves' Right to Revolt," he recalled Nat Turner's slave revolt, telling white readers that African Americans still remembered how Turner had been mercilessly tortured and killed: "He was stripped naked, and compelled to walk barefooted, some thirty yards, over burning coals, and, when he reached the end, he fell, pierced by a hundred American bullets!" Douglass then warned slave owners, "If you will imbrue your hands in the blood of your brethren, if you will crush and chain your fellow-men, do it at your own risk and peril!"[24]

Like Garrison, Douglass aroused not only the conscience of America but also the wrath of pro-slavery forces. Slavery supporters were furious that a black man had the audacity to speak with such defiance. The *New York Herald* demanded that Douglass be banished to Canada, and the *Albany Sunday Dispatch* denigrated Douglass as a "saucy nigger." The *Dispatch* encouraged readers to take action against Douglass, advising, "As a moderate sum of money would, doubtless, induce Douglass to go to Toronto or Kingston, in Canada, where he will be much more at home, the Rochester people will do well to buy him off."[25]

By mortgaging his home and soliciting financial support from England, Douglass continued publishing his paper, which in 1851 he renamed *Frederick Douglass' Paper*, for thirteen years—more than twice as long as any of its less militant predecessors.

So, by 1850, a sustained African-American press had emerged as an important source of racial pride and identity as well as a powerful instrument in the anti-slavery struggle. The evolution of the African-American press into a stable institution served several purposes. By providing firsthand descriptions of the brutality that defined slave life, the writing of Douglass and other former slaves destroyed the myth that southern masters were kind. In addition, the eloquence and high literary qualities of the work of women and men such as Stewart and Douglass undermined popular charges that black people were intellectually inferior. On a broader scale, creation of black abolitionist newspapers was a crucial step in establishing that the Abolition Movement would not be a phenomenon resting entirely on white shoulders.

Moving Abolition onto the National Agenda

Even though Americans historically have prided themselves on being a freedom-loving people, two of the landmark events in the history of this nation's first 100 years were armed conflicts. The Revolutionary War was the single most important event in eighteenth century America; the Civil War was the most important event of the nineteenth century. Both conflicts were fueled partly by economic factors—the American Revolution by colonial refusal to pay high taxes to the British, the Civil War by the incompatibility of the agrarian South with the industrializing North. In neither case, however, did economics alone propel citizens into open warfare, as emotional forces also played an essential role in igniting the conflicts. And, likewise, in both cases those emotional elements were articulated to the American people in the form of journalistic publications.

In the decades leading up to the war between the North and the South, the emotionalism was focused on the issue of slavery, and the journalistic force that placed that debate on the national agenda was the abolitionist press. Beginning in the 1830s, anti-slavery newspapers such as Rev. Elijah P. Lovejoy's *St. Louis Observer* and William Lloyd

Garrison's *Liberator* raised the consciousness of the nation to a sinful abomination in fundamental conflict with the ideals of democracy—and humanity. Garrison strategically positioned the *Liberator* at the center of the storm. The epitome of the activist editor, he calculated a formula by which his strident discourse, angry rhetorical conflicts with pro-slavery editors, and dramatic acts of public defiance would ensure that neither he nor his crusade would be ignored.

Between 1830 and 1850, the abolitionist press—black as well as white—succeeded in articulating and broadcasting throughout the nation the moral indictment of slavery that precipitated the Civil War and ultimately forced the "peculiar institution" into a dark corner of American history.

3

Slowing the Momentum for Women's Rights

In July 1848, a group of progressive-minded Americans announced a concept that some people considered every bit as revolutionary as colonists demanding their independence or slaves seeking their freedom. The American women and men who gathered in upper New York state said, simply and forthrightly, that liberty was not the province of men alone but also was—or should be—the birthright of women as well. The tangible product of their first historic meeting in Seneca Falls was a paraphrase of the Declaration of Independence reading, "We hold these truths to be self-evident: that all men *and women* are created equal." Despite the formidable resources, impressive commitment, sound logic, and noble purpose of this stalwart band of individuals, more than seven decades would pass before the crusaders were finally able to secure the fundamental right for American women to vote.[1]

One of the most serious impediments to the march toward gender equality was the same force that already had built a record as a highly influential institution in American history: the news media. For by the mid-nineteenth century, it had been firmly established that the Fourth Estate was a body overwhelmingly peopled by—and largely committed to serving—men. Threatened by the possibility that women might be rising from their second-class citizenship to command a share of the male power base, the men who dominated American journalism ignored the Women's Rights Movement or, when they did cover it, did so with mockery and disdain.

American journalism's oppressive treatment of women did not begin in Seneca Falls. From the beginning of the republic, the media had worked to limit women's role in society, with publications of the late eighteenth century systematically restricting half the population to a narrow existence that had become known as the women's sphere—essentially, the home. That strategy intensified with coverage of the Seneca Falls Women's Rights Convention in 1848 and remained firmly in place throughout the nineteenth century. Eventually, women's rights leaders decided they would have to follow the example of the abolitionists and create an entirely alternative publishing network—the suffrage press—in hopes of counteracting the male journalistic conspiracy that had blocked their progress. The feminists found that the male dictatorship was so pervasive, however, that even this separate communication network was impervious to it.

Confining the American Woman to Her Place

American women had begun making major contributions to society by colonial times, succeeding in such diverse fields as education, medicine, literature, law, and printing. Indeed, by 1777 Mary Katherine Goddard had become such a respected printer that the founders of the country sought her out to print the first official copy of the Declaration of Independence. Despite colonial women's many accomplishments, however, it became apparent after the American Revolution that women would not be beneficiaries of the rights of equality promised in the United States Constitution.

The founding fathers did not specifically state that women would be denied rights; they simply ignored them, failing to explore the possibility of defining women as part of "the people." Western political thought provided no context in which women had been included as part of the body politic, and this was one political convention that the male architects of democracy opted not to tamper with.

The average eighteenth century woman assumed her *place* in society based on her husband's identity. She was considered, by nature, to be incapable of serious thought or important decision making. In addition to not being allowed to vote, a woman could not retain property in marriage, even if she had owned that property before her wedding day. So in case of divorce, she retained neither the ownership of land nor the custody of children. She typically married at sixteen and gave birth to a child every two years through her forties. She usually lost a third of those children to early death, and she lost her own health—as well as her looks—by her mid-twenties.

Woman's limited role in society was promulgated through the editorial content in the publications of the era. Fundamental was the message that men's sphere encompassed all of business and politics, while women's sphere was restricted to the four walls of the home. This distinct division of roles had to be faithfully adhered to for the well-being of the country, according to the American media of the late 1700s and early 1800s, because women lacked the ability to succeed in the public world, as they were intellectually as well as physically inferior to men.

The primary publishing venue for disseminating these messages was the handful of women's magazines that emerged in the late eighteenth century. *Ladies Magazine*, founded in 1792, became the first American publication aimed exclusively toward women—although it was owned and published by a man. Other magazines, some exclusively for women and others for men as well as women, soon joined the Philadelphia monthly to create the first generation of periodicals that shaped the lives of American women—but did not advance their progress.

The narrow limits of women's abilities was a consistent theme in the magazines, through both their content and their paternalistic tone. Typical was an article in *Ladies Magazine* that bluntly stated, "The number of women who have solid judgment is very small." Another said of women, "Placed in a situation of difficulty, they have neither a head to dictate, nor a hand to help." *American Museum*, another magazine of the era, made the intellectual inferiority of women clear when it stated, "The author of nature has placed the balance of power on the side of the male, by giving him not only a body more large and robust, but also a mind endowed with greater resolution, and a more extensive reach."[2]

The message was that domesticity dominated women's very being because they were not capable of acting autonomously in the public sphere, and therefore only one path was appropriate for them: marrying a man. And once wed, a woman should place pleasing her husband above all other goals. *Ladies Magazine* announced, "To make her husband happy and contented will ever be her wish, not to say her greatest pleasure." Other magazines reinforced the message. *The Dessert to the True American* said women should "cultivate assiduously the arts of pleasing," adding that these were the "arts for which they are well qualified by nature." For women to refine this talent was crucial, the magazine contended, because pleasing others was the only way women could achieve a sense of fulfillment: "It is by the art of pleasing only that women can attain to any degree of consequence."[3]

The first generation of American women's magazines emphasized that it was essential for a girl to learn her proper place in society from an early age. *Ladies Magazine* deemed it essential for a young woman not to consider herself first, but always to place her father's, brother's, or husband's happiness before her own. The arbiter on women's roles stated, "A girl should be taught, that her peculiar province is to please, and that every deviation from it is opposing the design of nature." The magazine acknowledged—but certainly did not express regret—that this meant females should routinely subjugate their own desires. "A girl is to be taught that a degree of subjection is allotted her," the magazine said. "It is that state of subjection, for which nature has intended the female part of the creation, that makes it so necessary for girls to acquire a *habit of obedience*."[4]

While idealizing the docile woman who dedicated her life to pleasing her husband, the magazines criticized the woman who allowed temptations to interfere with her wifely duties. *Ladies Magazine* warned women that their natures dictated that they had to struggle constantly to resist woman's "almost irresistible inclination to pleasure" through such follies as shopping, dancing, playing cards, and gossiping. "The female nature constantly shows a greater proclivity to the gay and the amusive, than to the sober and useful scenes of life." And *Weekly Magazine* provided women with a checklist of some of the most common errors they committed when speaking; those mistakes ranged from women not "acknowledging his [a husband's] superior judgment" to women voicing their own opinions.[5]

Discrediting the Women's Rights Movement

The paternalistic tone that dominated late eighteenth and early nineteenth century magazines began to fade after the historic meeting in the summer of 1848. For as women made their first dramatic assault on men's political and economic stranglehold on American society, the Fourth Estate responded by replacing paternalism with unrestrained hostility.

The event that marked the beginning of the Women's Rights Movement in the United States unfolded in Seneca Falls, New York, because that small community was the home of Elizabeth Cady Stanton. The woman who ultimately became the movement's leading theorist, writer, and orator was born in Johnstown, New York, in 1815 and married abolitionist Henry B. Stanton. Her marriage was a happy one, but her husband's work often took him away from home, leaving her with their seven children and the boredom of homemaking in an isolated setting. Stanton initiated the Seneca Falls convention by placing a public notice in the *Seneca County Courier*: "A convention to discuss the social, civil and religious rights of women will be held in the Wesleyan Chapel, Seneca Falls, New York, on Wednesday and Thursday, the 19th and 20th of July."[6]

Some 300 people heeded Stanton's call. They included a large number of women, such as Lucretia Mott and Amelia Bloomer, whose confidence and organizational skills had been developed through their work within the Abolition and Temperance Movements. At the end of the two-day meeting, sixty-eight women and thirty-two men signed their names to a Declaration of Sentiments.

The signers directly challenged the concept of sex-segregated spheres. Their declaration read, "The history of mankind is a history of repeated injuries and usurpations on the part of man toward woman, having in direct object the establishment of an absolute tyranny over her." The twelve resolutions encouraged women to enter the professions and demanded that women be granted property and child custody rights.[7]

The most controversial resolution—the only one that did not pass unanimously—demanded woman's suffrage, stating: "*Resolved,* That it is the duty of the women of this country to secure to themselves their sacred right to the elective franchise." Only after an eloquent appeal by African-American leader Frederick Douglass did the resolution pass, and then only by a narrow margin.[8]

One of the less prominent statements in the Declaration of Sentiments was the comment that women's rights proponents would endeavor to enlist the press on behalf of their cause, while acknowledging, "In entering upon the great work before us, we anticipate no small amount of misconception, misrepresentation, and ridicule." How right they were.[9]

American newspapers responded to the convention with a toxic mixture of outrage, contempt, and mockery—all forms of social control designed to slow the advancement of women. Headlines ranged from "Women Out of Their Latitude" to "Insurrection Among the Women." The *Rochester Daily Democrat* vilified the demands as "impracticable, absurd, and ridiculous." The *Rochester Daily Advertiser* belittled the proposals by calling them "extremely dull," "uninteresting," and "hardly worth notice," while deriding women's rights advocates for attempting to transform the United States into a "petticoat empire." The *Mechanic's Advocate* in Albany criticized the resolutions as "impracticable, uncalled for, and unnecessary."[10]

Other newspapers contributed more disdainful comments. James Gordon Bennett of the *New York Herald,* one of the most influential newspapers in the country, called the Seneca Falls meeting a "Woman's Wrong Convention" that proved the country's "political and social fabric is crumbling to pieces," and the *Worcester Telegraph* in Massachusetts mocked the women at the meeting as "*Amazons*" who were "*bolting* with a vengeance." The *Philadelphia Ledger and Daily Transcript* asked antagonistically, "Whoever heard of a Philadelphia lady assisting to *man* the election grounds, raise a regiment, command a legion, or address a jury?" The paper summarized its position on women's rights perhaps more succinctly than any other journalistic voice of the era: "A woman is nobody. A wife is everything."[11]

The Seneca Falls convention was the first of many events designed to maintain the momentum of the Women's Rights Movement. By the early 1850s, Susan B. Anthony had emerged as an important complement to Stanton. Born in Adams, Massachusetts, in 1820, Anthony taught school for fifteen years before committing her life to reform efforts, beginning with temperance and abolition but eventually focusing on women's rights. Unmarried and willing to devote her abundant talents to the movement, Anthony brought to the movement, in particular, strengths as an intellect and organizer.

Stanton and Anthony combined their abilities to create a dynamic partnership at the head of the movement—Stanton forged the thunderbolts, Anthony hurled them. Hundreds of women's rights meetings, petition drives, and public lectures erupted all over the country during the 1850s, with many of them attracting thousands of supporters. The two women also organized a national convention almost every year from 1850 until the beginning of the Civil War in 1861. And after the war ended and the Fourteenth Amendment gave former male slaves the vote, the women intensified the campaign for their own enfranchisement.

Regardless of what the particular event was or where it took place, a flurry of hostile newspaper articles followed in its wake. The *Syracuse Star* derided an 1852 meeting in that city as the "Tomfoolery Convention," calling the three days of speeches and discussions a "mass of corruption, heresies, ridiculous nonsense, and reeking vulgarities which these bad women have vomited forth." After women attempted to take their campaign to the New York state legislature, the *Albany Daily State Register* angrily stated that women's rights advocates initially were amusing like "clowns in the circus" or "gentlemen with blackened faces." The newspaper then cast aside all sense of amusement, saying disdainfully: "The joke is becoming stale. The ludicrous is wearing away, and disgust is taking the place of pleasurable sensations, arising from this hypocrisy and infidel fanaticisms."[12]

In addition to trivializing the movement, the newspapers attacked feminists on the ground that they were abandoning their responsibilities in the home. Typical was a vitriolic article in the *Mechanic's Ad-*

vocate in Albany that excoriated women for attending women's rights activities "at the expense of their more appropriate duties." Because increased rights would destroy the traditional division between women's and men's spheres, the *Advocate* insisted, such a shift would "demoralize and degrade from their high sphere and noble destiny women of all respectable and useful classes, and prove a monstrous injury to all mankind. It would be productive of no positive good, that would not be outweighed tenfold by positive evil." James Gordon Bennett was a leader on this theme, thundering from the *New York Herald*'s editorial page that feminists were belying woman's true nature. He asked rhetorically: "How did woman first become subject to man, as she now is all over the world? By her nature, her sex, just as the negro is and always will be to the end of time, inferior to the white race and, therefore, doomed to subjection; but she is happier than she would be in any other condition, because it is the law of her nature."[13]

Newspapers carried this accusation of violating the laws of nature to the point that they equated supporting women's rights with committing a sin against God. The *Herald* screamed, "These ladies are, at least, trenching on immorality, and are in dangerous contiguity to, and companionship with, the most detestable of vices."[14]

The *New York Times* took the position that women already possessed so much political power that to grant them any more would deny men their equal share in governance. The *Times* editorial page lamented, "We regret to see how obstinately our American women are bent on appropriating more than their fair share of Constitutional privilege." The paper argued that if women insisted on securing voting rights, men would be forced to band together for their own political survival: "The time has come for the organization of a 'Rights of Man Association,' to withstand the greedy appropriativeness of womankind."[15]

In complete contradiction with that argument was another one that portrayed women as helpless and foolish children who had no idea what life was like beyond the protective environment of the home. The *New York Herald*, which soon became the movement's most inveterate opponent, referred to female leaders as having "weak and silly heads" and being "candidates for admission into lunatic asylums," saying the women obviously were misguided if they were eager to enter the wild-and-woolly world of politics. The *Herald* asked with mock disbelief: "What do the leaders of the woman's rights convention want? They want to vote and to hustle with the rowdies at the polls. They want to be members of Congress, and in the heart of debate subject themselves to coarse jests and indecent language."[16]

In an effort to discredit prominent leaders of the movement, newspapers attacked their unmarried status. Ignoring the fact that a nineteenth century wife had to devote such enormous effort to household chores that little time remained for activism, the papers characterized the single leaders, especially Anthony, as sexual freaks. The *New York Sun* wrote, "The quiet duties of daughter, wife or mother are not congenial to those hermaphrodite spirits who thirst to win the title of champion of one sex and victor over the other." The *Herald* added: "These women are entirely devoid of personal attractions. They are generally thin maiden ladies, having found it utterly impossible to induce any young or old man into the matrimonial noose."[17]

Newspapers routinely referred to women in the movement by such degrading terms as "poor creatures," "unfortunate women," "old maids," and "unsexed women," while calling men involved in the movement "Aunt Nancys," suggesting by innuendo that men who supported women's rights were either homosexual or totally dominated by their wives.[18]

Despite the scornful tone in virtually all mainstream newspapers that mentioned the subject of women's rights, Stanton believed all publicity was good publicity because it ultimately would help move women's rights onto the national agenda. Assessing the widespread coverage of the Seneca Falls convention, Stanton wrote in her personal correspondence: "There is no danger of the Woman Question dying for want of notice. Every paper you take up has something to say about it." Opting for the point of view that it was better to be deplored than ignored, Stanton continued: "Imagine the publicity given to our idea by thus appearing in a widely circulated sheet like the *Herald*. It will start women thinking, and men too; and when men and women think about a new question, the first step in progress is taken."[19]

Other women's rights advocates expressed similar sentiments. Lucretia Mott acknowledged in 1855 that the newspapers "ridiculed and slandered us" but was convinced, based on her work in the Abolition Movement, that the press goes "through three stages in regard to reforms; they first ridicule them, then report them without comment, and at last openly advocate them. We seem to be still in the first stage on this question [of women's rights]."[20]

Creating a Voice of Their Own

Visionary leaders such as Stanton and Anthony realized that in order for the Women's Rights Movement to succeed, the leaders would have to follow the example of the Abolition Movement and create their own alternative medium of communication.

In January 1868, Stanton and Anthony founded the *Revolution*. Based in New York City, the newspaper carried a masthead reading: "Men, Their Rights and Nothing More; Women, Their Rights and Nothing Less." As radical in content as in its title, the *Revolution* insisted that securing suffrage was merely the first step in the women's rights campaign. The paper argued, "The ballot is not even half the loaf; it is only a crust—a crumb." With Stanton as its driving editorial force, the *Revolution* espoused liberal views on a wide range of social issues, from abortion and prostitution to divorce and prison reform. Such controversial content alienated many potential readers and even more potential advertisers. Although the *Revolution* was initially funded by eccentric millionaire George Francis Train, its circulation never exceeded 3,000 and it ceased publication in 1870—surviving only two years and leaving $10,000 in unpaid bills.[21]

Not all feminists agreed on the breadth of the women's rights agenda, creating a major split in the movement. After Stanton and Anthony founded the National Woman Suffrage Association exclusively for women in July 1869, Lucy Stone and her husband Henry Blackwell formed the entirely separate and considerably less radical American Woman Suffrage Association in January 1870.

Stone then immediately founded *Woman's Journal*, a far less abrasive journalistic endeavor than the *Revolution*. The Boston-based *Woman's Journal* focused on suffrage and its importance to such middle-class efforts as establishing women's clubs and encouraging women to obtain higher educations. Rather than speaking in radical rhetoric, the *Journal* adopted the conventional journalistic writing style of an establishment newspaper. The bulk of the paper's contents reported on suffrage activities and legislative campaigns around the country, including verbatim transcripts of woman suffrage speeches and conventions. The newspaper's relatively moderate stands appealed to many Americans, giving *Woman's Journal* the support it needed to publish without a single interruption from 1870 through 1933, building a circulation of 6,000. What is more, the *Journal* was a real business, financed through a stock company, that achieved financial solvency.

The *Revolution* and *Woman's Journal* were by no means the only members of the suffrage press, as several dozen publications were created to spread the gospel of woman suffrage ideology. Most of them served local communities and were short-lived, as they struggled both for circulation and financial support during an era when most women had little independent income. The various journals also tended to be driven by an individual woman editor and aimed at an audience of middle- and upper-class white women. One exception was *Woman's Era*; the monthly newspaper was published and distributed nationally by Josephine St. Pierre Ruffin, a member of Boston's African-American elite, from 1890 to 1897. "The stumbling block in the way of even the most cultured colored woman is the narrowness of her environment," Ruffin wrote in *Woman's Era*. "It is to help strengthen this class and a better understanding between all classes that this little venture is sent out on its mission." A large number of the journals were published in the West, where many of the earliest advancements in woman's suffrage were made.[22]

It would be misleading, however, to suggest that the suffrage press was a major force in transforming American society's views on women's rights. Most of the publications did not build circulation figures beyond a few hundred, and the majority of those readers were already committed to the Women's Rights Movement. And unlike the fanatical William Lloyd Garrison and his *Liberator*, woman suffrage editors did not garner national attention by orchestrating spectacular public events—such as burning the Constitution during a Fourth of July celebration—or by provoking editorial screaming matches with mainstream editors who disagreed with them.

The most significant impact of the suffrage press was on the movement itself. The publications were able to bridge the gaps of time and space, providing an important tie that bound together women from different locations to create a grassroots social movement. During an era when mass transportation did not exist, a women's rights convention or lecture generally could not draw more than a few dozen people, but a journal could reach several hundred—including people living in rural areas. Once a publication arrived at a woman's home, it informed her of activities nationwide, articulated the ideology of feminist theorists, offered her arguments to use in her own community, and reinforced her sense of purpose. In fact, the very existence of a journal provided a tangible product that was vital to sustaining a long public campaign.

Intensifying the Attack

Even after many decades of women's rights activism, most of the mainstream press continued to express scorn toward the reform efforts. In fact, many of the male-dominated newspapers responded to the increasing power of women leaders not by tempering their campaign of ridicule and contempt, but by increasing the intensity and viciousness of their attacks.

During the final decades of the nineteenth century, mainstream newspapers focused much of their unrelenting assault on the personal characteristics of the most high-profile women. Typical was an article in the *New York Tribune,* the most widely read and respected newspaper in the country, that attacked the leaders, saying: "Our heart warms with pity towards these unfortunate creatures. We fancy that we can see them, deserted of men, and bereft of those rich enjoyments and exalted privileges which belong to women, languishing their unhappy lives away in a mournful singleness." That same year, the *New York World* sank to an equally low level of hate-filled rhetoric. One diatribe insulted everyone in the Women's Rights Movement by describing the women as "mummified and fossilated females, void of domestic duties, habits and natural affections" and the men as "crack-brained, rheumatic, dyspeptic, henpecked men."[23]

The most mean-spirited comments were written about Anthony. Newspapers continually ignored the substance of Anthony's discourse and focused instead on her appearance and her status as a "spinster." In 1866, even though Anthony was by that time a figure of international stature, the *World* demeaned her by referring to her by her first name, saying, "Susan is lean, cadaverous; with the proportions of a file and the voice of a hurdy-gurdy." In 1870, the *Utica Herald* in New York described Anthony in equally abusive language, asking: "Who does not feel sympathy for Susan Anthony? She has striven long and earnestly to become a man. She is sweet in the eyes of her own mirror, but her advanced age and maiden name deny that she has been so in the eyes of others." And in 1879, the *Richmond Herald* in Kentucky wrote, "Miss Anthony is uncomely in person, has rather coarse, rugged features and masculine manners."[24]

By the final decades of the nineteenth century, technical advances in paper and printing production had ushered a plethora of inexpensive magazines into the journalistic mix. Many of them attracted huge numbers of middle- and working-class readers by appealing to popular topics—including the various controversies involving women's rights. Articles such as "Manly Women" in *Saturday Review* and "Is Marriage a Failure?" in *Cosmopolitan* fueled the negative attitude toward the changing role of women.[25]

Perhaps the most incendiary of such articles was a series in *Nineteenth Century* magazine that painted a particularly unflattering portrait of the typical women's rights advocate as "that loud and dictatorial person, who suffers no one's opinion to influence her mind, no venerable law hallowed by time, nor custom consecrated by experience, to control her actions. Mistress of herself, the Wild Woman as social insurgent preaches the 'lesson of liberty' broadened into lawlessness." Like many journalistic voices before it, the magazine predicted that the rise of such women would be the downfall of civilization. The series also criticized women participating in such "violent" sports as golf and cricket.[26]

A drawing from Life *magazine depicted Elizabeth Cady Stanton as smug and grossly overweight, while portraying bespectacled Susan B. Anthony as grim and rail thin.*

Magazines exploited the emotional impact of images to lambaste women's rights advocates as well. Particularly adept at this technique was *Life* magazine, a forerunner of the photo magazine of the same name that would capture the imagination of the American public in the 1930s. The nineteenth century version of *Life* used line drawings to place the modern generation of liberated women in uncomplimentary poses. One showed a female minister preaching to an empty church; another depicted women smoking, drinking alcohol, and cavorting in a modern-day club for women. A two-page image in an 1896 issue was particularly memorable. It depicted an obese Stanton and a resolutely grim Anthony dressed in the uniforms of male naval officers in front of an all-woman Navy. The caption read: "The New Navy, about 1900 A.D."[27]

Victory Despite the Fourth Estate

After twenty years of separation, the two wings of the Women's Rights Movement united in 1890 to create the National American Woman Suffrage Association. The activists still, however, stood far from victory. Between 1870 and 1910, feminists waged nearly 500 campaigns in cities and states nationwide to place referenda before the voters, with only seventeen of those efforts actually even succeeding in bringing their issues to a vote.

Success did not begin in earnest until the early years of the twentieth century, when the Progressive Movement pushed reform and liberal social thought into the national spotlight. With regard to the Women's Rights Movement, this era of progress meant the feminist demands no longer seemed so radical compared to those of the men and women determined to remake American government and industry. The emphasis on efficiency and productivity that was key to the Progressive Movement manifested itself in a new generation of youthful leaders brimming with energy and pragmatic strategies centering on public agitation, direct confrontation, and political tactics. Sentiment and misty-eyed idealism would not prevent these hard-driving, resourceful women from achieving the first goal positioned squarely in their sights: woman suffrage.

The rise of the adept new generation was dramatically demonstrated in 1907 when Harriot Stanton Blatch, Elizabeth Cady Stanton's daughter, abandoned the stodgy National American Woman Suffrage Association to create what became the Women's Political Union. Adopting techniques from activist British women, Blatch broadened the American movement to appeal to working-class women and to organize the first suffrage parades, which immediately became a popular and productive device. Alice Paul, another young activist who admired the British model, began mobilizing public demonstrations to push hard for a Constitutional amendment. In 1913, Paul formed what later became the National Woman's Party. When her militant tactics led to women being harassed and even imprisoned, the American public finally began giving attention and support to the issue of woman suffrage. In the last phase of activism, Carrie Chapman Catt incorporated effective organization and political strategy into the movement. Catt's "winning plan," which she began in 1916, was a tactical and organizational masterpiece that pressured the House of Representatives into passing the Nineteenth Amendment in 1918. Two years later, after hard-fought battles in the Senate and then in the individual states, woman suffrage became the law of the land in August 1920—seventy-two years after the call had gone out at Seneca Falls.

Suffering from the Power of the Press

It was not until 1919 that mainstream American journalism finally began to treat the Women's Rights Movement as the major social and political revolution that it had for half a century promised to become. The majority of the press supported woman suffrage only after the Nineteenth Amendment had cleared the Senate and ratification by the states appeared inevitable. Until that time, establishment newspapers and magazines chose to portray the American woman as they had throughout the late eighteenth and early nineteenth centuries—as a physical and intellectual cripple who had to be cared for and protected much as a helpless child did. Even though such highly capable and remarkably resourceful women as Elizabeth Cady Stanton, Susan B. Anthony, and Lucy Stone were ably leading the intriguing and potentially far-reaching movement by the mid-nineteenth century, the American institution charged with informing the country's citizenry about social and political trends opted to treat this particular social movement—when it acknowledged the movement at all—with ridicule and hostility.

Coverage was so limited and so distorted that movement leaders had no choice but to create their own alternative means of communication. Largely because of the American woman's continued political, social, and economic repression, however, the woman's suffrage press—unlike the abolitionist press—was ineffective in shaping the public opinion of the majority of American society. Not until many decades passed and a new generation of militant activists took charge of the movement in the early 1900s did it finally begin to have the impact on the American mind that allowed women to secure the right of suffrage that they so clearly deserved.

The role American newspapers of the nineteenth century played in slowing the momentum for women's rights is an example of the press abusing the mighty power it wields. Had the Fourth Estate mobilized that power as a positive force in support of the Women's Rights Movement, there is no question that half the American citizenry would have been granted its rightful voice in the democratic process far earlier than ultimately was the case. Nor would the nineteenth century provide the only example of the American news media slowing women's march toward equality. Many observers have noted that the news media's attitude toward women's rights would not change until the few women involved in journalism advanced to positions as editors and other policy makers. Anthony created a vivid image supporting this point of view in 1893 when she told the *Chicago Tribune*: "If the men own the paper—that is, if the men control the management of the paper—then the women who write for these papers must echo the sentiment of these men. And if they do not do that, their heads are cut off."[28]

4

Attacking Municipal Corruption: The Tweed Ring

THE TWEED RING RULED New York City in the 1860s and early 1870s like no political machine before or since. Payoffs, kickbacks, padded contracts, extortion, election fraud—they were all part of what came to personify big-city corruption by profligate public "servants." William Marcy Tweed and the band of political henchmen who did his bidding ultimately stuffed their pockets with some $200 million taken from city taxpayers.

This crime against democracy was finally exposed by an unlikely antagonist: cartoons. For Thomas Nast's illustrations in *Harper's Weekly* gave the evil profiteering of the Tweed Ring a face, and that face appalled and enraged the people of New York. In a political crusade that spanned three years, the courageous editorial cartoonist attacked municipal corruption with a vengeance. By defying "Boss" Tweed when other journalists accepted Tweed's payoffs, Nast provided one of the earliest examples of the dramatic power that journalistic images can wield.

A year after Nast began attacking Tweed in *Harper's*, the *New York Times* joined the crusade, putting into words the accusations that Nast was communicating through pictures. When the *Times* published secret documents laying bare the extent of the ring's sordid activities, the series hastened the end of the corruption.

Nast deserves the most credit. The passion and impact of his unrelenting visual attacks stand alone in the annals of American editorial cartooning. Even Tweed himself ultimately came to acknowledge that

Nast had destroyed him, saying: "I didn't care a straw for the newspaper articles—my constituents didn't know how to read. But they couldn't help but see them damned pictures." This assault by a journalistic David on a political Goliath stands as a stunning example of how the news media have shaped history.[1]

Heyday of Corruption

After the Civil War, the United States underwent fundamental changes at a dizzying pace. Many of the changes had their roots in the confluence of three phenomena of immense dimension—urbanization, industrialization, and immigration. These powerful forces opened the door to wholesale corruption in politics as well as business, and an army of opportunists took advantage of the fluid situation for their personal gain, creating what became known as the Gilded Age.

William Marcy Tweed was born in New York City in 1823. After working briefly as a city fireman, Tweed entered ward politics and a career in the public realm. His ascendancy up New York's political hierarchy between 1864 and 1869 was eased by his membership in Tammany Hall, a classic urban political organization of the nineteenth century. The Society of Saint Tammany had been founded soon after the American Revolution as a social and patriotic club that vowed to oppose New York's moneyed interests. By 1850, however, Tammany Hall had created its own Democratic Party power base and had mushroomed into a potent force in city politics that skillfully manipulated the electorate.

Tweed, at the height of his control from 1869 to 1871, wielded enormous influence because of his many political and municipal connections. He was, simultaneously, the highest official of Tammany Hall, chairman of the New York Democratic Party Central Committee, a member of both the New York County Board of Supervisors and the New York State Senate, director of New York City's Department of Public Works, and construction supervisor for the New York County Court House. Also, in a blatant example of conflict of interests, Tweed had become one of the city's largest real estate magnates, with his property holdings valued at $12 million. In these various capacities, Tweed gained control of the state legislature, County Board of Supervisors, City Board of Aldermen, and the judicial network for the entire state.

"Boss" Tweed's actions were supported by a cabal of Tammany Hall cronies led by New York Mayor A. Oakey "Elegant Oakey" Hall, City Controller Richard B. "Slippery Dick" Connolly, and City Parks Director Peter B. "Brains" Sweeny. These four men had their thumbs on every facet of New York government, using their political muscle to make the city treasury their own.

Tweed's political strength was built on his uncanny ability to find a common denominator between the various levels of New York society. He could ingratiate himself to the most highly respected bankers and judges at the top of the social scale while simultaneously maintaining connections with low-level politicians, immigrant factory workers, and mindless ruffians.

Tweed maintained his position by handing out payoffs that came either directly or indirectly from the city treasury. Hundreds of thousands of dollars went to lobby the state legislature to ensure the laws it approved were those that the Tweed Ring wanted, and lesser sums bought votes at the ballot box and "judicial" decisions in the courtroom. Most of the payoffs for his constituents, who were overwhelmingly from the city's immigrant poor, came in the form of city jobs. The number of patronage positions Tweed doled out to keep the city's political machine well lubricated ultimately totaled some 60,000.

Tweed also developed an intricate kickback system to support this ever-growing political organization and amass an obscene quantity of wealth for himself and his associates. The unwritten procurement policy was that the ring received 65 percent of all city contracts. The contractors learned to take this policy into account when bidding for city projects.

The political boss spent his bounty with conspicuous abandon. In particular, his daughter's wedding became one of the marvels of the Gilded Age. Her wedding gown cost $4,000, with $1,000 going for accessories and $20,000 for food and drink. The lavish event was not all spending, however, as Tweed's political friends showered his daughter with some forty sets of sterling silver and fifteen sets of diamond jewelry. In all, the princess of the Tweed Ring received gifts valued at more than $100,000.

Though Tweed's abuse of the city coffers was an open secret in political circles, no one possessed sufficient power and independence—or want—to curtail it. But it was in his control over the newspapers that his success in averting public clamor was the most insidious. In 1862, New York aldermen passed a resolution to pay individual reporters $200 a year for "services" to the city, and in the expansive manner of Tammany Hall this figure had been increased tenfold. Even more fundamental to the administration's ability to influence the content of the newspapers was the city advertising budget. Tweed subsidized the largest papers in the city—the *World*, *Herald*, and *Post*—by annually placing some $80,000 worth of city advertising in each. During the ring's reign of corruption, the city treasury funneled $7 million to the newspapers in exchange for their silence.[2]

With the Fourth Estate joining the executive, legislative, and judicial branches all suppressed under the ring's mighty thumb, it seemed that no one had a meaningful response to Tweed's insouciant challenge: "Well, what are you going to do about it?"

Pictures Confront Politics

Thomas Nast was born in Germany in 1840, and his family immigrated to New York in 1846, drawn to America by the dual appeals of personal freedom and economic opportunity.

Young Nast showed an early talent for drawing and joined the staff at *Harper's Weekly* in 1862. The New York–based magazine assiduously aimed its content at common laborers, following the motto, "Never shoot over the heads of the people." This philosophy lifted the magazine's national circulation to 100,000, making it the largest publication in the country. As social and political cartoonist for *Harper's*, Nast soon proved himself to be an artist whose social commentary could move vast audiences. In 1864, the most important American art critic of the day, James Jackson Jarves, wrote: "Nast is an artist of uncommon abilities. He has composed designs of allegorical, symbolical, or illustrative character, far more worthy to be transferred in paint to the wall-space of our public buildings than anything that has as yet been placed on them. They evince originality of conception, freedom of manner, lofty appreciation of national ideas and action, and a large artistic instinct."[3]

During a *Harper's Weekly* career spanning more than twenty years, Nast crafted some 3,000 drawings. Perhaps the most legendary symbols to emerge from his pencil were the Republican elephant and Democratic donkey. Others to his credit included the cap and dinner pail to represent the working man and the classic Santa Claus with his rosy cheeks and jolly demeanor—one familiar to Tommy Nast during his childhood in Germany.

In the early 1860s, Nast focused on capturing the nobility as well as the tragedy of the Civil War. After the war had ended and Ulysses S. Grant was asked to name the person who was most responsible for saving the country, the general responded, "Thomas Nast. He did as much as any one man to preserve the Union and bring the war to an end." President Lincoln praised Nast as well, saying, "His cartoons have never failed to arouse enthusiasm and patriotism, and have always seemed to come just when those articles were getting scarce."[4]

Thomas Nast was one of the most influential political cartoonists in the history of American journalism. Reprinted by permission of the Library of Congress.

So by the late 1860s when the country was changing more rapidly than it ever had before, Nast was well positioned to begin an assault on the most corrupt city administration in the history of American politics.

Nast began his crusade in September 1869. Initial caricatures were aimed at Tammany Hall. One depicted New York Governor John Hoffman, a stalwart Tammany Democrat, with the slogan "'Peter the Great' Chief of the Tammany Tribe," suggesting Tammany leaders were taking on the tyrannical bearing of Russian czars. Tweed remained in the background of those early cartoons. In a scene showing self-righteous Catholic bishops giving the Pope huge trunks labeled "Tax Payers' and Tenants' Hard Cash," Tweed was depicted only as one of the many bishops—albeit one of the most corpulent.[5]

As Nast's crusade developed, however, Tweed's profile rose. In particular, Nast used Tweed's ostentatious symbols of power to redefine the corrupt politician's public image. Nast took the very marks of respectability and success that Tweed cherished, such as a $15,000 diamond stickpin, and made them exemplars of greed and crudity. Nast also dressed Tweed and his coconspirators in striped outfits reminiscent of prison uniforms. He consistently mocked Tweed as bloated, coarse, and gluttonous—a man who feasted on the richest of foods while the city's poor went hungry.

Through the relentless strokes of Nast's artful pencil, the dignity and spoils of political office were rendered liabilities. Nast made it first possible and then popular for the citizens of New York to laugh at the man whose iron grip controlled every element of their lives. Through the journalistic artwork that appeared week after week in *Harper's*, the public began to see Tweed no longer as a hero, but as a rapacious scoundrel.

The New York Times *Joins the Assault*

The fall of 1870 marked a turning point in the journalistic campaign against the Tweed Ring. Until that time, James B. Taylor had been a member of the board of directors at the *New York Times*. Because Taylor's New York Printing Company received massive advertising contracts from city hall, Taylor prevented the *Times* editorial staff from speaking out against Tweed. Instead, the *Times* joined other New York newspapers in reaping the financial profits of a cozy relationship with the ring. Late in the summer of 1870, however, Taylor died. A month later, the *Times* ran its first anti-Tweed editorial.

That accusation began with a pointed request, "We should like to have a treatise from Mr. Tweed on the art of growing rich in as many years as can be counted on the fingers of one hand." It then shifted to a personalized narrative style that readers could relate to: "Most of us have to work very hard for a subsistence, and think ourselves lucky if, in the far vista of years, there is a reasonable prospect of comfort and independence. But under the blessed institution of Tammany, the laws which govern ordinary human affairs are powerless. You begin with nothing, and in five or six years you can boast of your ten millions." The editorial ended with a sweeping indictment: "There is foul play somewhere."[6]

Meanwhile, *Harper's* kept up its barrage. Nast created one of his most inspired cartoons by translating into a compelling image the rumors that Tweed had bought his influence in the Democratic Party—using money from city taxpayers, of course. The caption read "The 'Brains,'" and the cartoon showed Tweed's rotund body with his head replaced by a bag of money marked with a huge dollar sign where his mouth should have been. Beneath the biting caricature, Nast placed Tweed's trademark retort: "'Well, what are you going to do about it?'"[7]

The harsh depictions angered Tweed, whose political instincts told him the journalistic attacks were gaining momentum. In particular, he became concerned about the impact Nast's cartoons could have on the New York working class that represented his political base. Tweed told his political cronies: "If those picture papers would only leave me alone, I wouldn't care for all the rest. The people get used to seeing me in stripes, and by and by grow to think I ought to be in prison." Tweed knew that in order for his despotic methods to continue, the press—especially Nast—had to be persuaded to end its crusade. He ordered his hired thugs: "Stop them damned pictures."[8]

First, Tweed sent a banker to tell Nast that local art benefactors so admired his work that they were offering him $100,000—twice his annual salary at *Harper's*—to travel to Europe and study art. Recognizing the offer as a thinly masked bribe to get him out of New York, Nast declined. The banker then upped the offer, first to $200,000 and then to $500,000. At this point, Nast terminated the discussions, vowing to put Tweed in jail. Before departing, the banker warned Nast, "Dead artists don't draw." Not long after hearing that statement, Nast noticed strangers loitering near his Manhattan home. So, for safety's sake, he moved his family to suburban New Jersey.[9]

When neither bribery nor intimidation succeeded in stopping Nast, Tweed tried extortion. Using his power over city contracts, the

THE "BRAINS"

THAT ACHIEVED THE TAMMANY VICTORY AT THE ROCHESTER DEMOCRATIC CONVENTION.

One of Thomas Nast's most famous cartoons depicted "Boss" Tweed with a rotund physique, a diamond stickpin, and a bag of money instead of a face. Reprinted from Harper's Weekly.

dissolute politician attempted to control Nast by squeezing the organization that published his magazine, Harper Brothers Publishing Company. All Harper bids to sell textbooks to city schools were rejected, and Harper textbooks already in the classrooms were thrown away—more than $50,000 worth of public property was destroyed. *Harper's Weekly* not only remained committed to Nast's crusade but incorporated Tweed's scheme into it. A cartoon showed Tweed knocking a Harper Brothers textbook from a student's school desk and cuffing the child. On the classroom blackboard were written the sarcastic words: "Sweed is an honest man" and "Tweeny is an angel."[10]

After the *Times* joined *Harper's* in the crusade, Tweed also tried to silence that publication. When *Times* publisher Henry J. Raymond died, his estate put one third of the company's shares on the market. In 1871, Tweed representatives attempted to buy the shares, hoping to quiet the opposition. The new publisher, George Jones, turned down the offer and found another buyer. When the *Times* turned up the heat even further, the ring went to Jones and offered $1 million for the newspaper's silence. Jones refused, telling his readers, "The public may feel assured that the *Times* will not swerve from the policy which it has long pursued, but that it will hereafter be more persistent than ever in its efforts to bring about those political reforms which the people require and expect."[11]

A Tammany Man Blows the Whistle

The *Times* made good on that promise in July 1871 when it entered into a secret arrangement with James O'Brien, a former supporter of the Tweed Ring who had served as city sheriff but who held a grudge against the ring for not treating him as well as he thought he deserved. The vengeful defector obtained copies of hundreds of documents from the city controller and gave them to the *Times*. Armed with the documents, the *Times* published a blockbuster series of articles and editorials that exposed a variety of criminal acts.

The first articles showed that the city was paying exorbitant rents for two dozen buildings purportedly used as National Guard armories. The *Times* reported not only that the city was paying $190,000 a year to rent buildings that were completely empty but also that the properties had a fair-market rental value of only $46,000. The *Times* reproduced documents that showed the profits were being funneled to James Ingersoll, Tweed's brother-in-law.[12]

The second and even more explosive round of stories focused on Tweed's fraudulent activities related to the construction of the new county court house. In 1854, an architect estimated the building would cost $250,000. Anyone involved in construction anticipates modest cost overruns, but no one could have expected that by the time the project was completed in 1872 the price tag would have skyrocketed to an incredible $12.5 million—fifty times the original estimate!

Every day for a month, the *Times* exposed one phenomenal misappropriation after another. Ingersoll's bill to the city for three tables and forty chairs: $180,000. A month's work by a single carpenter: $360,000. Carpeting: $566,000. Light fixtures: $1.2 million. Cabinets: $2.8 million. Furniture: $5.7 million.[13]

One of the most eye-popping expenditures was to plasterer Andrew J. Garvey. The *Times* spread the invoices for his courthouse work across its front page, showing that his total charges amounted to $2.9 million. Commenting on these figures, the *Times* editorial page wrote sarcastically of Garvey, "Andrew J. Garvey is clearly the prince of plasterers."[14]

The *Times* pulled no punches in either the terms it used to describe the greedy law breakers or the headlines it created to label the stories. The paper called the men "thieves of the ring," "swindlers," "municipal thieves," and the "city's plunderers," while describing their acts as "gigantic frauds" and "frauds upon the people." Headlines ranged from "Proofs of Theft" and "More Ring Villainy" to "The Betrayal of Public Liberties" and "How the Public Money Is Embezzled by the Tammany Rulers."[15]

Such hard-hitting news did not remain a local story for long. Within days of the first revelation, the nation's newspapers began reprinting *Times* stories, adding their own words of outrage. The *Philadelphia Press* said, "The wholesale robbery practiced by the Democratic government of New York city is being clearly shown us by the *Times*, which is pushing the work of exposure with commendable zeal." The *Daily Advertiser* in Boston began its summary of the disclosures, "The New York Times is doing New York and the whole country excellent service by its bold warfare on Tammany." The *Providence Daily Journal* weighed in with, "The exposure of the *Times* will have a wholesome effect upon State and Nation." The *Chicago Tribune* wrote, "The days of the Ring are numbered."[16]

The New York newspapers that received substantial advertising revenue from the city responded to the *Times* investigation very differently. The politically independent *New York Herald* published little about the exposé except to criticize the *Times* as being "sensationalistic" and "over-excited." The *Herald* went on to accuse the *Times*, which generally supported the Republican Party, of being driven primarily by the political harm the scandal would cause Democrats, "We are led to the opinion that its case is vastly exaggerated, and may be fairly suspected as a violent effort for a party sensation." The *New York Tribune* questioned whether the *Times* had acted with professional integrity in publishing financial accounts secured "surreptitiously."[17]

The strongest defense of Tweed and his allies came from the Democratic *New York World*, which reprinted none of the accusations. In fact, two days after the *Times* began its bruising exposé, the *World* thanked Tammany Hall for bringing "energy," "system," and "order" to the city. The *World* also castigated *Times* editors as "slanderers," "slam-bangers," and "radicals" intentionally overstating the negative aspects of the city's Democratic administration in order to divert the country's attention away from the "monstrous corruption" being carried out by President Ulysses S. Grant and other Republicans in Washington. The *World* wrote, "Abuse that is poured out like water day by day, that never ceases, that is never qualified by one word of praise, must be extravagant, and prompted by party bitterness rather than a desire for the public good."[18]

The *Times* responded to the rival papers by accusing them of being bought off by Tweed. The *Times* wrote: "We voluntarily rejected the City advertising when we found that it could only be had at the cost of gagging the paper. We demand to see a list of the amounts the city has paid to all newspapers during the last three years." To questions regarding the veracity of the material it reported, the *Times* challenged city officials to sue for libel if the information was incorrect. When no suit materialized, the *Times* argued that Tweed and his cronies had, thereby, admitted their guilt. "The Tweed Ring admits the truth of our charges and the accuracy of our figures," the newspaper crowed. "Let the public judge between us."[19]

Based on the flood of letters the *Times* received, the public clearly sided with the newspaper. One read, "In telling you that never before were the columns of your paper employed for a better purpose, I know that I am but echoing the sentiments of all honest and law-abiding citizens who desire to see the reputation of our City upheld." Other words of encouragement included, "Keep on and you will soon bury 'the Ring'" and "Thanks, thanks, a thousand thanks for your fearless articles. These fattening hogs have had too long a rest." Many letter writers identified themselves as former Tammany faithfuls who had abandoned the organization because of the press revelations; one defector wrote, "I hope you will continue persistently and fearlessly in the course you have taken."[20]

Reaching the Masses

The only criticism voiced in the hundreds of letters was a concern that the august *Times* was not reaching the New York laboring class. The *Times* took a big step toward speaking to that group when it printed 200,000 copies of a news supplement summarizing the charges against city officials. The most extraordinary aspect of the four-page special section was that, in hopes of reaching the city's huge immigrant population, it was written both in English and in German, marking the only time in the *New York Times's* century and a half of publishing that it was produced in a foreign language.[21]

The *Times* special supplement notwithstanding, Thomas Nast's work in *Harper's Weekly* was more successful at reaching a broad readership. Although the *Times*'s work was unparalleled in its detail and documentation, articles were not easily accessible to New Yorkers of lower educational levels. Indeed, the mind-numbing lists straight from account ledgers were difficult even for the most learned readers to comprehend. For many people, Nast's mode of communicating through images, therefore, was much more successful because the cartoons translated the *Times*'s complicated accounting and numerical evidence into passionate and outraged indictments that appealed to a citizen's basic sense of right and wrong. Because he trafficked in images rather than huge blocks of words, Nast also was able to overcome the language difference and high illiteracy rate in nineteenth century New York—even people who did not buy *Harper's* saw Nast's images being hawked by newsboys on street corners throughout the city.

Nast picked up the major themes in the *Times* charges and brought them to life in a way that only images could. An August 1871 *Times* editorial said pointedly, "What the public wants to know is *who stole the money*?" Nast's next cartoon showed Tweed and his chums standing in a circle, with each pointing to the man to his right. The caption read: "'Who Stole the People's Money?'—Do tell *N.Y. Times*." Nast amplified another *Times* headline—"Will it 'Blow Over?'"—by depicting Tweed and his accomplices as plump vultures standing on top of a pile of bones marked "New York City Treasury," "Law," "Justice," and "Liberty." The caption read: "A Group of Vultures Waiting for the Storm to 'Blow Over'—'Let us *Prey*.'"[22]

Triumph of the Press

As state and municipal elections approached in the fall of 1871, *Harper's* and the *Times* combined forces in an all-out attack aimed at catapulting the Tweed Ring out of office. One Nast cartoon showed a crowd of laborers looking into a safe labeled "N.Y. Treasury" but finding only pieces of paper marked "debts," while behind the safe Tweed and his cohorts toasted each other with glasses of champagne. The caption: "What are you going to do about it?" Another drawing, this one on the cover of the magazine, showed the four frightened men cowering as four nooses loomed in the background.[23]

Meanwhile, the journalistic crusade finally had aroused the New York citizenry to organize in opposition to the ring. When a public meeting was called to discuss the accusations *Harper's* and the *Times* had made, 3,000 men and women packed the hall. A Committee of Seventy evolved from the meeting, charged with investigating city officials. The committee's first act was to petition one of the city's few remaining honest judges for a court order to prevent officials from any further spending. Based on the cartoons and articles, the judge granted the court order.

The journalists maintained their pressure. On the eve of the 1871 city election, Nast co-opted Tammany Hall's signature emblem to his purposes. For years, corrupt politicos had used a ferocious tiger as a symbol of the Democratic administration's power. But now Nast transformed the mascot into the "Tammany Tiger" as a symbol of the Tweed Ring raging out of control and ravaging the city and its peoples. In a double-page drawing distributed two days before the election, Nast drew the tiger—with eyes glaring and jaws distended—in the Roman Coliseum where the arena was strewn with the mangled bodies of figures labeled "the law," "the republic," and "the ballot." While the savage tiger ripped the bodies apart, Tweed and his comrades in crime, dressed in togas reminiscent of the final days of the Roman Empire, looked on from their thrones high above the arena. The caption asked New York voters: "The Tammany Tiger Loose—'What are you going to do about it?'" The image was one of Nast's most powerful and most influential. Tweed's opponents reprinted it and distributed it broadly on election day, taking particular care that the image was visible in the city's poorest neighborhoods.[24]

Harper's generally allowed Nast's cartoons to speak for themselves, but on the eve of this momentous event the magazine reinforced the message in a dramatic editorial printed next to the drawing. It began: "The contest in New York is that of the whole country. It involves a great deal more than the punishment of individual swindlers and the recovery of more or less money. The question is whether free institutions can rescue themselves from corruption. If the utmost power of corruption can be baffled peacefully and legally, it will be the noblest vindication of the popular system in history." The editorial ended: "Forward, then, and God speed the right!"[25]

When the votes were counted, the ring had been swept from office. Tweed was the only Tammany candidate who won reelection, thanks to massive ballot fraud. Regardless of what illicit means Tweed had used, the victory was a hollow one because he was left without a single ally. The election was a staggering defeat for the ring. Nast's next

The Tammany Tiger Loose. —"What Are You Going To Do About It?"

This dramatic cartoon distributed throughout the city of New York on the eve of the 1871 city election depicted Tammany Hall as a savage tiger and helped turn the public against the Tweed Ring. Reprinted from Harper's Weekly.

cartoon showed Tweed as a naked Roman soldier surrounded by crumbling columns—the empire had fallen.[26]

Late in 1871, Tweed was indicted on a variety of fraud-related charges and named conspirator in a multi-million-dollar civil suit filed by the citizens of New York. In 1873, he was sentenced to twelve years in prison. Several of his political accomplices were tried as well, although most of them fled to foreign countries.

Tweed's final years unfolded with a series of bizarre twists. In 1876, he bribed his way out of jail and escaped to Cuba and then to Spain. His plan was foiled, however, because of his long-standing nemesis: Thomas Nast. American law enforcement officials, in hopes of locating Tweed, circulated an image of the fugitive to law enforcement officials in countries around the world. The particular image they chose was one from *Harper's* that showed Tweed, dressed in prison stripes, grabbing two young boys and shaking the last few pennies from their pockets. Spanish officials did not read English, but—ironically—arrested Tweed based on Nast's image, assuming the fat man in prison

Based on this Thomas Nast cartoon, Spanish law enforcement officials captured and deported "Boss" Tweed not for political corruption but for kidnapping. Reprinted from Harper's Weekly.

stripes was a "child stealer." So the officials arrested Tweed not for political corruption but for kidnapping.[27]

Spanish officials deported Tweed to New York, where he was returned to jail. The powerful kingpin did not fare well behind bars. Because Tweed had grown grossly overweight from indulging in too much alcohol and rich food, his health went the way of his power. He died in 1878, at the age of fifty-five.

The Journalistic Legacy

Harper's Weekly and the *New York Times* both received paeans for the leading role they played—by combining compelling visual images with relentless verbal attacks—in destroying William Marcy Tweed and his band of disreputable rogues. Ministers across the country showered the publications with flowery blessings from the pulpit; President Grant and rising star Theodore Roosevelt were among the many elected officials who sought to enhance their political fortunes by claiming close allegiance to the press heroes.

For *Harper's*, one of the most eloquent commendations came from its closest competitor, *The Nation*. The progressive magazine wrote: "To Mr. Nast it is hardly possible to award too much praise. He has carried political illustrations to a pitch of excellence never before attained in this country, and has secured for them an influence on opinion such as they never came near having in any country." In particular, the magazine praised the power of the image to reach the masses, saying of Nast, "It is right to say that he brought the rascalities of the Ring home to hundreds of thousands who never would have looked at the figures and printed denunciations, and he did it without once being weak or paltry."[28]

For the *Times*, the strongest applause came from other newspapers. The *Milwaukee Sentinel*'s words were typical: "Truth has been crushed to earth in the metropolis of 'these United,' which has been so long and so badly affected with the malaria of corruption and falsehood. The truth that 'truth will rise again' has been rendered clear. 'The *Times* to the rescue' has been heard; and, hearing the call, it has done its duty fearlessly and well."[29]

Readers also expressed exuberant appreciation for the heroic feat the publications had accomplished on their behalf. During the two years that *Harper's* pummeled Tweed, its circulation tripled, rising from a respectable 100,000 to a remarkable 300,000. In that same period, not only did the *Times* circulation increase 40 percent and the value of a share of its stock soar from $6,000 to $11,000 but the paper was set firmly on course to becoming the country's undisputed newspaper of record.

Far more important than what the destruction of the Tweed Ring meant for the individual publications, however, was the profound significance of what the victory said about American journalism. In a *Harper's Weekly* editorial praising not itself but the *Times*, the magazine wrote: "The significance of the political victory in New York can scarcely be exaggerated. The result is the triumph of a free and fearless press."[30]

The crushing defeat of the Tweed Ring showed the world that democracy could—when kindled by the noble institution of a free press—cleanse itself of an evil so pervasive that it infected all three official branches of government. History recorded an unequivocal example of the Fourth Estate fulfilling its role as government watchdog, as well as a stunning example of the news media clearly helping to shape history.

5

Journalism as Warmonger: The Spanish-American War

AT THE END OF THE nineteenth century, American imperialism and journalistic dynamism came together to create one of the darkest moments in the history of American journalism. The United States raced onto the global stage as a world power, eager both to flex its muscles and to expand its geographic and economic boundaries. Journalism bounded forward as well, driven by a desire to reach the surging population and by technological innovations that improved how news was pursued and packaged—the typewriter, telephone, half-tone engraving, and automated press among them.

The changing news business attracted entrepreneurs who saw journalism as an exciting frontier worthy of their creative talents. Two publishing visionaries in particular dominated the era and ultimately changed the profession, as well as the world: Joseph Pulitzer and William Randolph Hearst. After they revolutionized journalism, their bitter rivalry gave birth to the double-barreled brand of sensationalism known as yellow journalism. Its toxic formula—one part news to two parts hype—was devised to fuel the infamous Hearst-Pulitzer circulation war.

Yellow journalism took on a life of its own after Hearst began championing, mainly to boost circulation, the cause of Cuban rebels seeking to break the Spanish shackles that bound them to colonial status. As Hearst's campaign intensified and Pulitzer joined in, the Cuban crusade led to a level of irresponsible and unethical behavior that redefined the limits of the shameful acts the news media can commit—

from distortion and the staging of events to disinformation and the systematic manufacturing of news. The grotesque sensationalism that Hearst and Pulitzer practiced, especially their coverage of the 1898 explosion of the battleship U.S.S. *Maine,* created a high-pitched and bumptious jingoism and a national hunger for war. That public frenzy ultimately pushed the president of the United States to abandon his antiwar policy and thrust America into a war with Spain that, in a less hysterical climate, may have been avoided.

The *New York Evening Post* was among the newspapers that, on the eve of the Spanish-American War, denounced the yellow journals as "sinners," "public evils," and "a national disgrace." The *Post* wrote caustically: "Every one who knows anything about 'yellow journals' knows that everything they do and say is intended to promote sales. No one—absolutely no one—supposes a yellow journal cares five cents about the Cubans, the *Maine* victims, or anyone else." The *New York Times,* by this time setting a standard of excellence in American journalism, expressed a similar view. The *Times* acknowledged that the "freak journals" Hearst and Pulitzer published while "raving for revenues" possessed the combination of power and potency that they "might very well suffice to force a declaration of war." In an extraordinary call for legal restrictions on freedom of the press, the *Times* concluded, "It is a defect in the law that so reckless and dangerous a treatment of grave international questions should not be unlawful."[1]

Joseph Pulitzer Pioneers a New Journalism

Born in Hungary in 1847, Joseph Pulitzer came to the United States as a mercenary fighting for the North in the Civil War. While still in his teens, he drifted west and wrote for a German-language newspaper in St. Louis. By working ferociously, the reporter—taunted by his competitors as "Joey the Jew"—was able to buy one bankrupt newspaper and merge it with another to create the *St. Louis Post-Dispatch.*

Beginning in 1878, Pulitzer pioneered a new style of newspapering. This new approach targeted the masses of American humanity who previously had been ignored by the comparatively staid sheets of the older order. According to Pulitzer's revolutionary concept, newspapers should be cheap, should be written clearly and concisely, and should actively crusade in the community interest. What's more, the facts Pulitzer highlighted on page one were to be gathered and written with an emphasis on accuracy unknown to his journalistic predecessors. He vowed, "Accuracy is to a newspaper what virtue is to a woman."[2]

Pulitzer joined the Democratic Party and led St. Louis in such reform initiatives as exposing fraud at the polls, putting an end to high profits and poor service by gas and streetcar monopolies, and closing city brothels and gambling halls. Pulitzer built the *Post-Dispatch* into a financial success that pushed the once-penniless immigrant's annual income to $200,000.

In 1883, Pulitzer broke into the biggest market in the country, targeting his *New York World* at the huge new urban laboring class. The legendary "people's paper" was committed to being readable and sincerely dedicated to serving the masses by exposing fraud and fighting public evils.

Pulitzer's innovative enterprise was not, however, without controversy. Many erudite New Yorkers denounced the *World* as cheap and vulgar. They accused Pulitzer of introducing multicolumn illustrations and dramatic headlines—such as "Baptized in Blood" and "A Child Flayed Alive: A Brutal Negro Whips His Nephew to Death"—merely to shock readers. Pulitzer defended the techniques as essential to attracting more people to buy his newspaper and, therefore, read his progressive editorials.[3]

Critics be damned, Pulitzer catapulted the *World* into the largest newspaper in the country, soaring from 15,000 when he bought it to 250,000 four years later. The circulation growth was aided by creative techniques. After Jules Verne's novel *Around the World in 80 Days* created a national stir, Pulitzer sent "stunt girl" Nellie Bly on a global adventure to circle the world in seventy-two days. The pretty twenty-four-year-old's stunt was such a triumph that she later went incognito to investigate conditions in sweatshops and women's prisons.

Pulitzer expanded the definition of news into the world of sports and revolutionized the American newspaper by introducing women's pages brimming with articles on social etiquette, home decorating, and romantic advice aimed at female readers—the target buyers of the department stores that became major advertisers in the *World*.

William Randolph Hearst Stupefies the World

Born in California in 1863, William Randolph Hearst entered a world far different from that of Pulitzer. Hearst was the only son of a self-taught mining engineer who struck it rich in the silver mines of the Comstock Lode. George Hearst used his phenomenal wealth to buy a seat in the United States Senate and his son's admission into Harvard. But young Hearst was an indifferent student who drank too much and spent more time playing with his pet alligator and selling ads for the

Harvard Lampoon than he did studying. After sending his professors personalized chamber pots with each man's likeness drawn on the bottom, he was expelled.

Hearst, who idolized Pulitzer, worked briefly on the *World* and then persuaded his father to let him edit the *San Francisco Examiner*, a financially failing newspaper the elder Hearst had purchased to support his political career. Willie Hearst took to newspapers like Babe Ruth took to baseball. With Pulitzer as his model and his father's deep pockets at his disposal, Hearst hired the best staff money could buy and undertook ambitious and progressive crusades, including campaigns to lower city water rates and end the Southern Pacific Railroad's dominance of the Republican state political machine.

Hearst, like Pulitzer, appealed to the masses, telling his reporters: "There's a gripman on the Powell Street line—he takes his car out at three o'clock in the morning, and while he's waiting for the signals he opens the morning paper. Think of him when you're writing a story. Don't write a single line he can't understand and wouldn't read." Hearst hammered at injustice while highlighting murder and scandal. He was innovative in the breadth of his coverage, too, pushing sports and theater news to page one and hiring reporters exclusively to cover society and financial news.[4]

Hearst was a showman who set out to entertain and startle his readers every day. And when the actual news of the day was too dull, Hearst *created* stupefying events. He paid a young couple to be married in a hot-air balloon and hired hunters to go into the mountains to trap a grizzly bear and bring it to San Francisco—while writing exclusive stories for the *Examiner*. Readers became so eager to see what Hearst would come up with next that the publisher kept the city at a carnival pitch. He loved it, saying, "Putting out a newspaper without promotion is like winking at a girl in the dark—well-intentioned but ineffective."[5]

After eight years in Hearst's creative hands, the *Examiner*—he immodestly dubbed it "The Monarch of the Dailies"—had become a trendsetter in American journalism as well as a popular and profitable business. Circulation had jumped from 12,000 to 200,000.

The War of the Newspapers

Willie Hearst was a privileged and selfish young man who in 1895, at the age of thirty-two, realized his life's dream of competing with Joseph Pulitzer. Hearst's vehicle was the *New York Journal*, a scandal sheet that had been nicknamed "the chambermaid's delight" before

Hearst bought it and began pouring his inheritance into it. His earliest changes were dropping the price from two cents to one, introducing color printing, luring top advertisers away from the *World*, and raiding Pulitzer's stable of talented reporters, editors, and business executives.

Within a year, the *Journal* ranked as New York's second largest paper, trailing only the *World*. Hearst and Pulitzer then became engaged in the most notorious newspaper war in American journalism history. Editors filled their pages with gaudy, emotion-packed, devil-may-care stories that set out not merely to inform but also to entertain and shock. The Hearst-Pulitzer battle for readers and profits turned the high drama of life into a cheap melodrama and led to stories being twisted into the form best suited for sales by the howling newsboy—journalism without a soul.

The term "yellow journalism" evolved from one of the most memorable battles between the publishing titans. *World* artist Richard F. Outcault created the "Hogan's Alley" cartoon featuring a cast of tenement dwellers who lampooned such upper-class fads as golf matches and dog shows. The central character in each drawing was a grinning, snaggle-toothed urchin who wore a bright yellow nightshirt that earned him the name Yellow Kid. Hearst lured Outcault to the *Journal*, but Pulitzer had another artist continue to draw the popular cartoon. So when the newspaper war heated up, both publishers hired gangs of kids to plaster billboards, lampposts, and the sides of trolley cars with posters featuring the Yellow Kid. The mascot—impudent, mindless, and hyperactive with a manic gleam in his eye—came to represent the sensationalistic journalism that defined the era, and the concept of yellow journalism was born.

Among Hearst's innovations was hiring Annie Laurie as the first "sob sister." Laurie stressed the tragic and emotional side of stories. Sent to investigate the city hospital, the comely young woman dressed in shabby clothes and collapsed on the street. Taken to the city hospital, she was insulted and pawed by lustful interns who gave her nothing but an emetic of hot water and mustard. Laurie's indignant front-page exposé shook up the hospital and led to the firing of the head physician. In later stories, Laurie moved to Utah and lived with the Mormons to describe the realities of polygamy, worked in a fruit cannery to publicize the low wages and miserable working conditions women and migrants endured, and interviewed the madam of a house of prostitution to offer readers a voyeuristic peek into the underbelly of urban life.

By 1897, a mere two years after arriving in New York, Hearst had pushed the *Journal*'s daily circulation to 500,000—within striking distance of the *World*'s 600,000. It was in this highly charged atmosphere

The New York World's *mindless and impudent cartoon character the Yellow Kid has remained a symbol of sensationalistic journalism for more than a century. Reprinted from the* New York World.

of scrambling for the hottest scoop of the day that the *Journal* and *World* began to focus on the events that helped thrust the nation full tilt into international warfare.

The Battleground Shifts to Cuba

As the Industrial Revolution evolved, the United States grew eager to expand its boundaries and enlarge its international presence—and economic markets. Many imperialistic eyes turned south. By 1895, Cuban rebels were tired of their colonial status and were striking out at Spanish economic interests in Cuba by wrecking trains and burning sugar plantations. Americans sympathized with the underdogs who were struggling to break away from a European monarchy, and American businessmen saw the island eighty miles off the Florida coast as an attractive potential for territorial and economic expansion.

When Hearst heard that a few ragged rebels had elected a leader, the *Journal* heralded the men as—voila!—courageous freedom fighters struggling against Spanish oppressors. Hearst's praise conflicted with the U. S. State Department, which regarded the insurgents as insignificant because they controlled no port and no city of any size. But Hearst, who had a penchant for reducing complex phenomena to simple terms, cast the Cuban rebels as patriotic heroes thirsting for liberty. He told readers, "Their proceedings have been animated by the same fearless spirit that inspired the patriot fathers who sat in Philadelphia on the 4th of July, 1776."[6]

To champion the Cuban cause, Hearst painted an alarming portrait of Spanish brutality. One article stated, "The Spaniards stab to death all Cubans who come under their power." Another described Spanish soldiers dragging insurgents from a hospital and bayoneting them to death. *Journal* readers found the accounts compelling, even though the stories were based not on the firsthand observations of correspondents but on letters and statements from partisan Cubans who had recently fled to the United States.[7]

Pulitzer initially opposed American involvement in Cuba, but he soon shifted to complete support of it. Years later he admitted the sole motivation for his change of heart had been the opportunity for increased circulation.[8]

In December 1896, Hearst sent bon vivant reporter Richard Harding Davis and renowned artist Frederic Remington to Cuba. He paid each man $3,000 a month and expected material commensurate with the generous salary—the average monthly pay for correspondents at the time was $120. Remington initially responded that Cuba did not merit the coverage Hearst wanted to give it. According to legend, the artist sent Hearst a telegram: "Everything is quiet. There is no trouble here. There will be no war. I wish to return." The Napoleonic publisher replied: "You furnish the pictures and I'll furnish the war." Although historians question whether this verbal exchange ever took place, it accurately captures Hearst's style during the era.[9]

Davis and Remington soon produced the kind of journalism their power-drunk boss demanded. Davis reported that Spanish officers had boarded an American ship anchored off the Cuban coast and forced three pretty young Cuban women to submit to strip searches. Spread across five columns was a Remington drawing that showed a cluster of Spanish officers leering at a young woman's naked body as she stood helpless on deck. The incendiary headline: "Does Our Flag Shield Women?" The story set off a political firestorm. A congressman and senator introduced resolutions in their respective houses of Congress, denouncing the brutish Spanish officers and praising the *Journal* for bringing the incident to light. Disgruntled at being scooped, the *World* tracked down the women and published their strikingly different account. They had been disrobed and searched by a female officer in the privacy of a cabin—*not* by male officers on the deck of the ship.[10]

Although the *World* did not manufacture stories with the abandon the *Journal* did, Pulitzer also sent correspondents to Cuba and published sensationalized reports. One announced, "Old men and little boys were cut down and their bodies fed to the dogs." Another said, "The Spanish soldiers habitually cut off the ears of the Cuban dead and retain them as trophies." The *World* editorial page demanded that the American government take immediate action: "No man's life is safe. American citizens are imprisoned or slain without cause. Blood on the roadsides, blood in the field, blood on the doorsteps, blood, blood, blood! Not a word from Washington! Not a sign from the president!"[11]

The lurid coverage reaped the benefits the dueling newspapers wanted. By 1897, Pulitzer's circulation had climbed to 800,000 and Hearst's to 700,000. What's more, the *World*'s and *Journal*'s circulation figures and resources far surpassed those of any other newspaper in the country, and so hundreds of small papers reprinted the *World* and *Journal* stories—hyperbole and all.

Cuban coverage ranks as a disgraceful example of journalistic distortion. Cuban officials kept reporters away from the action because they wanted to control how the world perceived them. The reporters cooperated because they preferred to trade the primitive conditions of the jungle for Havana's palatial Inglaterra Hotel, complete with sterling silver serving trays and an abundance of exotic Spanish delicacies. So

Frederic Remington's drawing of Spanish officers forcing young women to submit to strip searches helped propel the United States toward war with Spain. Reprinted from the New York Journal.

each day reporters gathered around a rebel spokesman who fed them "eyewitness reports."

Helping the rebellion gain momentum, the *Journal* and *World* published accounts of battles that never took place and narratives of heinous atrocities that were pure propaganda. The *Journal* reported, under the startling headline "Feeding Prisoners to Sharks," that the Spanish tied the hands of Cuban civilians behind their backs and threw them into sections of the ocean with "immense numbers of sharks." The *Journal* also denounced the Spanish for attacking hospitals, poisoning wells, raping women, and roasting priests alive—none of which correspondents directly observed. *World* reporter James Creelman described the victims of an unconfirmed Spanish slaughter: "The skulls of all were split to pieces down to the eyes. Some of these were gouged out. All the bodies had been stabbed by sword bayonets and hacked by sabres. The bodies had almost lost semblance of human form." In each case, the only source was Cuban officials.[12]

The accounts aroused so much public attention that members of the United States Congress quoted from the *Journal* and *World* in floor debates concerning the Cuban insurrection. These hawkish legislators knew the grisly details would win support in Congress just as they were selling newspapers on street corners.[13]

Not everyone, however, was so positive about Hearst's and Pulitzer's activities. In early 1898, Spanish officials policing the Havana Harbor boarded Hearst's 138-foot yacht that carried his staff posted in Cuba. When they discovered several small artillery pieces on board, the Spanish immediately seized the boat. Hearst was outraged, publishing a February 12 article under a headline that announced the beginning of "The Spanish-*Journal* War." Hearst screamed not only at the Spanish but also at American Navy officers because they had allowed his yacht to be captured by a foreign power.[14]

"Remember the Maine!*"*

If news coverage of the Cuban rebels from 1895 to 1898 primed the weapons for warfare, coverage of the U.S.S. *Maine* disaster clearly pulled the trigger. American officials had anchored the twenty-four-gun battleship in Havana Harbor in early 1898 as a reminder that the United States was watching the Cuban conflict because of American business interests there. At 9:40 P.M. on February 15, 1898, the *Maine* exploded, killing 260 American sailors and shocking the entire nation.

The *Journal* and *World* exploited the American people's horror, pity, and anger to create warmongering coverage that still stands today as the epitome of the news media at their most truthless and most ruthless. Screaming headlines, misleading drawings, and shrill editorials laid the blame unequivocally on Spain—demanding that the United States immediately declare war.

In reality, it was preposterous to suggest that Spain destroyed the *Maine*. Spanish officials had desperately avoided bringing the United States into their conflict with Cuba because they knew the American navy would crush theirs. The *Maine* disaster was, in fact, the worst setback Spain could have suffered.

The cause of the explosion has never been definitively determined, but the most logical explanation is that the ship blew up accidentally. The *Maine* was part of the first generation of coal-powered warships with their coal bunkers located near the ship's magazines. Heat generated in the bunkers could have ignited the magazines and caused the ship to explode. During the previous year, a dozen such incidents had been reported on American ships—including sparks aboard the U.S.S. *Cincinnati* that ignited ammunition crates.

Regardless of who was responsible for the *Maine* explosion, Hearst pulled out all the stops. The most memorable of the *Journal*'s front pages remains a textbook example of distortion. The banner headline on page one read: "Destruction of the War Ship *Maine* Was the Work of an Enemy." Below the incendiary headline, Hearst ran a drawing of the *Maine* with cables leading from a submerged mine to a Spanish fortress on shore—a flight of fancy that many readers undoubtedly accepted as fact. No fewer than six additional headlines on page one carried an eye-popping "$50,000!" as the reward the *Journal* offered for evidence related to "the crime."[15]

The shrieking tone of the headlines for the next week testify that truth was the 261st casualty of the explosion: "The War Ship *Maine* Was Split in Two by an Enemy's Secret Infernal Machine," "War! Sure! *Maine* Destroyed by Spanish," "The Whole Country Thrills with War Fever," and "How the *Maine* Actually Looks As It Lies, Wrecked by Spanish Treachery, in Havana Bay."[16]

Hearst did not confine his warmongering to the headlines. He introduced a "War with Spain" card game with the object being to sink Spanish ships, and within a week after the explosion the *Journal* relayed 15,000 letters from readers to their congressmen demanding that the country declare war on Spain. The publisher also ordered three of his reporters in Havana to skulk about the city at night plastering walls with posters that read: "Remember the *Maine*!"[17]

Hearst's sensational coverage paid off. Three days after the explosion, the *Journal* became the first newspaper in American history to boast a seven-figure circulation, having surpassed the one million mark—and the *World*.[18]

Although Pulitzer was not as willing as Hearst to sacrifice truth on the altar of circulation growth, he also pushed hard for war. Immediately after the *Maine* tragedy, the *World* expressed skepticism that foul play had destroyed the battleship by placing a question mark at the end of its first headline: "*Maine* Explosion Caused by Bomb or Torpedo?" and highlighting President William McKinley's opinion that the explosion must have been the result of an internal explosion. But after the *Journal* insisted that the Spanish had killed the American

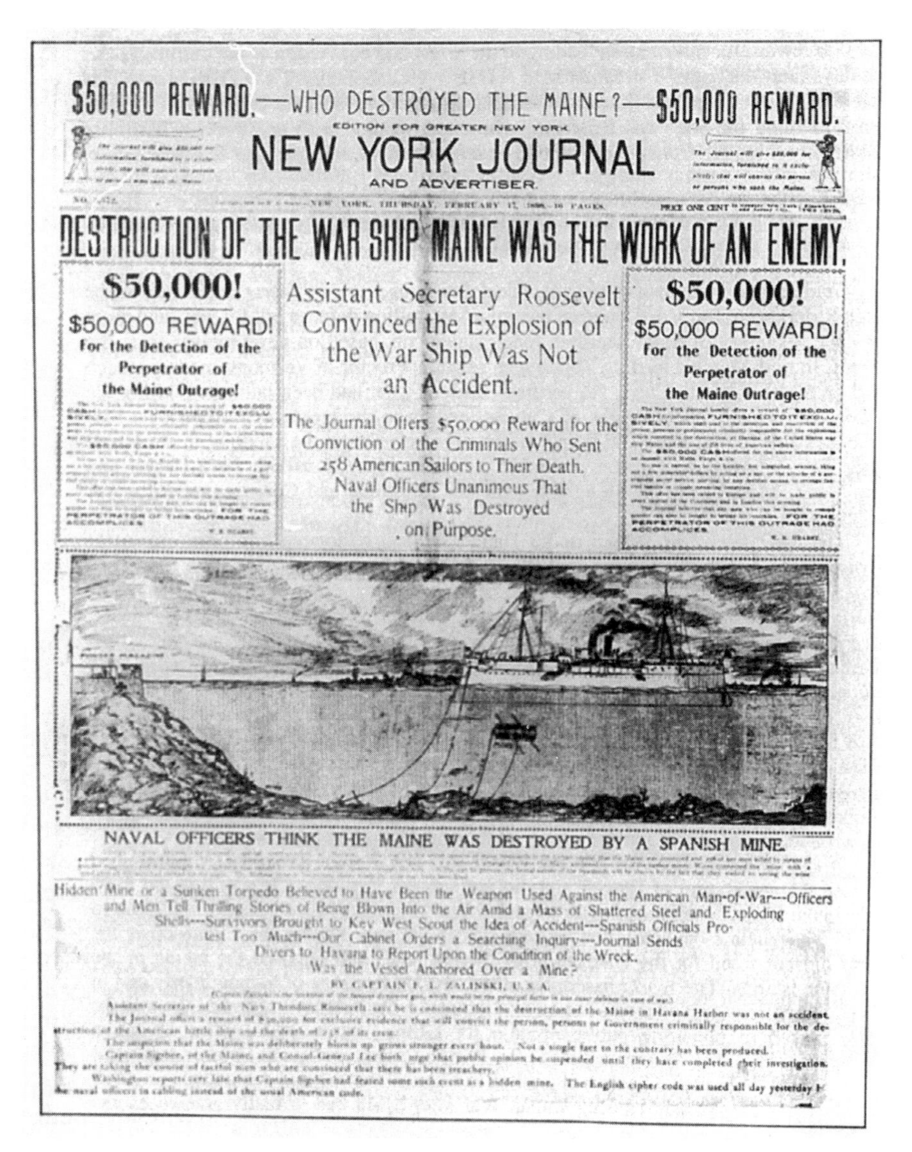

$50,000 REWARD.—WHO DESTROYED THE MAINE?—$50,000 REWARD.

EDITION FOR GREATER NEW YORK

NEW YORK JOURNAL
AND ADVERTISER.

NEW YORK, THURSDAY, FEBRUARY 17, 1898.—16 PAGES. PRICE ONE CENT

DESTRUCTION OF THE WAR SHIP MAINE WAS THE WORK OF AN ENEMY.

$50,000!

$50,000 REWARD!
For the Detection of the Perpetrator of the Maine Outrage!

Assistant Secretary Roosevelt Convinced the Explosion of the War Ship Was Not an Accident.

The Journal Offers $50,000 Reward for the Conviction of the Criminals Who Sent 258 American Sailors to Their Death. Naval Officers Unanimous That the Ship Was Destroyed on Purpose.

$50,000!

$50,000 REWARD!
For the Detection of the Perpetrator of the Maine Outrage!

NAVAL OFFICERS THINK THE MAINE WAS DESTROYED BY A SPANISH MINE.

Hidden Mine or a Sunken Torpedo Believed to Have Been the Weapon Used Against the American Man-of-War—Officers and Men Tell Thrilling Stories of Being Blown Into the Air Amid a Mass of Shattered Steel and Exploding Shells—Survivors Brought to Key West Scout the Idea of Accident—Spanish Officials Protest Too Much—Our Cabinet Orders a Searching Inquiry—Journal Sends Divers to Havana to Report Upon the Condition of the Wreck.
Was the Vessel Anchored Over a Mine?

BY CAPTAIN E. L. ZALINSKI, U. S. A.

Assistant Secretary of the Navy Theodore Roosevelt says he is convinced that the destruction of the Maine in Havana Harbor was not an accident.

The Journal offers a reward of $50,000 for exclusive evidence that will convict the person, persons or Government criminally responsible for the destruction of the American battle ship and the death of 258 of its crew.

The suspicion that the Maine was deliberately blown up grows stronger every hour. Not a single fact to the contrary has been produced.

Captain Sigsbee, of the Maine, and Consul-General Lee both urge that public opinion be suspended until they have completed their investigation. They are taking the course of tactful men who are convinced that there has been treachery.

Washington reports very late that Captain Sigsbee had feared some such event as a hidden mine. The English cipher code was used all day yesterday by the naval officers in cabling instead of the usual American code.

Although William Randolph Hearst immediately proclaimed the 1898 destruction of the U.S.S. Maine *"The Work of an Enemy," most experts attribute the tragedy to an explosion aboard the ship.*

sailors, the *World* did not remain skeptical—or rational—for long. Four days after the disaster, Pulitzer announced the findings of his own investigators: "*World's* Latest Discoveries Indicate *Maine* Was Blown Up by Submarine Mine." In fact, Pulitzer went further than Hearst by not only announcing that the Spanish had destroyed the *Maine* but *crediting* that discovery to his own newspaper's investigation. A page-one headline boasted: "*World's* News of the Evidence of a Mine Under the *Maine* Changes the Feeling Throughout the Country." Pulitzer adopted a tough stance on the editorial page as well: "We do not arbitrate with assassins. Two hundred and sixty of our brave sailors have been hurled to sudden and awful death. What more is needed? Is there no limit to our patience?"[19]

Overpowering the President of the United States

The most significant impact of the jingoistic campaign was not on readers but on the country's commander in chief. The *Journal*, with the *World* close behind, whipped public fury to such a fever pitch that the words initially uttered by voices of reason were drowned out by the din of screaming headlines.

After McKinley's measured statement that the *Maine* explosion must have been caused by the ship's own magazines accidentally igniting, the *Journal* attacked him. Hearst called the president's peace stance "cowardly" and dictated by Wall Street financiers who feared that war might upset the stock market. The *World* pushed McKinley as well, writing: "The army is ready. The navy is ready. The people are ready. And now the President says 'Wait!'—'Wait' for what?"[20]

McKinley judiciously refused to act until Navy investigators studied the remains of the ship. Hearst, in contrast, had no intention of being judicious. Three weeks before the report was released, he quoted anonymous sources as stating definitively, but ultimately incorrectly: "The disaster in Havana harbor was due to the explosion of a submarine mine. This mine was planted by officials of the Spanish Government."[21]

When the Navy report was released in early April, it concluded that the *Maine* had been destroyed by a mine. The findings were inconclusive, however, because investigators were unable to determine who had placed the mine in the harbor. Unstated was the fact that the Navy officials had not even considered the possibility that the ship's design had been at fault. For Navy officers to admit that their own branch of the military had allowed its battleship to blow up during the most sensitive mission it had been assigned in decades would have created the most humiliating incident in the history of the United States Navy.

When President McKinley, not a dynamic leader, continued to call for "deliberate consideration," the *Journal* and *World* turned up the heat. Hearst gave prominent placement to stories about McKinley's effigy being hanged in Colorado and burned in Ohio and Virginia. Hearst also sent his vast stable of reporters to interview the mothers of the dead sailors, quoting one as saying, "How would President McKinley have felt, I wonder, if he had had a son on the *Maine* murdered as was my little boy?" Pulitzer was less emotional but no less insistent, telling McKinley, "Stop deliberating and proceed to action."[22]

Amid such statements from a war-hungry press—and as McKinley saw his own and his Republican Party's popularity wane as public sentiment mounted for war—it became increasingly difficult to proceed with diplomatic efforts. McKinley felt relentless pressure as the press's rip-snorting frenzy for war swept across the nation. The entire country seemed to be seething under the daily onslaught of misinformation and sensationalism. The president clearly lacked the dynamism and personal charisma to sway public opinion in such a high-pitched environment.

Spanish officials made a determined bid for peace, giving every indication that they were willing to compromise in order to reach an amicable settlement. When the United States demanded that Spain abandon its controversial policy that separated noncombatants from the rebels, Spain agreed. And again when the United States demanded that Spain declare an armistice, Spain once more agreed. But despite these major concessions, war fever had become so pervasive that rational thinking no longer played a role.

To survive politically and stabilize the nation, McKinley had to support going to war. So he finally caved in to the pressure and adopted a pro-war stance. The might of the Fourth Estate had, in short, forced the president of the United States to capitulate on a matter of grave importance to humanity.

On April 19, the Senate narrowly passed a war resolution by a vote of forty-two to thirty-five, meaning only four more senators voting for peace would have swung the balance. The next day, the *Journal*'s victory was reflected in its four-inch-high headline on page one: "Now to Avenge the *Maine*!"[23]

On the Battlefront

After war was declared, Hearst and Pulitzer continued to maintain a hysterical pitch. Symbolic of Hearst's attitude was the question he began posing to his readers on the upper corners of page one: "How do you like the *Journal*'s war?"[24]

Hearst assembled a journalistic armada by chartering ten ships at a cost of $15,000 a day to shuttle news stories from Havana to the nearest telegraph station in Key West, publishing as many as forty editions a day during the height of hostilities. Unable to contain his oversized zeal, Hearst hired a luxury steamer for himself and sailed for the war zone with twenty staff members—the *World* sent only six—and a lightweight printing press that enabled him to publish a newspaper on Cuban soil. He claimed the *Journal-Examiner* was for the benefit of American soldiers fighting in the field, but the primary reason clearly was to reap favorable publicity back home.[25]

The master showman received additional positive press when he set up a trap to catch Pulitzer at blatant plagiarism. For this purpose, Hearst published a totally fallacious item that stated, "Colonel Reflipe W. Thenuz, an Austrian artillerist of European renown, who, with Colonel Ordonez, was defending the land batteries of Aguadores was so badly wounded that he has since died." The *World* took the bait and the next day published a slightly rewritten version of the item, "Col. R. W. Thenuz, an Austrian artillerist, well known throughout Europe, who, with Col. Ordonez, was defending the land batteries of Aguadores, was so badly wounded in the bombardment of Monday that he has since died. He performed many acts of conspicuous gallantry."[26]

The *Journal* pounced on the *World*, announcing that Colonel Thenuz had never existed and then gloating about how it had caught the *World* in an embarrassing journalistic faux pas. Thrilled with the success of his trickery, Hearst ran letters from newspaper editors condemning the *World* for plagiarism and published a tongue-in-cheek "In Memoriam" poem honoring the fictitious colonel. Refusing to allow the prank to die, Hearst proposed building a monument to the colonel. Readers joined in the frivolity by contributing burlesque sketches for the monument as well as making financial donations—including Confederate currency and Chinese yuan. Meanwhile, the humiliated *World* had no choice but to maintain a painful silence.[27]

Hearst, still the overgrown adolescent, had even more fun when he strapped on a pistol, grabbed a reporter's notebook, and covered the war firsthand—often on horseback. In one incident, the publisher and *Journal* reporter James Creelman were double-teaming the same battle when a bullet struck Creelman in the left arm and lodged in his back. The reporter later recalled waking up in a field hospital to see Hearst clutching his notebook, "his face radiant with enthusiasm. 'I'm sorry you're hurt,' said Hearst. 'But wasn't it a splendid fight? We beat every paper in the world.'" The story carried only Hearst's byline.[28]

American soldiers and sailors were not having nearly as much fun. U.S. military forces suffered badly from lack of experience and poor planning. Although the one-sided war lasted only four months, the toll in American lives surpassed 5,000. At war's end, Spain granted Cuba its independence and ceded the Philippines, Guam, and Puerto Rico to the United States.

From Hearst's point of view, the war was a glorious success. Not only did the United States thrash Spain but Hearst achieved the massive circulation he had dreamed of. By August 1898 when the fighting ceased, the *Journal* and *World* both were claiming figures of 1.25 million. The *Journal*, with lower ad rates, actually was still losing money. By war's end, Hearst had spent the entire $7 million he had inherited from his father.

Legacy of Shame

The Spanish-American War probably could have been avoided, as the Spanish gave clear signals that they were eager to negotiate. But the decision to go to war was not made entirely by diplomats or military leaders. For it was, more than any major American conflict before or since, a war fueled by the news media. If Hearst, with his tawdry flair for publicity and agitation, had not filled his pages with sensational stories . . . had not made the explosion of the *Maine* a symbol of Spanish treachery . . . had not urged thousands of citizens to write their congressmen . . . had not dragged the powerful *World* with him into journalistic ill-fame . . . had not pushed President McKinley to abandon his anti-war stance . . . had not whipped the public into such a war frenzy that senators no longer acted on the basis of reason but for political survival . . . there may have been no war.

Some historians have suggested that Hearst actually may have blown up the *Maine*. Just three days before the explosion, the *Journal* had declared its private war on Spain in response to Hearst's yacht being seized, while also screaming at the American Navy for not coming to its rescue. So blowing up the *Maine* would have been an act of revenge against both the Spanish, by thrusting the United States into the Cuban crisis, and against the American Navy. What's more, destruction of the battleship certainly boosted the *Journal*'s circulation. The Hearst-as-instigator theory received a huge boost in 1901 when James Creelman, Hearst's star reporter in Cuba, wrote mysteriously in his memoirs: "The time has not yet come when all the machinery employed by the American press on behalf of Cuba can be laid bare to the American public. Things which cannot be referred to even now were attempted."[29]

After the war, Hearst yearned to become president of the United States. Though that goal eluded him, Hearst served in the United

States Congress, played a decisive role in several presidential elections, and built a huge publishing empire. When he died in 1951, Hearst left assets of $160 million and a legacy of journalistic accomplishment overshadowed by journalistic shame.

Numerous participants in and scholars of the Spanish-American War have attributed much of the blame for the conflict to Hearst. Spanish Commander Valeriano Weyler said the catalyst was neither Spanish oppression nor Cuban rebellion: "The American newspapers are responsible. They poisoned everything with falsehood." Spanish Prime Minister Canovas del Castillo agreed, telling an American reporter, "The newspapers of your country seem to be more powerful than the government." John K. Winkler was among the many historians who have blamed Hearst for the war, saying, "The Spanish-American War came as close to being a 'one-man war' as any conflict in our history." Creelman agreed, saying point blank, "The *Journal* provoked the war." Joseph P. Wisan, who wrote a book about the press during the Cuban crisis, concluded, "The Spanish-American War would not have occurred had not the appearance of Hearst in New York journalism precipitated a bitter battle for newspaper circulation." Wisan continued, "The *Journal* and *World* used Cuba to achieve their prime purpose—an increase in circulation."[30]

Statements regarding Hearst provoking the war also came from the egotistical empire builder himself. His editorial-page editor wrote in his memoirs, "Hearst was accustomed to referring to the war, in company with the staff, as 'our war.'" The publisher summarized his own reflections on the war—and the mighty power of the news media more generally—in an editorial published in the *Journal* a month after the war ended. Hearst wrote, in his immodest fashion:

> The newspaper is the greatest force in civilization.
>
> Under republican government, newspapers form and express public opinion.
>
> They suggest and control legislation.
>
> They declare wars . . .
>
> The newspapers control the nation.[31]

6

Muckraking: The Golden Age of Reform Journalism

DURING THE SECOND HALF of the nineteenth century, the American economy experienced an unprecedented orgy of expansion. Propelled by hundreds of new inventions that made American offices and factories the most efficient operations in the history of the world, business and industry raced into the future at breakneck speed. Production figures doubled and redoubled, foreign exports soared, and the number and variety of factories boggled even the most visionary of minds. America, fueled by unbridled genius and energy, established itself as the nation of the future.

In politics, the Republican Party charged mightily onward to the chords of the "American System." This plan called for using the country's abundant resources, human as well as material, to transform the United States into an industrial giant, while protecting American business from foreign interference. Prosperity lay in adopting laissez-faire policies—which often meant adopting no policies whatsoever—while building more railroads, digging more mines, and increasing factory production by finding a new man who worked even faster than the last.

At the same time, however, the country had evolved into one that the Founding Fathers would not have claimed. For the world's democratic stronghold had been "let go," turned into a nation *of the corporation, by the corporation, and for the corporation*. Though industrialists and investors made enormous sums, the economic boom largely bypassed the common man. In particular, the hordes of new immigrants, drawn by the radiance of America's promise, were crowded into dark factories and foul slums. The nation founded on the bedrock concept of equality had deteriorated into a society dominated by a few gluttonously rich robber barons who feasted on life's pleasures while the teeming masses struggled to stave off starvation. The pungent odor of corruption had spread into politics as well; in government at all levels, the wholesale flouting of laws and the sprawling spoils systems rivaled those of the infamous Boss Tweed in New York some thirty years earlier.

But then, at the moment of greatest need, the Fourth Estate stepped into the fray. Armed with literary talent and investigative skill, reform-minded journalists boldly accused the nation of auctioning off its birthright for private gain. These progressive warriors exposed a stunning variety of crimes against democracy. They reported the rampant misdeeds of greedy industrialists and grafting politicians—from the local level all the way to the United States Senate—to show how the scofflaws had climbed to success not on the basis of their ability but by being ruthless and lawless. Other reporters revealed the vast differences between the fraudulent claims of patent medicines and the actual contents of the products, and still others exposed the unsanitary techniques used in preparing foods and the inhuman practices that helped boost American labor into a mighty force.

To the delight of their readers, the reporters provoked political, industrial, and social change not through erudite intellectual discourse but by describing the sordid details to create a new style of magazine writing that was as gripping as it was edifying—office clerks and shopgirls never knew business and politics could be so *interesting*. Fortunately for those relatively low-paid workers, technological advances in printing and paper production allowed magazines to lower their prices to an affordable level. Also contributing to the rise of the magazine as America's first truly national medium were the country's rapid growth—the population doubled between 1880 and 1900—and the advent of advertising as a stable institution standing on the shoulders of the plethora of new products, new businesses, and new competition. Responding to these forces, a panoply of popular magazines vied for attention with vivid and compelling exposés. In the early years of the new century, a dozen national magazines boasted a combined monthly circulation of a staggering three million copies—with individual articles sometimes so riveting that they pushed that figure to five million.[1]

The term that ultimately came to define this journalistic phenomenon was coined by President Theodore Roosevelt, who led the larger reform movement that the journalists helped to spark. During the Progressive Era, government attempted to reassert its control of business through myriad new agencies and regulations. The youthful and buoyant Roosevelt supported journalistic reform, but in one of the volatile moments that defined his personality he lashed out at the crusaders for finding nothing good about society but looking constantly at the negative elements—as if *raking muck*. The epithet took hold, and the golden age of reform journalism became known as *muckraking*.[2]

The contributions that these progressive journalists made to this country established a high-water mark that remains unsurpassed—in both breadth and intensity—in the epic drama of how the news media have shaped American history.

Attacking Municipal Corruption

Lincoln Steffens, an intellectual who wore spectacles and a string tie, is widely acknowledged as the first muckraker. After studying at the finest universities in the United States and Europe, Steffens joined the *New York Evening Post*, covering Wall Street and city police. Ten years later, in 1902, he switched to *McClure's*, the greatest of the muckraking journals.

Steffens then undertook the project that would make him a journalistic icon—investigating the state of municipal government in the United States. For three years he visited the country's largest cities to conduct detailed studies, first digging through public documents and then interviewing city officials.

He designed his first article, "Tweed Days in St. Louis," as a wake-up call to alert the American public to the immorality driving city officials throughout the country. Steffens's exposé of St. Louis politics and government reported that city aldermen had crafted a system of governance based on bribery and corruption. In the October 1902 article, Steffens said of St. Louis: "Taking but slight and always selfish interest in the public councils, the big men misused politics." He went on to describe how the wrongdoing spread. "The riff-raff, catching the smell of corruption, rushed into the Municipal Assembly, drove out the remaining respectable men, and sold the city—its streets, its wharves, its markets, and all that it had—to the now greedy business men and bribers." Steffens ended with a bitter tone, "When the leading men began to devour their own city, the herd rushed into the trough and fed also."[3]

Steffens did more than expose. For his blockbuster article gave St. Louis District Attorney Joseph W. Folk the public support he needed to prosecute dozens of city officials for a wide variety of offenses, from stuffing the ballot box to padding contracts. Folk was so successful, in fact, that in 1904 he was elected governor of Missouri. And all the time he continued to credit Steffens for building the popular support that allowed him to reform the city and then the state government.[4]

After publishing the St. Louis article, Steffens moved on to other cities, publishing blockbuster articles that exposed wrongdoing in Minneapolis, Pittsburgh, Philadelphia, Chicago, and New York City. Steffens then moved on to state governments, reporting the illegal and unscrupulous practices among government officials in Missouri, Illinois, Rhode Island, and New Jersey.[5]

Steffens's series was one of the most significant examples of the muckraking journalism that some dubbed the "literature of protest." With the laboratory scientist's eye for fundamentals, he traced how—in city after city, state after state—the quest for individual wealth and power infected governmental institutions, organized business, and the low-life criminal element to create a systemic world of graft much larger than its individual parts.

Contemporary newspapers and magazines lauded Steffens's series as a watershed. The *St. Paul Pioneer Press* praised Steffens's "keen deductions," and the *St. Paul News* called him "an investigator of ability and seriousness" and his series "the first to tell the plain, unvarnished truth about American municipal life." Many of the hosannas focused on Steffens's approach, applauding him for examining municipal corruption in remarkable depth. William Allen White, the revered editor of the *Emporia Gazette* in Kansas, wrote, "Mr. Steffens has made an important step in the scientific study of government in America. This work should be in every social and economic library, for it is a work of real scientific importance."[6]

The most tangible legacy of Steffens's journalistic work, published as a book titled *The Shame of the Cities*, was that it helped usher in the city-manager form of government. After Steffens revealed the corruption that inevitably occurred when elected politicians ran local government, cities such as Toledo, Cleveland, and Detroit opted to hire professional administrators who had training and experience in operating large organizations. And these men, in turn, began to reduce the political spoils system by requiring that job applicants possess formal credentials and pass standardized tests.[7]

Busting the Trusts

S. S. McClure, the Irish immigrant who founded the leading muckraking magazine, decided to tackle the enormous power of corporations by focusing on a single trust—tracing its history, leaders, and inner workings. For the trust, McClure chose Standard Oil, the country's oldest and largest monopoly that was supplying an astounding 90 percent of the oil to light American homes and power American factories. For the investigative reporter, he selected a serious-minded woman who looked more like a schoolmistress than a street-wise reporter: Ida Minerva Tarbell.

Born in the oil region of northwestern Pennsylvania, Tarbell grew up surrounded by derricks, tanks, and pipelines, and her father and brother earned their livelihood in refining. After receiving her bachelor's and master's degrees, Tarbell wrote for *Chautauquan* magazine on such progressive subjects as education and public health. She later specialized in biographies, writing a book about a female leader of the French Revolution and lengthy articles on Napoleon Bonaparte and Abraham Lincoln.

In the first installment of her monumental series "History of the Standard Oil Company," which began in November 1902, Tarbell described how the trust had achieved its position by John D. Rockefeller's shrewd and ruthless approach to competition. She revealed that he had created a system of secret—and illegal—agreements with selected railroads to give him preferential rates. Under the contracts, Rockefeller transported his oil exclusively via those railroads in exchange for rates equal to half what his competitors paid. The shipping cost discount made it impossible for other companies to compete with Standard Oil, driving the smaller operations out of business.[8]

Though the articles were packed with financial information, Tarbell's narrative style and abundant anecdotes made compelling reading. When she described the youthful Johnny Rockefeller, she showed that financial cunning had always been his defining trait: "When he was eight years old, he raised a flock of turkeys. The flock was a fine one, for the owner had given it close care, and it was sold to advantage. A boy of eight usually earns to spend. This boy was different. He invested his entire turkey earnings at seven per cent. It was the beginning of a financial career."[9]

Other anecdotes were equally engaging, telling of such sinister activities as bribery and violence—racy stuff then as now. She told of a Cleveland refinery owner whose bereaved widow went to Rockefeller and begged him for financial advice so she could feed her three children. Rockefeller assured her that he would help her; then he paid her $79,000 for a refinery worth $200,000. In another article, Tarbell described how Standard Oil officials paid the chief mechanic at a competing refinery to stoke the fire in a tank to such a high temperature that the safety valve blew off and thousands of barrels of oil were lost.

After her blockbuster exposé of Standard Oil, Ida Minerva Tarbell was proclaimed the Terror of the Trusts, "a modern-day Joan of Arc," and the Queen of the Muckrakers. Reprinted by permission of the Library of Congress.

She also told how Rockefeller's henchmen had paid the most valued employee of a competing East Coast refinery to move to California, forcing the company out of business.[10]

Publications throughout the country lauded Tarbell's work. The *Washington Times* said, "Ida M. Tarbell has proven herself to be one of the most commanding figures in American letters today," and the *Chicago Inter Ocean* called her series "absorbing." The *Louisville Courier-Journal* wrote, "This series of impartial narration has attracted wide attention, not only for the subject-matter, but for the vividness with which the light is thrown upon one of the most corroding ulcers of modern times."[11]

For readers of the era, learning about the internal operations of the great oil company was as exciting as reading a suspense story or heart-stopping romance. A typical letter to Tarbell read, "These articles are the *Uncle Tom's Cabin* of to-day, revealing the criminalities and outrages of the trust system." Another said breathlessly, "Keep it up."[12]

Some readers went beyond praising Tarbell to offer her information. A teenager who worked for Standard Oil had been assigned to burn office paper. Upon reading some of the documents, he realized they proved that Rockefeller paid railroad workers to misroute the cars carrying competitors' oil, causing serious delays and soaring costs. The teenager sent the papers to Tarbell, who used them—concealing the name of her youthful informant—as the basis for more accusations.[13]

Public enthusiasm was so great and material so plentiful that the series, initially scheduled for three articles, was expanded to eighteen. By the time the series ended in October 1904, Tarbell was being hailed as one of the most courageous women in American history—"a modern-day Joan of Arc," the Terror of the Trusts, and the Queen of the Muckrakers.

Tarbell's series, which McClure also published as a book, had profound impact on public policy. The first tangible result came in 1906 when Congress passed the Hepburn Act, making the penalties for preferential arrangements by railroads so severe that the practice quickly ceased. Then, after federal grand juries indicted Standard Oil on fraud charges, the United States Supreme Court ruled in 1911 that Standard Oil was violating the Sherman Anti-Trust Act. The high court then forced the mammoth monopoly to dissolve and become thirty-eight smaller companies.[14]

Tarbell's series—credited with boosting *McClure's* circulation from 350,000 to 500,000—had impact on the American social fabric as well. Ministers praised Tarbell from their pulpits. Historians commended her accuracy and thoroughness. *Public Opinion* magazine wrote, "There is not a single sign in the whole narrative of any other motive than an arrival at the truth." In the words of Louis Filler, who chronicled the muckraking phenomenon for history books, "The 'History of the Standard Oil Company' marked an epoch. Once it appeared, there could never be any further question about the existence or significance of trusts. The intricate message of Tarbell's masterpiece filtered down into the very consciousness of the average American citizen."[15]

Although Rockefeller avoided going to jail, the series damaged his image so severely that he hired the country's first publicity man, Ivy Lee, to improve his tarnished reputation. When the most renowned of the robber barons began making huge contributions to charities, the public again credited Tarbell, thanking her for opening the Rockefeller purse to the common good.

Most important, the series fulfilled McClure's goal of showing the public not only that many big businesses were corrupt but also that the Fourth Estate could force them to abide by the law. So Tarbell's journalistic triumph encouraged other muckrakers to investigate other monopolies. *McClure's* and *The Arena* exposed the railroads, and *Cosmopolitan* tackled the telephone and telegraph companies. *Hampton's* focused on the mining and sugar trusts, *Collier's* on liquor interests, *Everybody's* on the beef trust.[16]

Exposing the Realities of American Labor

A third major figure emerged at the vanguard of the reform-journalism movement when Ray Stannard Baker's byline joined those of Steffens and Tarbell in *McClure's* in early 1903. Baker was an earnest and tenacious young man who earned a reputation as the world's greatest reporter because he totally immersed himself in whatever subject he was studying.

In the early years of the twentieth century, that subject was American labor. Specifically, Baker examined the enormous power of labor unions. Although he was by no means anti-labor, Baker distrusted the unions, suspecting they had become as corrupt as the sprawling corporations they fought against. He was particularly concerned that the common worker was no longer allowed to make his or her own decisions regarding whether to join a union. So Baker painted the first authentic picture of labor racketeering and the strong-arm tactics that unions often employed to swell their ranks.

A novelist at heart, Baker built his articles around profiles of individual workers, each filled with concrete detail. In his first article, he focused on some of the 17,000 miners who in 1901 refused to enter the mines until their salaries were raised, creating a nationwide coal strike. Baker told how men who wanted to continue to work were coerced and harassed, how local merchants refused to sell groceries to the miners' wives, and how their sons and daughters were taunted by union members.[17]

Much of the highly personalized article focused on John Snyder, who continued to work so his wife and two babies would not go hungry. After Snyder left for the mines in the morning, Baker reported, crowds of union men would surround his house and yell insults at his wife. Baker then recounted how the woman had left the house one day to visit her mother, returning to find the house had been burned to the ground. Baker wrote sympathetically of the Snyders: "They searched in the ashes, hoping to find something left, but there was not even any remains of their cook stove, or sewing machine, or bed spring. Their house had been looted before burning, and the furniture had been distributed among their neighbors. While Mrs. Snyder and her mother were looking into the ruins, the crowd gathered and hooted 'Scab, scab!'"[18]

In other articles, Baker described how powerful union leaders had grown as lawless as medieval kings. He shined the spotlight on Eugene Schmitz of the Musicians' Union, who had ridden the power of the labor unions into politics to become the most corrupt mayor in San Francisco history. Baker wrote that the city had become the epitome of what was wrong with organized labor: "Here the grip of the union is most powerful, its authority most unquestioned, its monopoly most perfect." The consummate reporter, Baker supported his assertion with direct quotations. A prominent contractor told him, "The employers of San Francisco are flat on their backs. When a labor leader makes a demand, we give in without a word. We can't do anything else." Baker quoted another employer summarizing the status of the union men: "They own the town."[19]

Individuals and institutions concerned about the rising power of American labor recognized the value of Baker's exhaustive reporting. Colorado's labor commissioner reprinted Baker's articles verbatim as part of his annual report, and Harvard University required all economics students to read the articles.[20]

Numerous publications applauded Baker's work as well. The *Wall Street Journal* labeled his articles "remarkable"; the *New York Sun* chose the adjective "astounding." The *Providence Journal* wrote, "His presentation of the labor situation is remarkably just," and the *San Jose Mercury-Herald* cooed, "Mr. Baker tells his story fearlessly and without bias, protecting no interest and championing no cause but that of truth."[21]

Baker, like Steffens and Tarbell, did not merely expose wrongdoing but also helped to right the wrongs he discovered. In Baker's case, the most tangible impact of his articles came in 1906 when Mayor Schmitz in San Francisco, Baker's symbol of the labor boss gone bad, was indicted on five counts of extortion.

Among the muckrakers who followed Baker's lead to report on other problems with American labor was Rheta Childe Dorr, who focused on the plight of working women. First as women's editor of the *New York Evening Post* and later as a writer for *Hampton's*, Dorr sculpted vivid slice-of-life portraits to illustrate the hardscrabble life that women workers had to endure.

Dorr's parade of subjects entered the workforce in their teens but lost their vibrant youth to the long hours and arduous working conditions. Sadie was sent into a factory at the age of fifteen to pay the college tuition for her older brother; she stitched muslin underwear twelve hours a day, sewing some four miles of fabric each year. Edna worked as a waitress; she walked twelve miles a day carrying heavy trays of food, paying exorbitant fines if she broke a dish or spilled even a single drop of water. Anna was a widowed mother of four who labored fourteen hours a day in a hot, steamy laundry until she finally collapsed and died of pneumonia. Dorr later reprinted her articles in a book titled *What Eight Million Women Want*.[22]

Other muckrakers wrote about child labor. By 1900, some two million children were employed full time in the country's factories, mines, and textile mills. The working conditions these children—some of them as young as five—had to endure were not widely known outside the tenement neighborhoods that had sprung into place in large cities. The muckrakers soon changed that.

The ground-breaking articles on this subject appeared in *Cosmopolitan* in 1906 under the byline of Edwin Markham. Known as "the poet of the muckrakers," he wrote in a highly interpretive style bursting with indignation at a nation that would sacrifice its children for financial profit. Markham called child labor a "cruel and wasteful fungus that destroys the present and threatens the future," lambasting industrialists who forced children to work fourteen hours a day and screaming, "O Dollars, how diabolical are the crimes committed in thy name!"[23]

Along with his passionate prose, Markham reported facts that were nothing short of appalling. He revealed that mining companies sought young children because they could crawl into the smallest and most dangerous of tunnels. He also accused employers of routinely lying about the ages of their young workers, "Mills keep a look-out for the inspector, and at the danger signal the children scurry like rats to hide in attics, to crouch in cellars, behind bales of cotton, under heaps of old machinery."[24]

Markham's combination of emotional writing and hard-hitting investigative reporting paid off. By 1907, two-thirds of the states had enacted legislation protecting children, and in 1916 Congress banned from interstate transportation any products manufactured in factories that employed children. Much of the credit for protecting America's next generation went to Markham. One history of the period stated, "He helped to create a changed attitude toward child labor, and his studies gave impetus to child labor legislation."[25]

Awakening the Public to Dangerous Foods and Drugs

Another issue endangering the lives of children—as well as adults—was the poor quality of the food and medicine America was consuming. Because refrigerated railroad cars were now speeding perishable products hundreds of miles, the public was consuming, for the first time, a variety of food preservatives with such strange names as *borax* and *benzoate*. Drugs were of concern as well, with the health field overrunning with quacks selling patent medicines to the tune of $100 million a year. Some products promised to cure cancer, others to curb addiction to tobacco, and still others to enlarge female breasts. Most users had no idea that many "medicines" contained alcohol and "soothing syrups" were laced with morphine or cocaine. In reality, the widely used products were destroying the nation's health while transforming unsuspecting men, women, and children into drug addicts.

The most spectacular assault on the food industry began after the newspaper *Appeal to Reason* offered to pay an idealistic young writer named Upton Sinclair $500 to live among Chicago stockyard workers in order to write a series of articles describing the conditions he found there. Sinclair accepted the Socialist weekly's offer and spent seven weeks talking late into the night with meatpacking workers and their families, while also interviewing plant managers, doctors, lawyers, ministers, and social workers.

After the first installment appeared in February 1905, it became immediately clear that neither the food industry nor journalism would ever be the same. For Sinclair wrote his series "The Jungle" with the fire of a man who had witnessed human suffering at its most base level. In his shocking revelation, Sinclair reported that exhausted workers sometimes fell into the huge vats where meat was being canned—which meant that consumers were unknowingly eating human flesh. Sinclair wrote: "For the men who worked in tankrooms full of steam, their peculiar trouble was that they fell into the vats; and when they were fished out, there was never enough of them left to be worth exhibiting. Sometimes they would be overlooked for days, till all but the bones of them had gone out to the world."[26]

Some critics argued that Sinclair's popular series was not muckraking because it was written as fiction, but the author defended his work as journalism because it was based on intensive reporting. Sinclair said, "'The Jungle' will stand the severest test—it is as authoritative as if it were a statistical compilation." Readers agreed with Sinclair rather than his critics, as have the generations of students who have read the series in book form. In his standard history of the muckrakers, Louis Filler wrote that no work had "a nearer approximation of what was generally thought of as 'genius.' 'The Jungle,' from the moment it began to appear in the *Appeal*, was recognizably the literary sensation of the time."[27]

One reader was President Roosevelt. After completing the series, he sent his own agents to Chicago to confirm what Sinclair had written. And confirm they did. The agents' words were not as graceful as Sinclair's, but they told a strikingly similar story.[28]

The leader of the muckraking campaign against drugs was *Ladies' Home Journal*. Editor Edward Bok fired the first salvo in 1904 by urging readers to boycott patent medicines: "A mother who would hold up her hands in holy horror at the thought of her child drinking a glass of beer, which contains from two to five per cent alcohol, gives to that child with her own hands a patent medicine that contains from seventeen to forty-four per cent alcohol—to say nothing of opium and cocaine!" Along with the editorial, Bok printed a chart listing the alcohol content of forty popular patent medicines.[29]

Other magazines joined the *Journal*'s crusade. *Collier's* hired lawyer Mark Sullivan to lead its efforts. In one article, Sullivan reprinted the minutes of a meeting of the trade group that patent medicine manufacturers had organized. At the meeting, the presiding officer boasted that his advertising contract forced magazines and newspapers to oppose any proposed legislation that threatened to decrease his sales. An accompanying editorial said of Sullivan's exposé, "The article shows just how relentless a grip the Patent Medicine claw has upon the press of this country."[30]

In the same issue, *Collier's* boldly announced that it would no longer accept ads from patent medicine companies. This was a daring step for any magazine to take, as publications of the era bulged with page after page of ads promoting these products, providing the magazines with a major source of revenue. Nevertheless, the list of magazines that ultimately were willing to make the sacrifice was impressive, including not only *Collier's* and *Ladies' Home Journal*, but also *McClure's*, *Good Housekeeping*, the *Saturday Evening Post*, and *Everybody's*. The decision had serious financial consequences. A year after *Collier's* purged patent medicine ads from its pages, the magazine announced, "We spoke out about patent medicines, and dropped $80,000 in a year."[31]

Other offensives against patent medicines by *Collier's* appeared in a two-fisted series titled "The Great American Fraud." Samuel Hopkins Adams began, "Gullible America will spend this year some seventy-five million dollars in the purchase of patent medicines." Adams then detailed how the country would harm itself. "In consideration of this sum, it will swallow huge quantities of alcohol, an appalling amount of opiates and narcotics, a wide assortment of varied drugs ranging from powerful and dangerous heart depressants to insidious liver stimulants; and, far in excess of all other ingredients, undiluted fraud."[32]

In the articles that followed, Adams documented that specific patent medicines either endangered the lives of their users or failed to live up to the promises made in their advertising. He reported, for example, that Acetanilid promised to relieve headache pain but actually accomplished this feat by the extremely risky practice of causing a person's heart to stop temporarily. Adams also reported companies publishing statements based on no scientific evidence whatsoever. He revealed that "the great international scientist, Pauli," whom the makers of Liquozone claimed had studied the product, actually was a piano maker named "Powley" who lived in Toronto, Canada.[33]

Like *Harper's Weekly* during its campaign against Boss Tweed, *Collier's* recognized the power of images. The magazine's full-page cartoon titled "Death's Laboratory" became a symbol of the hollow promises and deadly results of drug fraud. The drawing was dominated by a skull branded with the words "The Patent Medicine Trust—Palatable Poison for the Poor." The skull's teeth were bottles of patent medicine, and its cheeks were bags of money. Papers strewn in front of the skull read: "Slow Poison for Little Children" and "Baby's Soothing Syrup—Opium and Laudanum."[34]

By 1906, *Ladies' Home Journal* believed the muckrakers had raised public awareness to the point that it could take proactive measures. Bok printed "An Act To Regulate the Manufacture and Sale of 'Patent' Medicines," urging readers to clip out the simulated bill and send it to their congressmen in Washington. The editor who had initiated the crusade two years earlier now insisted, "This and other magazines have done their parts: the remedy of the fearful evil they have laid bare is in the hands of the people: in *your* hands. The question is: Will *you*, now, do your part?" Another editorial ended: "The Time Has Come for YOU to Act!"[35]

Readers responded with speed and volume. They flooded the White House and Congress with thousands of copies of the sample bill along with letters demanding that the government protect American

Collier's
THE NATIONAL WEEKLY

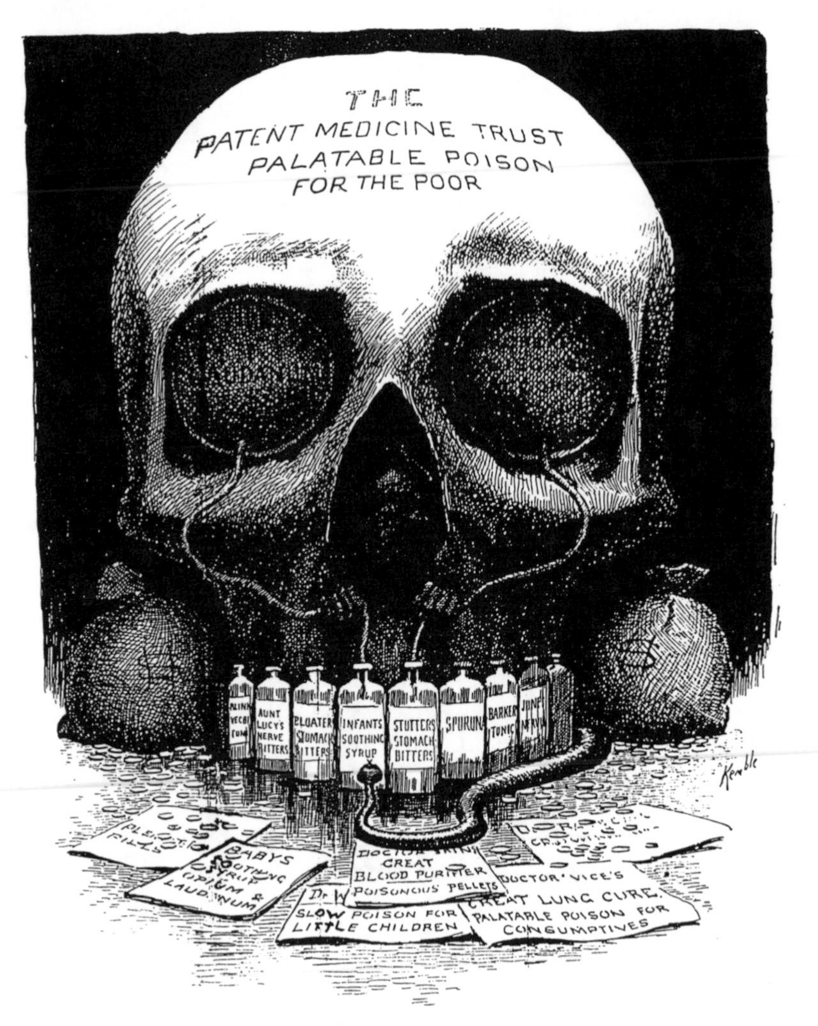

DEATH'S LABORATORY

A ghoulish drawing from Collier's *magazine came to symbolize the deadly patent medicine fraud at the turn of the century.*

consumers from unsafe drugs. In his annual message to Congress, President Roosevelt advocated a law regulating food as well as drugs; senators immediately introduced such legislation, as well as a bill to require inspection of meat. Propelled by public indignation, Congress passed the Pure Food and Drug Act, requiring all medicines to be analyzed and approved by the Department of Agriculture, and the Meat Inspection Act, requiring all meat to be examined before it was sold. Respected publications such as the *New York Times* joined prominent historians in calling the laws direct products of muckraking.[36]

Exposing "Treason" in the United States Senate

In the early years of the twentieth century, the upper house of Congress was widely known as the most reactionary body in America. Elected by state legislatures rather than directly by the people, senators were political puppets who were bought and paid for by Standard Oil and the other corporations that drove the national economy.

As muckraking rose to its zenith, the conservative nature of the Senate—widely known as the "millionaire's club"—stood in stark contrast to the reform movement sweeping the country. For the senators opposed, frankly and aggressively, each and every initiative the muckrakers championed. Only when public sentiment grew to leviathan proportions—as when the muckrakers agitated for regulation of patent medicines—did progressive measures break through the sturdy walls of the Senate.[37]

The man who ultimately challenged this formidable institution was no minion himself: William Randolph Hearst, the bad boy of American journalism, purchased *Cosmopolitan* in 1906 and began pouring money into it, eager to exploit the popular muckraking phenomenon and the soaring circulation it attracted. The author Hearst chose to conduct his exposé of exposés was David Graham Phillips, already a successful novelist.

The series debuted in March 1906, beginning: "The treason of the Senate! Treason is a strong word, but not too strong, rather too weak, to characterize the situation in which the Senate is the eager, resourceful, indefatigable agent of interests as hostile to the American people as any invading army could be, and vastly more dangerous." The article went on to lambaste the interests that "manipulate the prosperity produced by all, so that it heaps up riches for the few; interests whose growth and power can only mean the degradation of the people, of the educated into sycophants, of the masses toward serfdom."[38]

That premiere article focused on New York Senators Chauncey M. Depew and Thomas Collier Platt. Phillips, calling Depew the "archetype of the sleek, self-satisfied American opportunist in politics," disclosed that the senator received $50,000 a year from dozens of corporations in return for political favors. Of Platt, the reporter said he had a "long and unbroken record of treachery to the people in legislation of privilege and plunder."[39]

The accusations reverberated throughout the country, and the series was a runaway success. "Glory Hallelujah!" cried one letter praising *Cosmopolitan*'s courage and service to the public. The writer continued, "You have found a David who is able and willing to attack this Goliath of a Senate."[40]

In later installments, Phillips documented how senator after senator—Nelson W. Aldrich of Rhode Island, Arthur Pue Gorman of Maryland, John C. Spooner of Wisconsin, Joseph Weldon Bailey of Texas, Stephen Benton Elkins of West Virginia, Joseph Benson Foraker of Ohio, William B. Allison of Iowa—played leading roles in an enormous conspiracy to circumvent the needs of the people. Phillips eventually documented that seventy-five of the ninety senators were controlled by corporations.[41]

The series provoked vehement protests and denunciations from the accused. Hearst and Phillips both received hundreds of threatening letters and were repeatedly castigated on the Senate floor. But "The Treason of the Senate" continued, as did public interest. In June, *Cosmopolitan* boasted that its circulation had more than doubled since the series had begun three months earlier, jumping from 200,000 to 450,000.[42]

Phillips was not satisfied, though, simply to create a sensation or ensure the defeat of a few senators. He produced a barrage of irrefutable facts because he wanted readers to realize that the corruption infecting the Senate was not a temporary illness that could be cured by removing the current senators. Instead, he pointed his accusatory finger at the cause of the corruption: state legislatures selecting senators. And then, in the last of his nine articles, he proposed a solution: The voters of each state should elect senators directly.[43]

"The Treason of the Senate" demolished the walls that previously had seemed impossible to penetrate. A dozen senators were defeated in 1906, more in 1908 and 1910. By 1912, all seventy-five of the senators Phillips had exposed were gone. The final triumph in the high-risk crusade came in 1913 when a constitutional amendment transferred the election of senators from state legislatures to the American people. Political observers cited Phillips's stunning series as the catalyst.[44]

Muckraking: An Unparalleled Legacy

In synthesizing the era of reform concentrated in the first dozen years of the twentieth century, noted historian Arthur M. Schlesinger wrote: "Aggressive and sensational measures were required to awaken the nation from its lethargy and to rejuvenate the old spirit of American democracy. To this mission a new generation of Americans dedicated themselves. The protest first found expression through the popular magazines."[45]

Schlesinger is one of many scholars of the Progressive Era who has lavished praise on the muckrakers for their leading role in helping the nation recover from a dark period in its history. As these scholars have pointed out, the reform journalists spearheaded the campaign of investigation and agitation that ultimately set the nation on a more admirable course as it marched boldly into the twentieth century—the American Century. Some historians have focused on documenting the governmental reforms rightly credited to the crusading journalists. Arthur and Lila Weinberg wrote, "Muckraking was directly responsible for such initiatives as the Pure Food and Drug Act, direct election of senators, and city and state reform." Others have lauded the seminal impact that Ida Tarbell and her fellow trustbusters had on American business. C. C. Regier wrote, "The whole tone of business in the United States was raised because of the persistent exposures of corruption and injustice." Still others have made more sweeping observations about the muckraking phenomenon. Vernon Parrington described the muckraking era as "a time of brisk housecleaning that searched out old cobwebs and disturbed the dust that lay thick on the antiquated furniture," and David M. Chalmers said, "Their analysis of national life probed deeply into the vast changes that had taken place during the previous half-century. With their criticism the muckrakers lay the groundwork of public concern which resulted in many reforms."[46]

The reform impulse that the muckrakers ignited ultimately triggered a list of specific activities that was both long and broad. In city after city, corrupt municipal officials were replaced with men and women with professional training and experience. John D. Rockefeller's vice grip on the oil industry was broken, followed by the busting of other trusts that dominated the railroad, mining, liquor, sugar, and beef industries. Labor racketeering was exposed, as were the deplorable conditions that American industry forced workers—including women and children—to endure. The public was made aware of the fraudulent claims and harmful ingredients of food products and patent medicines, prompting federal legislation to protect consumers. Likewise, the unscrupulous profiteering in the United States Senate was revealed and a constitutional amendment was enacted to reform that body.

Despite this formidable list of achievements, a truly comprehensive roll call of reform-oriented journalism would be longer still: *Everybody's* exposés of the inner workings of the stock market and fraud among life insurance companies, *McClure's* articles on scandal in the United States Post Office, *Collier's* assault on the autocratic leaders of the House of Representatives, *Leslie's* report on the shocking number of accidents on the nation's railways, *American Magazine*'s denunciation of society's shameful treatment of African Americans, *The Independent*'s crusade in opposition to lynching and in support of woman's suffrage, and *Hampton's* attacks on organized religion.[47]

Nor is it possible to acknowledge the thousands of words of commendation heaped on the muckraking journalists by a grateful public. Comments praising Lincoln Steffens and Ida Tarbell were particularly abundant. Author Max Lerner wrote, "If we valued our historical figures according to their usefulness in creating a richer and healthier American culture, men like Lincoln Steffens would be heroes to be celebrated in every school and college." Historian Allan Nevins described Tarbell's series on Standard Oil as the "most enduring achievement" of the Progressive Era.[48]

More praise came for the work of the muckrakers as a whole. A professor at a European university gushed, "I find the articles to be the ideal literature of a free republic. They lash hard, cut deep—every blow drawing blood. It is by constant exposures of public evils that such evils are minimized." *The Independent* said in tribute to muckraking, "All right thinking men must rejoice that the literature of exposure came into existence when it did. It has accomplished a great purpose, and the American people will be sounder—more sincere, more fearless in right doing—henceforth because of it. The public conscience has been awakened." Perhaps a Wisconsin man said it most succinctly when he wrote to the reporting staff at *McClure's*, "Your names shall be immortal."[49]

For a final appraisal of this splendid chapter in the evolution of the news media's relationship to American history, it may be best to return to Schlesinger's concluding comments about muckraking. He said the journalistic phenomenon played a profoundly important role in saving democracy from the clutches of the robber barons and returning it to the common people who rightly governed America: "The most beneficial effect of the literature of protest was the moral awakening of the masses. In growing numbers they gave their support to a new group of political leaders who fought to restore government to the people."[50]

7

Defying the Ku Klux Klan

IN THE FALL OF 1915, a strange spectacle unfolded near Atlanta when William Joseph Simmons led a dozen men up a rocky trail on the imposing granite crest of Stone Mountain. As the night wind whipped the American flag that the men carried, Simmons ignited a pine cross that lit up the Georgia sky. Against this theatrical backdrop and with *Bible* in hand, the former preacher led the men in a vow of allegiance to the Knights of the Ku Klux Klan.

That dramatic ceremony expanded, during the next decade, into a nationwide organization that inflamed America's social and political landscape, providing a mooring to the thousands of frightened and disoriented Americans who had been uprooted by the rapid changes that erupted during the 1920s. The KKK offered them a sense of fraternity, a commitment to self-defined traditional American values, and a long list of people to blame for the social upheaval—Catholics, Jews, blacks, and recent immigrants.

The Invisible Empire became a force to be reckoned with. Texas klansmen elected one of their own to the United States Senate. In Arkansas, the KKK was so powerful that it held its own primaries to decide which of several robed brothers to support in the general election. Oregon KKKers captured the governorship and enough of the legislature to ban parochial schools. The klan elected two senators in Colorado and both senators as well as the governor in Indiana. In 1925, the klan invaded the nation's capital as 40,000 robed figures paraded down Pennsylvania Avenue.

Then the tide turned. By the end of the decade, the klan's power had faded into history—at least for the time being. The Invisible Empire's decline can be attributed partly to its lethal combination of violence, politics, and exploitative leadership, as well as its failure to produce the results it promised. But as during so many other chapters of American history, another critical element was the Fourth Estate. For while much of the American press either supported the klan or remained silent on the topic, a handful of newspapers crusaded against the Ku Klux Klan with all their might.

The seminal anti-klan campaign began in 1921 with a blockbuster exposé in the *New York World*. The series documented the organization's immorality and violence in riveting detail. Another assault evolved two years later when the *Commercial Appeal* in Memphis combined compelling front-page cartoons with relentless reporting in a courageous effort to defy the klan in that Tennessee city. Even deeper in the South, Alabama's *Montgomery Advertiser* concentrated its blistering attack, delivered largely during 1927, on the editorial page. The anti-klan efforts of these three newspapers earned them national acclaim as well as Pulitzer Prizes, the highest honor in American journalism.

Each of these valiant journalistic voices helped destroy the most powerful nativist organization in American history. United States Representative Peter F. Tague told a congressional hearing called to investigate the klan, "It has only been through the searching investigation of the great newspapers of the country that the evidence has been brought to the surface." Ku Klux Klan scholar Kenneth T. Jackson expressed a similar sentiment, saying, "Opposition from the newspapers severely damaged the Klan."[1]

Sweeping the Nation

Confederate veterans organized the original Ku Klux Klan in 1866 in hopes of preventing former slaves from exercising their recently acquired rights and to keep in check the carpetbaggers who invaded from the North. Within three years, they felt they had completed their work, and the KKK ceased to exist.

After Simmons revived the klan in 1915, his band of white-robed followers remained minuscule until 1920 when two enterprising promoters recognized the klan as a financial gold mine. Edward Young Clarke and Elizabeth Tyler persuaded Simmons to pay them one-fourth of the ten dollars each new member paid, an arrangement that ultimately yielded the recruiters the handsome sum of $30,000 a week. Propelled by Clarke's ambition and Tyler's craftiness, klan membership soared to four million by 1924. In addition, the Invisible

Empire mushroomed into a national phenomenon, exploding in numbers and influence throughout the West, Midwest, and Northeast, while continuing to grow in the South as well.

Clarke and Tyler urged their 200 recruiters to fill their rhetoric with such loaded phrases as "just laws," "pure womanhood," "100 percent Americans," and "the tenets of the Christian religion"—all crafted to communicate that the country was being overrun by enemies within. KKK recruiters promised to provide better schools, improve law enforcement, and hold fast to the traditional values being threatened by the socially permissive Roaring Twenties.

Klan growth was aided by the prevailing mood among many Americans. President Woodrow Wilson's heartfelt pledge that World War I would make the world safe for democracy had produced a palpable idealism among the American people, but the armistice had failed to deliver the millennium. When the United States Senate repudiated the League of Nations and Europe was again reduced to a gaggle of squabbling nations, Americans became disillusioned. In addition, the all-out war effort was not easily put aside; wartime hatred for the Germans was transformed into a peacetime suspicion of everything foreign—which the KKK eagerly capitalized on.

For the most part, American journalism did not stand in the way, as most newspapers quavered in fear of the klan's burgeoning power. Unwilling to challenge the klan and its broadening network of support, editors either covered the public events and official announcements of the KKK as they did those of other fraternal organizations or maintained a stoic silence regarding this secret society that each day was growing larger and more powerful.

The New York World *Hurls a Hand Grenade*

The first and most comprehensive journalistic crusade in defiance of the klan was a no-holds-barred exposé in the newspaper that Joseph Pulitzer had built to legendary proportions. The *New York World* promoted its September 1921 blockbuster with full-page ads that screamed, in three-inch letters: "Ku Klux Klan Exposed!" The ads carried quarter-page drawings of hooded figures as well as heart-thumping promises: "In Vivid, Picturesque Detail the World Will Tell the Story of the Purposes, the Ambitions, the Activities of the Ku Klux Klan."[2]

What the ads promised, the series delivered. The opening article characterized the klan's growth as a financial scam that had bilked members out of $40 million in initiation fees and charges for klan regalia. "The Knights of the Ku Klux Klan, Inc.," the sensational story read, "has become a vast enterprise, doing a thriving business in the systematic sale of race hatred, religious bigotry, and '100 percent' *anti-*Americanism."[3]

Anticipating more drama to come, *World* readers clamored for the next issue, creating a moment of rare excitement in New York journalism. Even before the first copies rolled off the presses a few minutes past midnight each morning, a crowd of eager readers gathered beneath the World Building's golden dome to grab the next installment.

The series continued full throttle day after day for three solid weeks, boldly and relentlessly answering tantalizing questions about the mysterious organization, much as Ida Tarbell had told the public about Standard Oil two decades earlier—but with considerably more flash.

The *World* received its biggest boost from former klan officer Henry R. Fry, who had joined the KKK thinking it was a fraternal order like the Elks or Odd Fellows. After learning the organization was founded on bigotry and hatred, however, he quit—and then gave the *World* hundreds of documents. Rowland Thomas, a novelist at heart, pored over the material and then wrote about it with passion and unrestrained zeal, knowing that all of America was eager to hear every detail.

Although the exposé was written in a sensational style, the *World* was as committed to destroying the klan as it was to building its own circulation. To ensure the series had maximum impact, the *World* syndicated it to eighteen dailies around the country. With such major voices as the *Boston Globe* and *Pittsburgh Sun* in the East, *St. Louis Post-Dispatch* and *Cleveland Plain-Dealer* in the Midwest, *Seattle Times* and Oklahoma City *Oklahoman* in the West, and *New Orleans Times-Picayune* and *Dallas Morning News* in the South reprinting the articles, the series held more than two million readers spellbound each day.

The series missed nothing. One article reported that Simmons advocated a return to chattel slavery, and another quoted lawyers saying the klan oath was illegal because it required members to obey the Imperial Wizard even when his orders conflicted with the United States Constitution. Still another meticulously recorded the name and address of 214 recruiters—from E. Y. Clarke, Imperial Kleagle, Suite 501 Flatiron Building, Atlanta, to W. S. Coburn, Grand Goblin, 519 Haas Building, Los Angeles—much as a newspaper might report the names on an FBI most wanted list.[4]

To guarantee that the series held the public's attention, editors packaged each installment with compelling artwork. Accompanying one article was a facsimile of the application form each member completed—with questions reading "Were your parents born in the United States?" and "Are you a Jew?" Other eye-popping images were created by reproducing some of the letters the *World* received from anonymous klansmen. One hand-scrawled letter reprinted on the front page read, "You will seal your death warrant. Watch out—you nigger lovers." Another letter, marked with a skull and crossbones, said, "KU KLUX KLAN—DEATH ULTIMATUM to the WORLD—You will have the pleasure to receive the necessary punishment for the publication of your series of articles regarding the Secrets of our powerful and holly [sic] ORDER. BEWARE."[5]

One of the paper's most explosive articles revealed the immorality of the organization's two master recruiters. The *World* reported that during a 1919 raid on a house of prostitution, Atlanta police had identified the drunken occupants of one bed as Tyler, who was widowed, and Clarke, who was married—but not to Tyler. A judge found them guilty of disorderly conduct.[6]

In a desperate attempt to protect the KKK's reputation, Atlanta klansmen immediately purchased all 3,000 copies of the *World* available in the city on the day the Clarke-Tyler story broke. When that effort failed and word of the peccadillo spread, klan officials accused the *World* of libel, swearing the Atlanta Police Department had no record of such an arrest and threatening to file a $10 million libel suit against the paper.

When Thomas returned to Atlanta to reexamine the records, he discovered that the incriminating pages had been cut out of the police file. Thomas had, during his earlier investigation, procured certified copies of the records, but the incident demonstrated that the klan's reach extended even to Atlanta law enforcement officers. It was fortunate that Thomas had secured the copies, as it was only after he produced them that the klan withdrew its threat of a libel suit.

As the klan cowered, the *World* went beyond reporting. In one proactive effort, the paper contacted New York public officials and forced them to go on the record either opposing or supporting the klan. Because their comments would become part of the *World*'s devastating exposé, the officials had little choice but to criticize the klan, thereby providing the newspaper with public statements it could revive when the Invisible Empire tried to make inroads into New York City. In response to the paper's inquiry, the president of the borough of Brooklyn said, "The Ku Klux Klan is an un-American movement," and New York City's police commissioner railed, "There is no room in America for an organization of religious and racial bigots." The *World* kept up the pressure for officials to take formal action against the klan. After several weeks of the paper's incessant badgering, the New York Board of Aldermen finally adopted a resolution condemning the KKK.[7]

The *World* climaxed its campaign with a withering summary of klan violence. Thomas began the article with impassioned rhetoric, saying of the klan, "For the forces of the law it substitutes terrorism, replacing trial and punishment of offenders with anonymous threats and masked infliction of vengeance." Next to the dramatic prose ran a tabulated list of outrages attributed to the Invisible Empire: four murders, twenty-seven tar and featherings, forty-one floggings—a total of 152 violent acts.[8]

Readers applauded the bold journalistic venture. One woman gushed, "I consider *The World*'s revelations regarding the Ku Klux Klan a public service of the highest type." An attorney wrote of the paper, "I wish it every success in its efforts to suppress this organization." The president of an organization of recent immigrants spoke for thousands when he said, "The League of Foreign Born Citizens congratulates the *World* upon its public service in vindication of the hope that America will remain the land of liberty without distinction of race, creed or nationality."[9]

As a result of the series, the United States House of Representatives launched an investigation of the klan. A mere two weeks after the exposé ended, Representative Peter F. Tague of Massachusetts opened the hearings by eulogizing the *World* and placing the series into evidence. Representative Leonidas C. Dyer of Missouri added his commendation, "I want to express to the *New York World* my great appreciation of the work it has done in bringing the facts to the attention of the public."[10]

As further evidence of the pivotal role the *World* had played, the congressmen called Rowland Thomas as their first witness. But Thomas took the high road, refusing to reveal any information that had not already appeared in print and saying simply, "We attempted always without bias to get an accurate statement of the facts."[11]

Thomas's brief comments were eclipsed by three days of theatrical testimony by the man who quickly emerged as the star of the hearings: Imperial Wizard William Joseph Simmons. Before his testimony began, Representative William Upshaw of Georgia set the stage. One of the first klansmen elected to Congress, Upshaw extolled Simmons effusively, "Knowing his sterling character as I do, I am prepared to underwrite his every utterance as the truth of an honest, patriotic man."[12]

Charming and courtly, sixty-year-old Simmons portrayed himself as a kindly Southern gentleman who had been viciously maligned by a mercenary northern newspaper. Dignified and impeccably dressed, he spoke eloquently of the KKK's benevolent purposes as a defender of America and swore the klan did not participate in violence of any sort, asserting the outrages attributed to it had been committed by criminals hiding behind klan robes. After refuting all charges, Simmons dramatically swore: "Here in the presence of God, before this committee of one of the greatest law making and deliberative bodies in the world, and standing in the shadow of the Capitol of our great nation, I say to you, gentlemen, that if the Ku Klux Klan was guilty of a hundredth part of the charges that have been made against us, I would forever disband the klan in every section of the United States." After delivering his statement with ultimate flair, Simmons collapsed in a faint.[13]

Besides defending the klan, Simmons used his time in the spotlight to attack the *World*. Reinforcing a racial stereotype of Jews, the Southern Methodist minister raised his nose slightly before telling the congressmen: "The attacks against the klan were originated and started by the *New York World*, which is owned and controlled by a Jew, Mr. Pulitzer, whose main purpose is circulation and revenue."[14]

Simmons's testimony was a triumph. By using the techniques of a showman and blatantly appealing to prejudice, he shifted public opinion regarding the klan. After three days of his oratory, many members of Congress and much of the American populace ceased to see the KKK as a demon and suddenly saw it as a hapless victim. In this new climate, Representative Upshaw introduced a bill stating that if the klan were prosecuted, similar investigations would be conducted of the Knights of Columbus, the Freemasons, and other fraternal societies. The klan hearings quickly ended.

This surprise development was soon followed by an even more shocking one. For in one of the more ironic twists in the history of American journalism, the *World* soon discovered that its bold campaign had totally backfired. The New York editors gradually came to learn the painful lesson that legions of news people of every generation have been forced to accept: Editors often are out of touch with their readers.

In this instance, the *World* editors finally had to acknowledge that their sensational crusade ultimately had not destroyed the klan but—quite the opposite—had given it a tremendous boost. For by reporting the KKK's insidious acts of bigotry and violence, the series described in glorious detail the exact elements of the klan that potential members found so appealing. The widely printed series, in fact, gave the klan its first national publicity—free of charge. Before these masses of frustrated Americans read the series, many of them had never heard of this secret society that offered members a way to fight change while hiding under the anonymity of hoods. By the end of the series, KKK recruiters were finding thousands of worried citizens, especially in the West and Midwest, who were not outraged by what they read but were eager to join the klan. Hundreds of zealots even clipped the application form straight from the *World*, filled it in, and mailed it to Atlanta with their membership fee. Historians have stated that while the series increased the *World*'s circulation by 100,000, it also boosted klan membership by several thousand.[15]

So as the *World* basked in the glory of winning the 1922 Pulitzer Prize for public service for its series on the klan, the newspaper could not ignore the fact that its reporting had spurred the growth of the organization and that Simmons's dramatic performance on Capitol Hill had stymied the momentum to stop the klan. The Invisible Empire clearly was a formidable force that would not be defeated merely by one series of newspaper articles.[16]

The Commercial Appeal *Engages in Hand-to-Hand Combat*

The next major battlefield in the klan-newspaper war unfolded in 1923 in Memphis, where Ku Klux Klan membership exceeded 10,000.

The city's major newspaper, the *Commercial Appeal*, gave the klan no quarter, with editor C.P.J. Mooney criticizing it as a profit-making scam. He also condemned the klan's use of vigilante violence as a means of terrorizing the city's African Americans, Catholics, and Jews. "The law is the soul of the nation," Mooney wrote. "No aggregation of individuals has a right to take unto themselves the duties of judges and juries."[17]

Even more effective than the editorials were the bruising front-page cartoons drawn by J. P. Alley, who portrayed klansmen as cowardly fiends hiding behind masks and bedsheets as they preyed upon the powerless. One showed a brawny man towering over a frail woman lying helpless on the ground as the man lashed a bullwhip across her back. The caption: "His 'noble work,' done in the dark!" Another showed a hooded klan member being ordered to unmask. In the next frame, the face was revealed as grotesquely ugly. The caption: "No wonder he puts a sack over that mug!" One of the most memorable of Alley's drawings juxtaposed a man draped in a white bedsheet and wearing the label "100% American" against a uniformed World War I veteran whose military duty had cost him one of his legs; the soldier smirked, angled his thumb toward the robed figure, and said sarcastically, "I'm unworthy—my religion ain't right!"[18]

This editorial cartoon by J. C. Alley took a light approach to depicting the ugliness of religious and racial bigotry. Reprinted by permission of the Memphis Commercial Appeal.

"I'M UNWORTHY—MY RELIGION AIN'T RIGHT!"

This biting Commercial Appeal *cartoon by Alley captured the absurdity of the KKK hating all Catholics—even disabled World War I veterans. Reprinted by permission of the Memphis* Commercial Appeal.

Klansmen recognized the potential damage of the drawings and sent Alley threatening letters. Undaunted, he not only continued his attack but depicted the intimidation tactics in a cartoon. It showed Alley sitting at his desk when a hooded figure approached him, knocked him off his chair, and threatened him with a huge club. Another frame showed Alley opening a letter to find the word "Warning." But the final frame showed Alley back at his desk, hard at work. The caption: "The Trials of a Cartoonist."[19]

The *Commercial Appeal*'s reporting staff concentrated its efforts on showcasing the internal struggles that befell the klan as the organization showed increasing signs of dissension from within. When klansmen Hiram W. Evans and J. A. Comer challenged Simmons's leadership, the newspaper transformed the conflict into front-page news. Reveling in the vicious infighting, the *Commercial Appeal* milked the story for all it was worth. One article read, "Charges of 'money-grabbing' made by J. A. Comer, grand dragon of the realm of Arkansas, were answered by similar charges by Emperor Simmons, who referred to several 'deals' in which Comer profited." Another article quoted Simmons calling Evans a "coward" and saying the klan was "tottering" under the new leadership. When the national officers charged each other with misusing funds and filed breach of promise suits against each other, those actions were immediately catapulted onto page one as well.[20]

The *Commercial Appeal*'s animus toward the klan did not derive from a progressive world view. For at the same time that the newspaper was taking up the cudgel against the klan, it supported anti-evolutionists while refusing to endorse a federal anti-lynching law. The newspaper's opposition to the secret order evolved from Mooney being Catholic and from his fear that the klan's stirring up of black Memphis would disrupt the status quo of white dominance. In one anti-klan editorial, Mooney stated patronizingly: "Ordinarily the white people of the south and the negro get along very well. It's only when an 'emperor' or a labor agent or something similar butts in that trouble ensues."[21]

Regardless of the *Commercial Appeal*'s motivation, the war between the klan and the *Commercial Appeal* intensified when the Invisible Empire became the key issue in the 1923 city election. After Mayor Rowlett Paine rejected invitations to join the klan, the hooded society nominated W. Joe Wood for mayor and four other klansmen for the Memphis City Commission. In a blatant act of intimidation, the klan placed its campaign headquarters directly across the street from the Commercial Appeal Building.

The KKK raised the campaign to a fever pitch, with nightly meetings in the Lyric Theater where Wood and his fellow candidates stood on either side of a white floral cross while 2,000 klansmen crowded together to hear speakers decry the pope and international Jewish bankers. During the rowdy meetings, every mention of the klan brought applause and a thunderous stomping of feet, but any reference to Mayor Paine or the *Commercial Appeal* drew boos and curses.

As the election neared and tension built, national klan leaders descended on the city, with Evans predicting a klan rout. Intimidation tactics mounted as well, with the klan's *Tri-State American* newspaper warning voters, "If you fail to fulfill the duty you owe to your family, the Ku Klux Klan will banish you and report your negligence to the duly constituted authorities." Mayor Paine was continuously threatened, too, as crosses were burned in his yard almost nightly.[22]

Mooney wrote somberly, "The eyes of the nation are on Memphis," and the *Commercial Appeal* went into a full-court press. When Louisiana law officials investigated possible klan involvement in the deaths of two men in that state, the accusations covered page one, as did a Philadelphia man's legal effort to dissolve the klan. And when the Invisible Empire's top publicity agent shot the organization's chief counsel in Atlanta, the *Commercial Appeal* made the incident its lead story three days in a row, spawning such fiery headlines as: "Bloody Climax in Klan Feud" and "Victim and Slayer in Klan Blood-Feud."[23]

On election day, the editorial page carried two rhetorical denunciations of the klan, and page one offered three stridently anti-klan articles, including accusations of a tar and feathering in Texas and the beating of an elderly woman in Alabama. On that crucial day, Mooney reserved the back page for a dramatic statement from the local veterans organization. One side of the page showed a white-robed klansman, the other a World War I soldier. The two-inch-high headline asked: "Which? The Men Who Wear the Hood or the Men Who Wore the Uniform?" The statement was signed "The Vets Club Campaign Committee."[24]

But the most effective editorial element in that election day issue appeared on the front page, where Alley created one of his most arresting cartoons. The eloquently simple drawing showed a man's hand covered in a white glove so the thumb and each finger looked like a klansman wearing a pointed white hood, the middle finger labeled "Mayor" and each of the other four marked "Commissioner." On the shirtsleeve were written the words "Imperial Wizard of Atlanta." The cartoon's message was clear: If local klan candidates were elected, they would be mere puppets of the KKK's diabolical campaign to make

THE SINISTER HAND.

"HALT, MEMPHIS!"

Appearing on the day of the crucial 1923 city election, this searing J. C. Alley cartoon helped defeat the KKK in Memphis by suggesting that if klansmen were elected, the city actually would be run from KKK headquarters in Atlanta. Reprinted by permission of the Memphis Commercial Appeal.

hatred America's driving value. The caption: "The Sinister Hand. 'HALT, MEMPHIS!'"[25]

Election day chaos was unparalleled. Klansmen distributed literature outside every polling place, and police sent riot alarms from fifteen precincts. When the ballots began to be counted, a mob of 400 klansmen demanded that the counting be in public. The men forced election officials into the street, surrounded them, and insisted that they count the ballots by the light of a huge bonfire. When the police arrived, they managed to secure the ballot box and move it to the courthouse in a police car—only by agreeing that a klan leader could keep the box constantly in his sight. Even then, dozens of automobiles filled with angry klansmen followed threateningly behind the police car.

Despite the rousing political rallies, intimidating tactics, and election-day antics, the klan was soundly defeated. Mayor Paine and his commissioners were reelected with 60 percent of the vote. When Paine led his followers in a jubilant victory parade through downtown, he stopped in front of the Commercial Appeal Building and directed the band to serenade the newspaper in honor of its decisive role in the election.[26]

In fact, when the results were announced, the entire nation seemed to breathe a sigh of relief. The *New York Times* hailed the election as "the biggest black eye the klan has yet received" and showered much of the credit on the *Commercial Appeal*. The most substantial paean, though, came from another New York institution when the School of Journalism at Columbia University awarded the *Commercial Appeal* the 1923 Pulitzer Prize for public service. The citation lauded the newspaper's "courageous attitude in the publication of cartoons and the handling of news in reference to the Ku Klux Klan."[27]

The Montgomery Advertiser *Wages War in the Deep South*

Though the *World*'s and *Commercial Appeal*'s anti-klan crusades were courageous, a third newspaper deserves even more applause. For this journalistic voice waged its battles in what, during the 1920s when the Ku Klux Klan was at its peak, can only be described as the belly of the beast: the Deep South.

Both Simmons and Evans came from central Alabama where the *Montgomery Advertiser* was published, helping build the state into a southern stronghold. The Alabama branch of the Invisible Empire reached the zenith of its political power in 1926 when it sent Hugo Black to Washington as senator and elected Bibb Graves governor.

The most sinister sign of the klan was not in polling places, however, but in secluded spots on country roads. For in response to what Alabama klansmen perceived as the reprehensible moral decay of the 1920s, they imposed a self-defined code of personal behavior that they enforced through acts of physical violence. Specifically, klansmen meted out their vigilante justice through floggings. Exactly how many men and women were kidnapped and lashed with bullwhips will never be known, but the figure was at least in the hundreds—possibly in the thousands. Many victims were beaten because the klan objected to their gambling or drinking habits; others suffered solely because of their color, religion, or ethnic background.

In 1927, the lone journalistic voice raised in opposition to flogging was that of Grover Cleveland Hall, editor of the *Montgomery Advertiser*. His editorials often recounted the appalling details of specific incidents, such as a mob of masked klansmen descending on Arthur Hitt, a respected African-American farmer, and "beating him unmercifully" until he sold them his farm for $80, even though the mineral-laden land was worth ten times that amount. Hall wrote, "It is perfectly outrageous that a negro or any other person should be bullied and frightened into sacrificing the fruits of a lifetime of toil in order to save his life." Hall ended the editorial with the dramatic question "How long, O Lord, how long?"[28]

The violence could be stopped, Hall argued, if a state law prohibited people from wearing masks: "The flogging evil cannot be effectively grappled with until it is made unlawful in Alabama to wear disguises in public places, and made a felony for men thus disguised to attack citizens of this state."[29]

Hall did not, however, speak for all of Alabama journalism. Many newspapers supported flogging, commending the klan for providing the moral leadership that, the papers argued, public officials were not. In its defense of the klan's vigilante activities, the *Alabama Christian Advocate* argued that flogging victims deserved the treatment they received, saying, "They are menaces to their communities." Many newspapers that refused to criticize flogging did not hesitate to attack the *Advertiser*. Calling Hall's editorial crusade "hysterical paroxysm," the *Monroe Journal* wrote, "Just what good purpose the *Advertiser* imagines might be served by unrestrained denunciation of this particular form of criminality we fail to fathom." The *Evergreen Courant* made the same point, asking, "Why raise such a howl?"[30]

Hall would brook no compromise. Instead of backing off, he adopted the additional tactic of reprinting the statements of outrage that began to appear in the Northern press as word of the floggings spread. An item that initially appeared in the *New York Herald Tribune* screamed, "When a mob of masked men invades a citizen's home at night, renders him helpless and then takes his wife out of bed, ties her to a barrel in the front yard and flogs her, is there any punishment within the law too drastic for the crime? We doubt it." One that first appeared in the *Milwaukee Journal* asked of Alabama, "Aren't there enough men down there to say that there must be an end to this bigotry and intolerance and brutality? Isn't there someone strong enough to lead a successful movement to blot out this new monstrosity?" The *New York Times* wrote indignantly that it should surprise no one that floggers were not indicted, "The floggings are attributed to the salutary moral forces of the Ku Klux Klan, the ruler of Alabama." Hall reproduced each negative characterization of Alabama along with his own comments about how the klan was damaging the state's reputation.[31]

By the end of the summer of 1927, Hall had succeeded in stirring public sentiment to the point that public officials could no longer ignore the KKK's violence. On the local level, police began investigating floggings and making arrests. When they did, Hall trumpeted the news in huge headlines. When seven men were charged in one county, five in another, and three in a third, the editor opted not to write three small items but pulled all the arrests together to create a major story showcased under the banner headline "Fifteen Persons Jailed in Lash Probe" and to laud the arrests with a flurry of editorials such as "Alabama's Good Name Vindicated." With the one-two punch of blockbuster news stories and rousing editorials, Hall ensured that the actions were branded into the public consciousness with such intensity that law enforcement officials had no choice but to prosecute the floggers. And when the men were tried and sentenced, Hall pulled out all the stops to provide headlines as well as editorial hosannas. He hailed one decision with the banner headline "Clayton Gets 8 to 10 Years as Flogger" as well as a twenty-inch story and photos of the flogger, victim, and judge—all on page one. On the editorial page, the editor was elated, saying, "We rejoice that Alabama has redeemed itself."[32]

Public opinion prompted action in the state legislature as well, for the elected representatives from throughout Alabama who came to the capital city also were influenced by Hall's crusade. Progressive legislators in both houses introduced tough anti-mask bills calling for exactly what Hall had advocated: to outlaw masks and robes such as those worn by KKKers, and to stipulate that masked floggers would be tried as felons. Hall threw his editorial weight behind the proposals: "The bills are an honest effort to go to the heart of the evils that have grown out of the use of hood and robe. They are designed to end terrorism in Alabama."[33]

Klansmen in the legislature, however, responded to the tough proposals by mounting a formidable defense. When Governor Graves sided with the pro-mask legislators, the fate of the anti-mask proposals were sealed. They were soundly defeated.

But Hall's battle with klan legislators had only just begun. In hopes of silencing the editor, klansmen in the state house proposed what became known as the "muzzling" bills. The sponsors of the reactionary bills said they would protect the state's national reputation, which the men argued had been severely damaged by the unfavorable publicity that Hall's crusade had propagated throughout the country. As evidence, the legislators cited the various editorials from newspapers such as the *Milwaukee Journal* and *New York Times* that Hall had reprinted.

To quiet the *Advertiser*, the legislators proposed broadening state libel laws to an unprecedented degree. According to the bills, any newspaper that published information that was deemed to be false and damaging to the state would be fined $25,000. The diabolical element of the legislation concerned who would do the deeming. Specifically, a widely circulated paper such as the *Advertiser* could be sued in every county where it circulated. That meant the decision about whether a particular statement was libelous could be decided by a jury of klansmen in any remote county in the state. In addition, the bills stipulated that no higher court could alter the verdict of the original jury. And, finally, the law would be retroactive to the previous year, meaning the *Advertiser* could be fined for all the negative statements it had made about the KKK during the anti-mask campaign.

Hall's criticism of the proposed legislation was ferocious. "A ruthless machine, drunk with power and maddened by editorial darts and flings, strikes at its foe, the press—and hits the friend of man, namely: The constitutional safeguard of freedom." He railed against the legislation, pointing out that it directly violated the First Amendment: "These bills are designed to kill freedom of the press in Alabama. They are a malicious, tyrannical, outrageous scheme to bulldoze and punish a free press."[34]

Despite Hall's searing attacks, Governor Graves lobbied hard for the muzzling bills, calling anti-klan legislators to his office for private meetings. National and state klan leaders swarmed to Montgomery to lobby for the legislation as well. The bills moved through the House

Judiciary Committee and onto the House floor, prompting what the *Advertiser* labeled "a four-hour battle which transcended in heat and passion legislative battles for a score of years." The final vote could not have been closer. But with forty-eight in favor and forty-eight opposed, the bills failed.[35]

Hall was recognized for his courage in defying the klan when he was awarded the Pulitzer Prize. The citation read, "Grover Cleveland Hall, *Montgomery Advertiser*, for his editorials against gangsterism, floggings, and racial and religious intolerance."[36]

Turning Back the Ku Klux Klan

The Pulitzer Prize is print journalism's highest honor, but newspapers truly dedicated to fulfilling their role in a democratic society find even greater reward in having positive influence on their communities. The *New York World*, Memphis *Commercial Appeal*, and *Montgomery Advertiser* all found themselves in that position, as each valiant journalistic voice ultimately had the satisfaction of knowing that it had delivered a body blow of no small impact.

Although observers have acknowledged that the *World*'s blockbuster series boosted the klan's growth in the West and Midwest, they have praised the ultimate positive impact it had on New York City. For the newspaper's proactive effort in getting city officials on the record as opposing the klan played a pivotal role in stopping the klan from gaining a foothold in America's largest urban center. The KKK enjoyed a high profile in New York state, with strong chapters in Albany, Buffalo, Schenectady, Syracuse, and Utica, but recruiters failed utterly in their efforts to attract New York City residents into their membership. The *Commercial Appeal* did the same, as the klan's defeat in the 1923 Memphis elections became a model of how the citizenry of a city could halt the klan—if the city was blessed with a courageous newspaper. Likewise, the *Advertiser* earned praise for its role in stopping the klan's rise to power in the state capital; Alabama's largest city, Birmingham, became a KKK stronghold, but the Invisible Empire failed miserably in efforts to become a power in Montgomery, the state's second largest city.[37]

Scholars who have studied the Ku Klux Klan also have extolled the Fourth Estate more broadly, lauding its vital role in keeping the klan in check. David M. Chalmers wrote in *Hooded Americanism* that the newspapers had more impact on the klan than any other force, and Kenneth T. Jackson wrote in *The Ku Klux Klan in the City* that the beginning of the country's resistance to the 1920s klan can be dated precisely to the newspaper campaigns.[38]

American journalism historians have echoed these praises. John Hohenberg wrote in *The Pulitzer Prize Story* that the anti-klan coverage "shows what digging and documenting can do to a seemingly powerful organization." One of the most effusive tributes to journalism's offensive against the klan came in the 1930s, in the immediate wake of the klan's decline, when Silas Bent wrote in *Newspaper Crusaders: A Neglected Story,* "That the klan is widely discredited, and in most places is an object of ridicule, is due to the drubbing administered it by the newspapers." He continued, "In no public issue have the newspapers of this country exhibited sounder editorial sense than in regard to the Ku Klux Klan. In few instances have they worked more effectively and boldly for the general good."[39]

8

Father Coughlin: Fomenting Anti-Semitism via the Radio

DURING THE 1930s and 1940s, a virulent anti-Semitism pervaded American society. Jews were unacceptable to many employers and unwelcome at many universities and social clubs. Jokes about "kikes" and "Yids" were commonplace, and oceanside beaches posted signs stating "No Dogs or Jews Allowed." Bigots such as Senator Theodore Bilbo and Representative John Rankin, both of Mississippi, openly expressed their hatred for Jews in the halls of the United States Congress. More than 100 civic organizations around the country publicly blamed Jews for the economic ills oppressing the nation. In 1939 a Roper opinion poll found that 53 percent of Americans believed restrictions against Jews were fully justified, and in 1942, in the midst of World War II, when respondents to another opinion poll were asked which groups represented the greatest threat to the American way of life, the three top answers were the Germans, the Japanese, and the Jews.[1]

Such flagrant hostility toward a segment of society does not emerge of its own accord. The American news media helped fuel anti-Semitism, with many newspapers openly supporting the various acts of discrimination. Anti-Semitic papers such as the *American Gentile*, *National American*, and *American-Ranger* spewed bigotry on American street corners with headlines such as "Communism Is Jewish" and "Jews Defile Our Christmas!"[2]

But the single most influential anti-Semitic spokesman in the country was a Roman Catholic priest who each Sunday afternoon took to the radio airwaves and spit a hateful venom across America.

Father Charles E. Coughlin had a voice like honey, but his message was pure poison. Between 1926 and 1940, his weekly radio broadcast routinely reached fifteen million listeners and sometimes attracted an extraordinary forty-five million—more than a third of the country's population. *Social Justice*, the magazine Coughlin published, boasted a weekly circulation of one million, and he also reprinted his radio talks as pamphlets sent without charge to his ardent followers. On both the airwaves and in print, Coughlin's fundamental message was the same: Jews are evil, money-hungry conspirators who have infiltrated American life and are destroying every value that Christian people hold sacred.

Emergence of the Radio Priest

Charles Edward Coughlin was born into a middle-class family of Irish heritage in Ontario, Canada, in 1891. A brilliant student, he was educated in Catholic schools and received a bachelor's degree from St. Michael's College and a divinity degree from St. Basil's Seminary, both in Toronto. Ordained in 1916, he quickly earned a reputation as an articulate and dynamic orator.

In 1926, Father Coughlin was called to a challenging task. Bishop Michael J. Gallagher of Detroit had decided to build a shrine to Saint Therese, and he chose Father Coughlin to be pastor of the new church. The post was a demanding one, as the Detroit suburb chosen for the shrine, Royal Oak, was a working-class community pockmarked with vacant lots and abandoned buildings. As an innovative means of expanding his congregation, Father Coughlin approached Detroit radio station WJR and asked to broadcast a weekly sermon based on the news events and issues of the day.

From the moment Father Coughlin stepped to the microphone on October 17, 1926—wearing his priestly vestments and standing at the altar of his church—his experiment with the untried medium of radio was a glorious success. Within a few months, thousands of letters and financial contributions were flowing into Royal Oak, Detroit newsmen anointed Coughlin the "Radio Priest," and in 1930 the young cleric signed a contract to speak nationwide on the Columbia Broadcasting System.

Because the country was floundering in the morass of the Great Depression, the radio commentator initially concentrated much of his discourse on economic matters. And economics soon led him into politics. His powerful voice rose in indignation as he assailed the bankers for causing the country's fiscal woes. The week that Father Coughlin

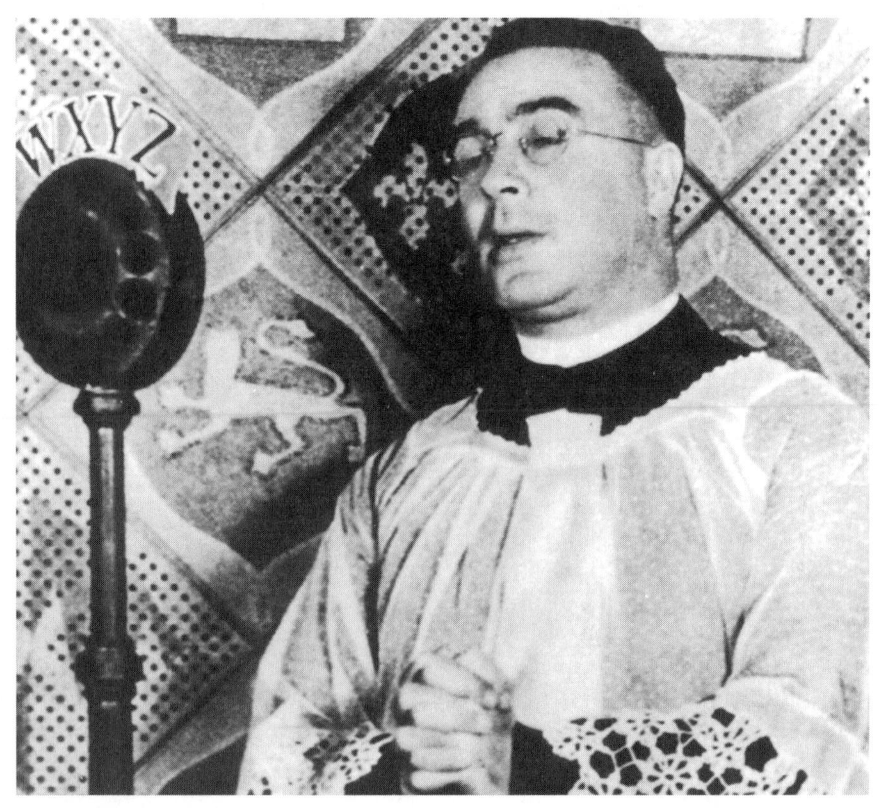

Although Father Charles E. Coughlin could look and sound like a gentle parish priest, his anti-Semitic venom was harsh and hateful. Reprinted by permission of the Library of Congress.

stepped into politics by castigating President Herbert Hoover as "the banker's friend, the Holy Ghost of the rich, the protective angel of Wall Street," listeners so loved the potent rhetoric that they flooded Royal Oak with 1.2 million letters.[3]

By 1932, the Radio Priest's weekly commentary had become so popular that he was employing 100 clerks to process 80,000 letters a week, and Royal Oak had to build a post office expressly to handle his mail. The young priest with the mellifluous voice was riding high on a wave of public interest in the newest mass medium. Radio prices plummeted with technological advancements in the early 1930s, making it possible for 70 percent of American homes to be equipped with a radio, the communication medium hailed as the "miracle of the age." By mid-decade, Coughlin's Sunday broadcast had become one of the most popular programs on the air.[4]

People crowded around their radios partly because of the magnificent oratorical quality of Coughlin's golden voice, which was touched with an Irish brogue and which scholars have described as "warm," "inviting," "mellow," "manly," "rich," "vibrant," and "electric." The Radio Priest's ability to reach his audience was aided by other characteristics as well. One biographer wrote, "His success was a result of his extraordinary skills as a radio performer, his ability to make his sermons accessible, interesting, and provocative."[5]

Eager to exploit the new medium, Father Coughlin learned that sprinkling his script with colloquial terms such as "swell," "damn," and "lousy" made his presentation even more engaging. He also spiced up his talks with ringing assertions and righteous fury, becoming a master at coining memorable phrases—"Christ or chaos," "the New Deal is God's deal," "Roosevelt or ruin."

The simplistic phrasing appealed to the masses of farmers, laborers, and industrial workers who waited eagerly for Coughlin's weekly visit into their homes. Crushed by the Depression that had stolen their expectations of social and economic mobility, these working-class Americans—particularly those of Irish and German descent—responded by the millions to Coughlin's radio magnetism. By 1933, listeners were sending some $5 million a year to "the messiah of Royal Oak," providing him with abundant funds not only to build and operate the shrine but to plan bold new ventures as well. Having no desire to accumulate wealth for hedonistic purposes, Father Coughlin used some of the money to establish a relief center where Depression victims could come for food and clothing, and he also erected a mammoth new shrine church with seating for 3,500 and a seven-story granite and marble tower with an immense crucified Christ across one side.

But Father Coughlin generated controversy as well. Not every listener applauded his vitriolic attacks on the nation's political leaders and economic institutions, and persons of authority began to question the priest's tactics. Al Smith, a Catholic and former governor of New York, told the *New York Times* in 1933, "When a man addresses so great a number of listeners as Father Coughlin, he assumes the responsibility of not misleading them by false statements or poisoning their judgments with baseless slanders." Opting to avoid trouble, CBS refused to renew Coughlin's contract and NBC declined his request to pick it up. Screaming that the networks were denying his freedom of speech, Coughlin hired his own stations and paid for the connecting phone lines himself to form his own network of sixty stations stretching from Maine to Colorado.[6]

In 1934, Coughlin moved into direct political action by creating the National Union for Social Justice. "I call upon you," he told his listeners, "to rise above the concept of an audience and become a living, vibrant, united, and active organization, superior to politics." Within a year, the National Union had eight million members.[7]

By 1935, Coughlin's convictions included strident opposition to communism, partly because anticommunist rhetoric struck a responsive chord among his followers. He adopted an alarmist tone, arguing that communists were plotting a bloody revolution to overthrow the American government and way of life.

That same year, Coughlin demonstrated that he could mobilize his followers to political action. Opposing a plan to create a World Court, he asserted that the organization would benefit only the "satanic international bankers" he blamed for America's economic woes. Coughlin urged his listeners to block the proposal, which President Franklin Roosevelt supported, by contacting their members of Congress. Coughlin's appeal produced an extraordinary 200,000 telegrams bearing more than one million signatures. The deluge was so massive that it overwhelmed the country's telegraph companies, forcing them to halt their operations temporarily. Congress was stunned by Coughlin's power, and the World Court suffered a crushing defeat. Both the *New York Times* and President Roosevelt himself credited Coughlin with killing the proposal.[8]

As Coughlin's power grew, so did his dissatisfaction with Roosevelt. The solution to America's lack of money, Coughlin said, was simply to print more currency. The president opposed the inflationary proposal as shortsighted; Coughlin argued that F.D.R. was a pawn of the international bankers. When Roosevelt continued to turn a deaf ear to Coughlin, the radio commentator broke from Roosevelt, coining new epithets—"The New Deal is a raw deal!" and "We can't have a New Deal without a new deck!"

In 1936, Coughlin expanded beyond the radio waves and began to commit his rhetoric to the printed word as well, founding his own weekly tabloid magazine. *Social Justice* printed the scripts from his broadcasts in addition to other essays and news items supporting his political, social, and economic philosophy.[9]

By the same year, Coughlin also had grown into a national political force, as *New Republic* magazine credited him with single-handedly ousting two congressmen from Ohio and engineering a humiliating defeat for the Cleveland Democratic machine. Bolstered by these successes, he became the driving force behind a third political party formed to capture the White House. Ineligible for the presidency because of his Canadian birth, Coughlin chose Congressman William Lemke, a North Dakota Republican, to head the Union Party ticket. Drawing enthusiastic crowds as large as 30,000 as he campaigned from coast to coast, the Radio Priest boldly asserted that if his party did not win at least nine million votes, he would retire from broadcasting. When Lemke pulled only about one-tenth that number, Coughlin withdrew from radio.[10]

Having tasted real power, however, he did not remain silent for long. In early 1937, his golden throat once again found its place on the American airwaves when he created a new forty-seven-station hookup that spanned the continent. Aware that his miserable failure in the election meant he would have to find a new theme if he hoped to hold the attention of his listeners, Father Coughlin focused on the position that ultimately would have devastating impact on American society.

Promoting Anti-Semitism

Although anti-Semitism had not been a mainstay of Coughlin's early commentaries, he had mentioned "Jews hoarding gold" and "bad international Jews." He also had communicated his hatred through innuendo and stereotyping. In 1933, he referred to "the story of the modern Jew" and in his very next breath made the statement, "It is all related in one sense to our present misery"—referring to the Great Depression. In the same talk, he continued, "This afternoon, my friends, I propose to speak upon a subject that is related to money," and then spent the entire program summarizing the history of the Jewish people. In an early *Social Justice* article, he said without elaboration: "There is a Jewish question. It is just as unfortunate that it exists in the social world as it is that cancer exists in the physical world."[11]

The Nation was the first publication to document Coughlin's bigotry. In 1934 the magazine called him "the most vicious single propagandist in the United States, having planted an anti-Semitic seed in the fertile minds of his millions of followers." The liberal magazine went on to castigate the Radio Priest as a blot on the profession of journalism, saying: "Father Coughlin illustrates perfectly the way of the demagogue. He deals in half-truths—that half of any truth which appeals most to the emotions." The *New York Times* followed suit, comparing Coughlin to Louisiana Senator Huey Long by characterizing both men as "demagogues," "rabble rousers," and "false prophets" whose national influence was due to their "shameful eagerness to play on prejudices."[12]

Additional comments suggesting Coughlin's bigoted feelings toward Jews came during the 1936 presidential campaign. In a Cleveland speech, he spoke of the "challenge of American Jewry" and referred to Jews as "the money-changers" and "traffickers in gold," stereotyping

Jews as being driven to acquire wealth. In the same speech, which garnered Coughlin his photo on the cover of *Newsweek*, he implied that Jews were not patriotic, saying, "I challenge every Jew in this nation to tell me that he does or does not believe in the principle of 'love thy neighbor as thyself.'"[13]

After the Union Party's humiliating defeat, Coughlin upped the volume on his anti-Semitism. In early 1938, he created the Christian Front. The all-male organization consisted of local chapters called "platoons"—with many people flinching at the concept of a clergyman using such a blatantly military term. The Christian Front excluded Jews from its membership, which was 100 percent white and 90 percent Catholic. Local chapters organized "buy Christian only" movements in dozens of American cities. Platoons attracted thousands of frustrated people to meetings where the major activities became drinking beer while praising Coughlin and cursing the man they condemned as the unofficial leader of American Jews—Franklin Delano "Rosenfeld."[14]

Intensifying the Bigotry

In 1938, Coughlin reprinted the spurious "Protocols of the Elders of Zion" in *Social Justice*. Originally published in Russia at the turn of the century, the forged documents purported to detail a plot by Jewish leaders to destroy Christian civilization and impose financial slavery upon the entire world. Coughlin's first installment from the "Protocols" quoted the unnamed organizer of the plot as telling his fellow Jews: "We shall soon begin to establish huge monopolies, reservoirs of colossal riches, upon which even large fortunes of the goyim (gentiles) will depend to such an extent that they will go to the bottom together with the credit of all the States on the day after the political smash."[15]

The "Protocols" went on to describe how Jewish leaders planned to saddle gentiles with tremendous debts and described a strategy to repress the economic status of non-Jews by encouraging workers to become dependent on alcohol. The documents said: "In order that the true meaning of things may not strike the goyim (gentiles) before the proper time, we shall mask it under an alleged ardent desire to serve the working classes and the great principles of political economy."[16]

In his comments accompanying the material, Coughlin argued that the world Jewish community's plans proposed in the "Protocols" had been carried out to create the Great Depression. Coughlin wrote: "The author of this document foresaw many years ago how to create want in the midst of plenty and how to agitate the thoughtless masses. This has been accomplished under the agency of the New Deal." He said his purpose in reprinting the "Protocols" was to defend God, saying, "The tyranny, oppression and needless poverty in the world are not of God's devising but are the results of planning by men who hate and detest the Christian principles of brotherhood."[17]

Coughlin immediately reinforced the new blatancy of his anti-Semitism through a series of other accusations. In the first, he asserted that Jews were prime players in a global conspiracy to ensure that communism would dominate every country in the world. This was followed by Coughlin's contention that Jewish bankers had plotted and financed the 1917 revolution that had overthrown Czar Nicholas of Russia, which he characterized not as a revolt by the peasants but as a "mad slaughter of Christians."[18]

The country responded to Coughlin's fallacious remarks with outrage. Rabbi Stephen S. Wise, leader of the World Jewish Conference, said, "Coughlinism is the deadliest form of anti-Semitism in America today." A front-page story in the *Detroit Free Press* bluntly labeled the priest's Sunday broadcasts "his weekly attack on the Jews" and lambasted his total disregard for accuracy, saying, "Father Coughlin is giving still further evidence of his congenital inability to tell the truth."[19]

Defending the Nazis

In late 1938, Coughlin took a stand that was nothing short of fanatical—even for a man widely known for his extremism. For in the legendary broadcast, the priest *defended* the Nazi persecution of Jews. According to Coughlin's bizarre scenario, it was the Jews's alleged introduction of communism into Russia that had propelled the Germans to devise the concept of Naziism as a desperate attempt to save Germany from communism. Coughlin told listeners, "Communism was a product not of Russia, but of a group of Jews who dominated the destinies of Russia." Repeating the word "communism" a dozen times to exploit the visceral hatred most Americans felt toward the antithesis of democracy, Coughlin argued that communism had to be stopped, regardless of the price—including committing atrocities against Jews. He bellowed: "Naziism is a defense against communism!"[20]

Many radio stations that had broadcast Coughlin's shocking defense of the Nazis immediately denounced it as disgracefully incendiary. WMCA in New York led the protests in what the *New York Times* cited as the first time in the history of American journalism that a radio station had publicly condemned one of its own speakers. Immediately after Coughlin's broadcast, the station told its listeners, "Father Coughlin has uttered certain mistakes of fact." WMCA then directed Coughlin to submit his future scripts to the station forty-eight hours before he aired them. When Coughlin refused, WMCA dropped him from its schedule. Several other stations then did the same.[21]

But most of Coughlin's foot soldiers stood by him. After he defended Nazi persecution of Jews, 6,000 New Yorkers gathered outside the WMCA studio to show their support of his views. The crowd cheered each time Coughlin's name was uttered and booed at every mention of Roosevelt. After the station refused to air his broadcasts, his faithful supporters organized massive picket lines in front of the station, with 2,000 people demanding their favorite radio voice not be silenced.

During his next commentary, Coughlin offered listeners yet another outlandish accusation by asserting that Jewish bankers had financed the Russian Revolution. For evidence, he cited a report he claimed had been produced by the United States Secret Service. The day immediately after the broadcast, however, federal officials denied that any such report existed. A statement released by the Treasury Department, which oversees the Secret Service, stated, "No such report was ever made by the United States Secret Service."[22]

By publishing the Treasury Department's denial as well as the growing criticism of Coughlin, the country's newspapers also may have inadvertently fueled the Radio Priest's anti-Semitic campaign. For just as the *New York World*'s 1921 exposé had spread details about the Ku Klux Klan to a wider audience, major newspapers unintentionally may have provided the same service for Coughlin by quoting lengthy passages of his anti-Semitic venom. When reporting the controversy between Coughlin and WMCA, for example, the *New York Times* published a twenty-one-inch story that reproduced numerous quotations from Coughlin, including, "Be not indulgent with the irreligious, atheistic Jews." *Times* editors as well as many of their readers undoubtedly found these statements heinous, but readers who were struggling with economic problems in their daily lives may well have found the rhetoric appealing.[23]

As Coughlin became increasingly fanatical, he openly embraced the fascist philosophy. He denigrated the American system of political parties as an outdated "mobocracy" and insisted that the political system in the United States should be replaced with a corporate state based on the Italian model.[24]

Because Coughlin's comments had degenerated into irrationality, many Catholic leaders renounced him. In a broadcast aired on thirty-four radio stations, the president of the American Bar Association,

Frank J. Hogan, said: "We Catholics cannot permit men of ill will to preach bigotry and anti-Semitism without raising our voices in protest. Some Americans have swallowed hook, line, and sinker the falsehood that the Jews are in league with the Bolshevik tyrants of Russia. I raise my voice against the spread of this lie." Cardinal George Mundelein of Chicago tried to distance the Catholic Church from Coughlin. In a statement read nationwide over NBC, Mundelein said, "Father Coughlin has the right to express his personal views on current events, but he is not authorized to speak for the Catholic Church, nor does he represent the doctrine or sentiments of the Church."[25]

Despite the strong words of criticism, Coughlin was not deterred. In the Catholic Church, a priest is responsible only to his immediate superior, and Bishop Gallagher remained Coughlin's strongest ally. Indeed, the denunciations seemed only to fuel the Radio Priest's anti-Semitic crusade. In 1939, he sent a letter to *Social Justice* subscribers saying: "America is suffering from the rule of those who are opposed to our Christ. Let's be militant and fight these people to the bitter end, cost what it may. Our Christ Who was crucified was no weakling when He drove the money changers from the temple by physical force. The day has come when we must stand up and fight for all that we hold dear."[26]

The growing crowd of Coughlin detractors—many of them Christians—were willing to fight as well, at least with words. The *Chicago Catholic Worker* published an open letter to Coughlin, addressing him as "the patron of prejudice" and accusing him of having become "psychotic on the question of Jews." The letter continued, "Your controversial Russian revolution statements justify a senseless, un-Christian attitude toward Mrs. Cohen, the delicatessen lady around the corner, and Meyer, the insurance collector." *Christian Century*, a Protestant weekly, condemned Coughlin for "attempting to arouse and play upon the animus of anti-Semitism" and being "Hitlerish in outlook, in method and in the effect he produces."[27]

The comparison to Adolf Hitler did not offend Coughlin, for the priest repeatedly—in perhaps his most radical stand of all—expressed *admiration* for the demonic dictator. Coughlin lauded Hitler as the "savior of peace and civilization" because he opposed communism. The priest wrote: "Hitler is to be admired. He has made of Germany the defeated a new, united, great nation. He has brought back to his father-land the pride of industrial achievements and scientific improvements." Even after Hitler invaded—many observers used the term "raped"—Austria and Czechoslovakia, Coughlin continued his absurd support of the satanic German leader.[28]

"Inciting to Riot and Civil War"

In his radio commentary in July 1939, Coughlin took yet another shocking step, considering his position as a man of God, by endorsing violence as a completely appropriate response to the social ills that, according to him, had been instigated by Jews. The hatemonger said: "The Christian way is the peaceful way until—until—all arguments have failed, there is left no other way but the way of defending ourselves against the invaders of our spiritual and national rights. And when your rights have been challenged, when all civil liberty has succumbed before the invaders, then may Christians meet force with force."[29]

Members of the Christian Front translated their leader's words into acts of intimidation and physical violence. In cities across the country, Coughlin followers smashed the windows of Jewish-owned stores and scrawled graffiti on the front doors of Jewish homes. Young men who called themselves "Coughlin storm troopers" pushed Jews off sidewalks, battered them with verbal insults, and baited them into Nazi-like street brawls where brass knuckles and knives were the weapons of choice. Jewish parents were afraid to send their children to school because gangs of young hooligans beat up every Jewish boy they caught alone. Police reported hundreds of cases of lone Jewish women, children, and elderly men being beaten by gangs of hoodlums who proudly identified themselves as "Father Coughlin's brownshirts." For Jews, American streets and subways were no longer safe.

Typical were the unrepentant statements of two New York thugs after they had been convicted of repeatedly attacking Jewish women. The men defiantly told a courtroom that they hoped "to see Jewish blood flow all over America" and wanted "every Jew in the United States hanged." In response, Magistrate Henry Curran spoke sentiments being felt, on the eve of World War II, by decent women and men across America: "With the world on fire, this is playing with matches, starting fires within our country. It's got to stop. These people who call themselves the Christian Front are dragging Christianity through the dust."[30]

Coughlin critics formed an organization called Friends of Democracy, seeking to have the priest removed from the air. They wrote the National Association of Broadcasters that Coughlin's endorsement of violence was clear evidence that he was using the airwaves "for the purpose of inciting to riot and civil war, and stirring up racial prejudice and hatred among the American people." The letter continued: "We urge that provision be made immediately to cancel Father Coughlin's contracts." Coughlin's detractors argued that his commentary was not protected by the First Amendment, which courts had interpreted as not protecting acts that incite violence.[31]

In October 1939, the National Association of Broadcasters adopted new rules designed to stop Coughlin. Specifically, they allowed contentious issues to be discussed only during free programs a station designated for debating the various sides of issues or during paid programs that used an open-forum format. By denying individuals the right to buy radio time to advocate controversial positions, the new rules clearly were aimed at removing Coughlin from the airwaves.[32]

And that they did. Several large stations immediately canceled Coughlin, and dozens of others waited until their contracts expired and then opted not to renew them.

Public opposition to Coughlin intensified in January 1940 when FBI agents in Brooklyn arrested seventeen members of the Christian Front and charged them with conspiring to overthrow the United States government. According to the FBI, the men had been plotting to murder several Jewish leaders as well as a dozen members of Congress. Agents, who found large quantities of rifles and explosives in the homes of the Christian Front members, further accused the men of plotting to seize several city post offices and armories.[33]

Coughlin, in another ultra-extremist decision, did not denounce the arrested men—but defended them. He praised them as a "fine body of New York Christians" and said: "I freely choose to be identified as a friend of the accused. It matters not whether they be guilty or innocent; be they ardent followers of the principles of Christianity or the betrayers of them, my place is by their side. There I take my stand."[34]

With Coughlin's future on the radio in doubt, the logical course of action would have been for him to temper his rhetoric. Coughlin was so obsessed with his hatred of Jews, however, that rational thinking no longer played a role in his decision making. So he continued his wild accusations, asserting that the American Civil War had not been fought because of slavery—but to seek freedom from Jewish bankers. Coughlin wrote, "Below the surface ran a current of intrigue that ended with the assassination of Abraham Lincoln *because he was determined that the United States be free from the bondage of the international bankers.*"[35]

By September 1940, the number of stations that were willing to defy the National Association of Broadcasters rules and air Coughlin's hate-filled diatribes was too small to make it economically feasible for the Radio Priest to continue to broadcast. So after fourteen years on the American airwaves, Father Coughlin left the radio. He did not go quietly, protesting, "I have been retired, temporarily, by those who control circumstances beyond my reach."[36]

Translating Hate Speech into Print

After being pushed off the radio, Coughlin shifted his anti-Semitic commentary to *Social Justice*. Indeed, his hate speech was even used as a technique for selling the magazine on city street corners. Newsboys were told to hawk copies by calling out "Buy your copy of *Social Justice*. Down with the Jews!" Distributors also told the boys to break into a loud wail whenever a potential customer walked by and, when asked why he was crying, to reply, "A big Jew hit me."[37]

In February 1942, with the United States fighting in World War II, Coughlin began another phase of his bigotry by announcing that Jews had engineered the entire war. According to him, the momentum for war had begun in 1933 as an outgrowth of the alleged Jewish-communist alliance. Because Jews wanted the Communist Party to take over Germany, he said, they created an anti-German propaganda campaign in the United States aimed at pushing America into the war. *Social Justice* stated, "A worldwide sacred war was declared on Germany not by the United States, not by Great Britain, not by France, not by any nation; but by the race of Jews." Coughlin used this chapter of his anti-Semitic crusade to argue once again that the Nazis were fully justified in persecuting Jews.[38]

Coughlin's assertion that Jews had started World War II was the straw that broke the camel's back. As early as the mid-1930s, United States Attorney General Francis Biddle had begun monitoring Coughlin's activities, and by 1939 FBI Director J. Edgar Hoover had taken personal charge of the investigation. The most damning piece of evidence was a sworn statement from Aleksi Pelypenko, a secret agent of the United States government who had posed as an Axis agent, that Coughlin had worked for the Nazis in early 1941 to disseminate anti-Semitic propaganda in the United States.[39]

After the United States entered the war, men like Coughlin who previously had been considered crackpots could no longer be tolerated. Because his hatemongering undermined the war effort, federal officials took direct action to quiet him. FBI agents drove a fleet of moving vans up to Coughlin's shrine and seized both his personal papers and business records. And in April 1942, Biddle charged *Social Justice* with violating the Espionage Act and Postmaster General Frank C. Walker barred the newspaper from the mails on grounds that it was seditious.[40]

But it ultimately took authorities of the Catholic Church to silence Coughlin. Biddle sent a representative to Detroit Archbishop Edward Mooney, saying that if Coughlin's public statements did not stop immediately, the federal government would charge him with sedition, which would lead to a high-profile and extremely embarrassing ordeal for the Church. In May 1942, Mooney ordered Coughlin to cease all nonreligious activities or be defrocked. *Social Justice* never appeared again, and Coughlin left the public eye.[41]

From 1942 until he retired in 1966, Coughlin served quietly as a parish priest in Royal Oak. Only the most persistent of news organizations succeeded in persuading him to make any statement whatsoever, such as when *Life* magazine managed to extract the brief quotation, "It was a horrible mistake to enter politics." Father Coughlin died in 1979.[42]

Influencing the Social and Political Landscape

Although it is not possible to establish a direct cause-and-effect relationship between Father Charles E. Coughlin's hate-filled rhetoric and the spread of anti-Semitism through American society, he clearly had significant impact on the minds of the American people.

As early as 1935 and the World Court debate, Coughlin demonstrated his ability to impel millions of voters to political action. In defeating the proposal to create a global legal body, the Radio Priest had even triumphed over the president of the United States. Observers of the American scene also asserted Coughlin's far-reaching influence. *Fortune* magazine wrote in 1934, "Coughlin is just about the biggest thing that ever happened to radio." The *Chicago Catholic Worker* said in its 1939 open letter to Coughlin: "You are the most powerful Catholic voice in the United States today. You are a definite, undeniable force on the American scene. Your opinions sway millions."[43]

Coughlin was not merely powerful, but he was also widely feared as one of the nation's most notorious extremists whose populist support could spell danger at the voting booth. Some political analysts have even gone so far as to suggest that Coughlin and the threat of his reactionary power forced President Roosevelt to shift dramatically to the left and introduce stridently liberal political measures in 1935. According to these observers, New Deal legislation such as "wealth taxes," the Social Security Act, and the Wagner Act guaranteeing collective bargaining rights were direct results of Coughlin.[44]

An audience sometimes soaring to forty-five million Americans gathered around the radio to hear Coughlin each Sunday afternoon from 1926 to 1940, and at least one million of them made the further commitment of subscribing to *Social Justice* and reading Coughlin's harsh words in print. With such a huge and fervent audience listening to his every word, Father Coughlin clearly had a profound impact on closing the minds and hardening the hearts of American society toward the world Jewish community. One biographer wrote, "His crisp voice, his vibrant personality, and his message were wonderfully suited to the time in which he lived and to the new medium which was sweeping the country." More than any other man or woman of the early days of this first electronic medium, the priest-turned-demagogue perfected the formula that successfully touched the very souls of his listeners. The story of how he spread anti-Semitism provides students of journalism history with a stunning example of the power of the radio to propel change—not necessarily by appealing to the best in human nature.[45]

9

Creating "Rosie the Riveter": Propelling the American Woman into the Workforce

WORLD WAR II WAS a watershed event in the evolution of the American woman. The demands that the international conflict made on the people of the United States offered women opportunities for new and expanded roles, profoundly changing the traditional social order. For when ten million working-age men donned military uniforms, a severe labor shortage developed in both the private sector and the rapidly expanding defense industries. Faced with a critical need for manpower, the nation turned to *woman*power.

Women heeded the call. As millions of them entered the labor force for the first time, artist Norman Rockwell's classic *Saturday Evening Post* cover of Rosie the Riveter—young and beautiful, but also strong and confident with a powerful rivet gun resting across her muscular thighs and a copy of *Mein Kampf* under her feet—aptly symbolized the phenomenon for the American public. Many women worked in industrial jobs directly related to the wartime build-up, laboring in airplane plants, shipyards, and munitions depots. Others worked in offices both inside and outside the government, serving most often as typists, secretaries, and personnel managers. Many women wore military uniforms, joining the branches of the Army and Navy created for women, frequently as nurses. This surge in wartime employment radically altered the face—not to mention the shape—of the nation's workforce. In 1940, twelve million American women worked outside the home;

four years later, that number had jumped to nineteen million—an increase of a staggering 58 percent.[1]

Such a sea change was, like so many other events in American history, hastened by the Fourth Estate. Newspapers, news magazines, and radio stations gave working women unprecedented quantities of positive coverage. In concert with the federal government's intense effort to persuade women to join the workforce—largely by appealing to their sense of patriotism but also by paying them higher salaries than they had ever earned before—American journalism became a willing venue for propaganda. This was one occasion when the Fourth Estate very clearly served as a handmaiden to the government. News organizations prodded, coaxed, and cajoled the public into supporting the concept of women working outside the home—an idea that middle-class America previously had refused to embrace. Newspapers and news-oriented magazines abandoned all traces of their traditional adversarial role vis-à-vis the government and constantly reminded American women that their brothers, husbands, and sons were in danger of death because they lacked the wartime goods that women could supply.

Although the primary motivation for news organizations nudging American women into the workforce was to support the government and the war effort, the campaign ultimately had other beneficiaries as well. The flood of positive images of working women prompted non-working women to expand their vision of what life could offer. This caused millions of women to consider—many of them for the first time—striving to find fulfillment not in cleaning toilet bowls or ironing their husbands' shirts but in operating a fifteen-ton crane or readying a machine gun for the field.

Some scholars question the long-term impact of women joining the workforce during World War II, pointing out that many of them were forced to give up their jobs when the soldiers came home—again, with a tidal wave of support from the news media. And yet, there is no question that the phenomenon altered the consciousness of a generation of American women as well as the expectations of their daughters. Millions of women suddenly joining the labor force was a turning point for the larger American society, too, because it began to be acceptable for women to combine the dual responsibilities of the home and the workplace. Most important, Rosie the Riveter herself gained a new level of confidence because she learned not only that she could fill GI Joe's shoes but also that doing so made her feel good about herself and her newfound place in society. Journalist Dorothy Thompson summarized the point at the time, saying, "There is no example in which a class or group of people who have once succeeded in expanding the area of their lives is ever persuaded again to restrict it."[2]

Calling All Women

World War II was, more than any military conflict before it, a battle of production. The Germans and Japanese had a ten-year head start on amassing weapons and wartime equipment, and the Allies suffered major material losses at Dunkirk and Pearl Harbor. The United States had to play catch-up, for victory clearly would go to the side with the most airplanes, battleships, guns, and ammunition. Production was essential for victory, and women were essential for production. *Business Week* said it succinctly: "Our entire manpower problem is most acutely a problem in womanpower."[3]

Encouraged by a four-alarm call by the government's propaganda machine, the nation's news media dutifully called for action. Radio proved to be the most successful venue in Seattle, where the city's multitude of defense plants created an acute labor shortage. So the local chamber of commerce appealed to independent station KJR and created a twice-weekly program called "Jobs for Women." Each fifteen-minute broadcast began with general commentary on the importance of women to the war effort and then aired descriptions of specific jobs available—listing physical requirements, location, hours, and wages. It worked. After a mere four weeks, 2,200 women had joined the Seattle workforce, and city officials gave the radio station 100 percent of the credit.[4]

Nationwide, though, national newspapers and magazines did the lion's share of the communicating. In many cases, the headlines told the story. Examples from the *New York Times* included "Needed: 50,000 Nurses" and "Woman Mans the Machine"; the *Christian Science Monitor* followed suit with "Calling All Women" and "It's Woman's Day Right Now." The news magazines did their part as well. *Newsweek* weighed in with "Output: Ladies Welcome" and "More Women Must Go to Work as 3,200,000 New Jobs Beckon," and *Time* cried "Nightingales Needed" and "The Ladies!" The broad array of public affairs magazines also chimed in with offerings such as "The Margin Now Is Womanpower" in *Fortune* and "Why You Must Take a War Job" in *American Magazine*.[5]

Some publications were so committed to increasing the number of working women that they supported a short-lived proposal to *force* women to work outside the home. *The Nation*'s 1942 cover story—titled "Shall We Draft Women?"—argued that compulsory employment for all able-bodied American women was a perfectly reasonable idea. "No one can say just what proportion of the needed women can be obtained by appeals for voluntary enlistment. Few authorities believe that enough qualified women workers can be obtained by this means," the magazine argued before finally blurting out impatiently, "We might as well face facts."[6]

Most publications did not go that far, but their messages were clear. "Forecasts show that about four million people who have never worked before must be enlisted in the labor force in 1943," *Fortune* wrote. "They will have to be mostly women because nearly all the men are already working or fighting. There is no alternative." The article went on to toss a dash of guilt toward those women who had not yet left the security of their homes, saying, "Resorting to 'idle' women becomes the only way."[7]

The *New York Times* joined the campaign. Rather than *telling* women readers to march out of the kitchen and onto the assembly line, however, the nation's most widely respected newspaper preferred to *show* readers how working women were making a difference. A fall 1941 article said of American women: "They are helping to build dive bombers for the Navy; they are making time fuses for high explosive shells in government arsenals; they are filling and sewing powder bags in a dozen newly built plants; they are turning out millions of rounds of machine-gun and small-arms ammunition." As the story gained momentum, it took on a cheerleading tone, offering women readers a long list of examples of how they could join up, "When the Boeing company began to expand its production of Flying Fortresses, it raided seamstress and tailor shops for women who could line the big cabins with felt and then cover the felt with a patent material." *Times* editors surrounded the affirming copy with photos that drove home the point, showing determined women of all ages working diligently at their tasks. The images carried captions such as "For precision work, women's fingers are often defter than men's" and "Where a leak may mean death, the job must be thoroughly done."[8]

The *Times* joined the other publications in running strident pleas for women workers that read like they had been written by government public relations flacks. One began, "Of our many war problems, one of the most acute is the need for graduate trained nurses. There are nurses now with American troops in Ireland, in Iceland and in Bataan, with fox holes dug beside their sleeping cots; there were four on Wake Island when the Japs got there. And many thousands more are needed." The recruitment brochure–style rhetoric continued, "To any working person, one of the greatest sources of satisfaction and of resultant prowess is the sense of being needed and in demand." The article was surrounded by photos of student nurses sitting in a classroom and trying on their white caps for the first time.[9]

Life *magazine's Margaret Bourke-White immortalized these diligent American women operating powerful acetylene torches in the iron works in Gary, Indiana. Reprinted by permission of* Life *magazine.*

Glamorizing the "Girls"

Before World War II, a woman working outside the home generally carried the stigma of economic necessity. A man's wife or daughter bringing home a paycheck suggested that the man was a failure, unable to provide for his family. Eliminating this deeply ingrained perception was no easy task, but the American news media put forth a valiant effort to do just that. One of their most effective strategies was to glamorize the American working woman.

A full-page article in the *Christian Science Monitor* declared proudly that women were doing their part in the war effort by shifting "From French Heels to Slacks." That headline ran above a three-column photo that could just as easily have appeared in *Vogue* or *Glamour*. It showed a trio of beautiful young women with broad smiles on their faces as they walked confidently forward, arm in arm, above the caption: "In Jumper, Jodhpur, and Slacks They Work . . . on recess from tire-changing duties in Washington." The accompanying article continued the upbeat tone, beginning, "The American 'glamour girl' is about to have her popularity crown usurped by the woman in overalls." The article went on to wax admiringly of the millions of women who were redefining what it meant to be fashionable. "Short skirts, full blouses, and flowing bobs get caught in wheels and presses. Open-toed shoes pick up loose filings. French heels trip over cables and tools. Slack suits and low-heeled oxfords are almost a necessity in factory jobs." The article did not stop with merely praising the fashion choices of working women but went on to celebrate—prescient for an article written in 1942—their cultural impact as well, "The metamorphosis in women's dress will be accompanied by an even greater change in the nation's thinking about women and jobs outside the home." In another feature, the *Monitor* made assembly-line workers sound like such Hollywood stars as Betty Grable, describing them as "alluring Grable-like damsels, clad in slacks and bandannas, and oozing glamour from every pore."[10]

Newspapers glamorized working women in their news stories as well. In an article about how women were changing factories, the *New York Times* managed to slip in the names of two of the country's top women's fashion designers: "In shops where delicate, dainty precision work is done, Lilly Dache can design a fetching bonnet to keep the hair from catching in the machinery. Molyneux can do a dashing uniform in gay colors and light fabrics." The *Times* repeated the technique in an article reporting on the huge number of women working in arsenals and aircraft plants, this time creating an image that made assembly-line work sound like applying makeup or filing fingernails: "Under fluorescent lights they sit at benches that might well be dressing tables, and work with tools no larger than a manicure set." In another article, this one reporting on the huge influx of workers into the nation's capital, the *Times* succeeded in making working in Washington sound like living in a sorority: "The Federal Triangle at 5 o'clock in the afternoon looks more like a college campus after 3 o'clock classes than the center of the nation's capital." Photos accompanying the article did not show female workers crammed into studio apartments, but attractive young women dancing in a Washington nightspot above the caption "Evening Out."[11]

The nation's news magazines helped glamorize working women as well. When *Time* published an article about the increasing number of government agencies requiring their employees to wear uniforms, it quoted from *Vogue*, the arbiter of women's fashion, "The uniform stands for our new spine of purpose, our initiative in getting women working, splayed out into hundreds of different jobs, to find talents which have been mossed over." *Life* jumped on the glamorizing bandwagon with a photo essay titled "Girls in Uniform" that gushed, "The woman worker in a war industry has acquired some of the glamor of the man in uniform. In labor's social scale, she belongs to the elite. At the very top is the girl who works in an airplane factory. She is the glamor girl of 1942." The article, surrounded by photographs of beautiful working women, went on to describe America's newest "glamor girl" as arriving at the factory at 6:30 A.M., "her hands smooth, her nails polished, her makeup and curls in order." *American Magazine* took the trophy for glamorizing working women via photos when it spread an image of four leggy young women across two pages to illustrate an article titled "Glory Gals." The three-paragraph article about the Women's Ambulance and Defense Corps was dwarfed by the titillating image of the women—dressed in scanty khaki shorts—frolicking in the surf, as if they were finalists in the Miss America pageant.[12]

Newsweek's commitment to glamorizing the female labor force came across loud and clear in an article describing how the war had swollen the ranks of Washington newspaperwomen, with the number of women admitted to the Senate and House press galleries rising from thirty-three in 1940 to seventy-three in 1943. A *Newsweek* reader must have found it difficult to reconcile the conventional image of the disheveled reporter with the descriptions of "tall, blond, and imposing" Esther Van Wagoner Tufty, who reported for Michigan papers but had been "mistaken for royalty during a trip to Europe," and Lee Carson, an International News Service reporter who had been dubbed "the siren of the women's group" because she wore "dressy clothes, high-heeled shoes, theatrical hairdos, and liquid make-up that gives her face a mask-like appearance resembling that of a Balinese dancer."[13]

Praising Working Women

Although the glamorized descriptions gave the impression that working women looked like Hollywood stars, news organizations made sure their articles lauded the talents and productivity of the women as well. The *Newsweek* article about women journalists, for instance, ended with a statement clearly tailored to reassure male readers, "The younger generation of newspaperwomen is composed of women who can do a man's job but still look like women." *Time* magazine also complimented the professional skills of women journalists, though labeling them with terms that would not be acceptable today. "The newshens cover almost everything," the magazine stated. "A girl reporter at the Interior Department was first to dig out the 'Big Inch' faulty-pipe story. The Associated Press's young Flora Lewis was 24 hours ahead on the State Department's embargo of oil shipments to Spain."[14]

The leading voices in American journalism had positive words for working women outside their field, too. By late 1942, *Newsweek* was boasting that women were working—and well—in virtually all areas of defense production, stating admiringly, "Depending on the industry, women today make up from 10 to 88 per cent of total personnel in most war plants." *Time* boasted that a female worker "can turn out half again as much work as a man," and the *New York Times* began a story with the assertion, "All responsible people connected with industry today agree that women are equal to men as far as being able to do almost any industrial job."[15]

In particular, the news media repeatedly applauded women's superior finger dexterity that enabled them to assemble the tiny, intricate parts that went into the airplanes and battleships that had to be built if the United States hoped to win the war. The *New York Times* quoted the spokesperson for one shipyard saying women excelled in other factory jobs as well: "Women of all ages are among our best welders and shipfitters. A Danish woman welder of 53 can match the record of the best man we have found."[16]

Radio joined the newspapers and magazines in trumpeting women's abilities. A station in Portland, Oregon, sponsored a "Working Women Win Wars Week." A typical script had the announcer declaring that women possessed "a limitless, ever-flowing source of moral and physical energy, working for victory." After a second voice asked why the country needed female workers, the announcer responded, "You can't build ships and planes and guns without them."[17]

When it came to highlighting women's strengths, *Business Week* was out in front. The magazine went far beyond praising women's dexterity, pointing out that they also were better than men at jobs requiring repeating the same task for a prolonged period or observing small details. That made women better not only at assembly-line work but also at inspecting products to ensure high quality and testing all types of war materials—from trucks and tanks to machine guns and aircraft cannons. In a story about women miners in Colorado, the magazine crowed, "In one mine, women wielded an 8-pound sledge in the best of manlike tradition." In early 1945, the business weekly even succeeded in locating a small manufacturing firm that was staffed entirely by women. Strato Equipment Company designed and produced high-altitude pressure suits for military pilots without a single male employee—except for the male mannequin that modeled the suits.[18]

News organizations touted the high marks women workers received regarding their work habits, too. Laudatory articles pointed out that women had proven to be easier to supervise and less likely to be involved in accidents or to damage tools and machinery. The *Times* quoted a shipyard spokesperson as saying, "We have found the women punctual on the job. They get to work on time. Not a single woman has been tardy even once and the foremen noted it appreciatively. Perhaps it is their long habit of getting the children off to school on time."[19]

Balancing Two Different Worlds

Because fully one-third of the women who joined the World War II labor force were mothers, the nation's newspapers and magazines committed themselves to reassuring the public that women could efficiently balance their responsibilities in the home with those in the workplace.

The quintessential article appeared in the *New York Times* under the headline "Woman War Worker: A Case History," although it could just as easily have read "Wonder Woman: A Case History." It began, "Alma is a pretty woman," and then proceeded to describe a woman with "real pink cheeks" and an "extremely feminine build" who managed to excel at her war plant job while also taking care of her husband and three children—also mentioning, of course, that "Alma didn't complain much." Indeed, her remarkable daily schedule did not allow for such luxuries.[20]

Alma—her last name was not given—began her day by arriving home from her nightshift job at the plant just in time to get Sally, Billy, and Tom Jr. off to school. After making her own breakfast and cleaning up the kitchen—"wondering how [her husband] Tom managed to use so many pots just to make cereal and eggs, and *why* he *always* had to spill grease on the floor"—she would fall into bed for an hour of sleep until it was time to prepare lunch for the children. After feeding the six-, eight-, and nine-year-olds and washing the lunch dishes, she tumbled back into bed until the children returned from school. Then she rose again to clean the house and prepare dinner so it would be on the table when Tom got home. After doing the dinner dishes and helping the kids with their homework, Alma slept for another hour before Tom woke her at 10 P.M. She consistently arrived at the plant an hour early because, she explained to the *Times* reporter: "Tom never went to bed until she left. As he needed a lot of sleep, she figured it was best to come on over to the plant early and not keep him up." Alma survived on five or six hours of sleep a day while spending forty-eight hours a week on her job, which required her to stand and operate a large machine that spit out tiny aircraft parts. Her only day off was Sunday, which she spent doing the week's laundry.[21]

The *Times* story ended with a textbook example of a passage crafted to inspire other American wives and mothers to march into the workforce: "When Alma measures the dullness and loneliness of a housewife's job against the interest and companionship of a production job, she inevitably concludes she does not wish to be a housewife or a housemother. She wishes, and will fight, to be a working wife and a working mother." Melodramatic music would have provided a fitting background for the maudlin prose: "Alma is going to be present in the machine shop from here on out, come war, peace, or high water. She has the energy. She has the ability." The story had built to a timeworn cliché that was delivered in the final sentence: "Where there's a will, it finds a way."[22]

Other articles were dotted with supportive statements and rosy images to reassure mothers, as well as society in general, that it was possible—not to mention *patriotic*—to balance the dual responsibilities of home and work. The *Christian Science Monitor* wrote: "Nursery schools are being set up in connection with most of the big defense plants, where mothers can leave their children in good hands. Plant authorities are usually willing to give a woman the shift that allows her to be home at the time her family needs her most." Another feature communicated the same reassuring sentiment: "Housewives are invited to choose their own hours at the Raytheon Company. They may select any four- or five-hour shift they like between eight in the morning and five o'clock at night. This obviates any hesitation on the part of the homekeeper on the ground that she would be neglecting her family by taking a job, since this arrangement enables her to get home at night before the children return from school."[23]

Redefining Women's Work

By World War II, magazines had been telling women for a century and a half—since *Ladies Magazine* was founded in 1792—that the *woman's sphere* was defined by the four walls of her home. The campaign to attract women into the wartime labor force, however, required that a very different message be communicated. With the fate of democracy hanging in the balance, newspapers and magazines embraced the new concept with gusto, encouraging women to expand into myriad new directions.

American Magazine led the initiative. The public affairs magazine set the tone when it announced, "A woman, when she gets hopping mad or when she senses a peril to the things she loves, can do darn near anything." It then took the next step of showcasing the fields in which "hopping mad" women were breaking new ground. An article titled "Amazons of Aberdeen" reported that not a single woman had been allowed to work at the Maryland testing grounds in 1941, but three years later 400 women were making sure Uncle Sam's guns and ammunition were working properly before the boys at the front received them. The article raved: "The girls fire big berthas, drive tanks over shell-torn terrain, toss 60-pound shells around as if they were biscuits. Tough babies, these gals? Well, hardly. Most of them are housewives, many of them mothers, one is a grandmother." Photos showed women in a variety of positions—driving a tank, operating a .30-caliber machine gun, towing a truck out of the mud.[24]

Other publications also championed women expanding into male bastions. The *New York Times* urged forestry officials to hire more women, pointing out that their keen powers of observation would enable them to spot fires better than men could. The *Christian Science Monitor* pushed for the Army to make better use of Private Marie McMillin than merely to have her sew parachutes when she had been, in civilian life, the world's top female parachute jumper—having completed 396 jumps, one of them from one plane to another at an altitude of 2,000 feet. *Time* campaigned for more women doctors by pointing out that only 6 percent of medical students in the United States were women, compared to 85 percent in Russia.[25]

Another major theme in the campaign to expand the definition of *women's work* was to increase the jobs open to African-American women. The war represented a second emancipation for black women, who always had worked outside the home but, because of the increased acceptance of working women, were now able to advance into higher-paying jobs beyond working as domestics. The drive for victory should outweigh the racism that pervaded many industries, *Newsweek* argued, as black women were as capable of working in aircraft plants and shipyards as white women were.[26]

Expanding jobs available to black women was a constant theme in *Opportunity*. The national African-American news magazine saw World War II as a doubly important event in the evolution of its female readers. "For many Negro women the idea of a 'career' outside the 'cook kitchen' looms for the first time as a reality," it stated. "They are pounding on the door of American Democracy, asking to be let in." *Opportunity* reported on the success African-American women were experiencing in various jobs, including as registered nurses and mechanics. The reporter writing one article was so pleased that an African-American woman had been hired in the electrical repair department at LaGuardia Airport that she used the first-person point of view, "The girl, the foreman told me proudly, was an excellent worker and 'one of the best men in the shop.'"[27]

Amid the long list of women pioneering in new jobs during the war, no one had a higher profile than the epitome of the intrepid new American woman: Margaret Bourke-White. Already highly regarded because of her breathtaking 1930s *Life* magazine photographs that transformed factories into Gothic cathedrals, she gained new visibility by becoming the first woman correspondent accredited to the Army Air Force. In addition to covering the fighting, Bourke-White also served as the model for the Army's first set of uniforms for women correspondents—which included a pink party dress for special occasions.

One of Bourke-White's most exciting stories of the war evolved from the military brass refusing to allow her to fly to North Africa, saying airplanes were too dangerous for women, and her subsequent decision to go by sea instead. When her troopship was torpedoed, she wrote firsthand from a lifeboat filled with women war workers. Bourke-White's *Life* article on the harrowing experience featured not only stunning photos but also a poignant description of the life-and-death realities of wartime. "We were bobbing farther away from the big ship," she wrote. "Just as a soldier let go of the raft to reach for a rope from the lifeboat, a wave flung the raft against him and cracked his skull. The skipper dived overboard, caught hold of the soldier and the two were dragged back into the lifeboat. Before the night was over, the soldier had died."[28]

Capturing the Moment in Pictures

Bourke-White's photo credit line was the most famous to appear in the nation's news publications, but it was by no means the only one. For at the same time that newspapers and magazines were nudging women into the workforce through their inspiring words, they also were using images for that purpose. By the 1940s, journalists had become well aware of the ability of high-quality photographs to touch the emotions of the American public. Taking their lead from Rockwell's homespun image of Rosie the Riveter, editors filled their pages with photographs of thousands of dedicated American women, virtually every one of them wearing Rosie's confident expression—and a good number of them in her trademark bib overalls as well.

Life, with its large format and status as the nation's first photographic news magazine, set the standard. Bourke-White's stirring account of her rescue at sea came to life with a half-page photo at the beginning of the article. It showed a rescue plane circling above a crowded boat filled with women waving, cheering, and frantically raising the V-salute.[29]

Bourke-White's artistic approach to industrial photography defied the mere two dimensions of a magazine in her "Women in Steel" photo essay, as her depictions of the heroic women workers painted them as far too strong and powerful to be captured on a printed page: Florence Romanowski poured molten-hot liquid steel into molds as white-hot sparks burst like fireworks on every side. Elizabeth Laba heated the iron ingots in her oven to 2,300 degrees. Rosalie Ivy, described in the caption as "a husky Negro laborer," mixed a special mud to seal the casting hole that molten iron would flow through on its way to the blast furnace. One page of the photo essay resembled a high school yearbook, showing nine faces lined up and peering out toward the reader. Bourke-White's camera had transformed each face into a dramatic symbol of the pride and faith that were leading the American working woman toward victory. The portraits communicated the women's character and determination, while the captions told their individual stories in shorthand style: "Blanche Jenkins, 39, is a welder at Carnegie-Illinois, buys a $50 war bond each month. She has two children." "Lugrash Larry, 32, a laborer in Blast Furnace Department, has four children. Husband works in Billet Mill." "Victoria Brotko, 22, is a blacksmith's helper. She took her twin brother's job when he joined the Marines."[30]

Bourke-White was drawn to women who were rugged and robust, but most photographers of the era—the vast majority of whom were men—preferred more feminine beauties. For the photos to accompany his "Girls in Uniform" photo essay, *Life* photographer J. R. Eyerman focused on Marguerite Kershner, a shapely brunette who meticulously applied rouge, eye shadow, and red lipstick before arriving at the factory. The caption below one of her half dozen photos read: "Although Marguerite looks like a Hollywood conception of a factory girl, she and thousands like her are doing hard, vital work." In keeping with journalism's commitment to glamorizing the American working woman, Kershner also was shown enjoying an active social life by bowling, roller skating, and horseback riding.[31]

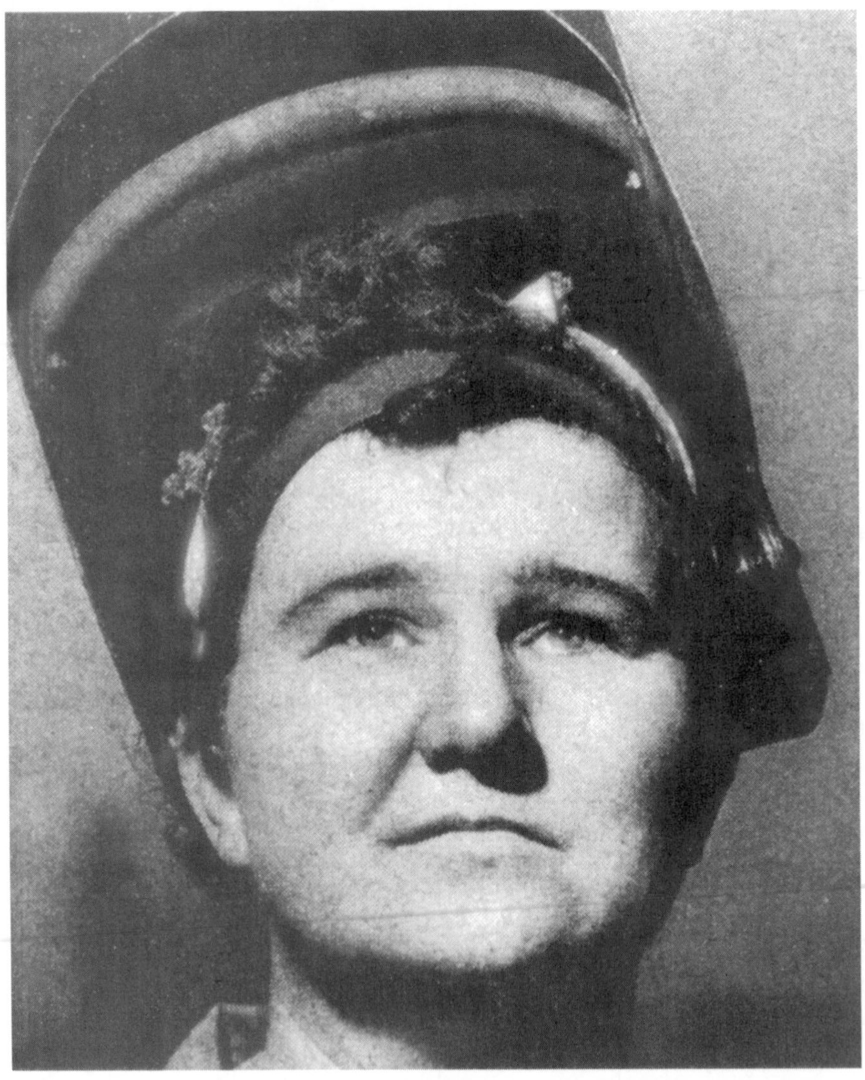

Blanche Jenkins—wife, mother, welder—was one of the hundreds of American women raised to heroic status through the artistry of Life *photographer Margaret Bourke-White. Reprinted by permission of* Life *magazine.*

Regardless of the publication, and whether the woman was as ravishing as a film star or as ugly as the proverbial mud fence, the single most recurring image was of the American woman at her work station, focusing with relentless determination on her given task. Whether *Time* published a medical story debunking rumors that riveting caused breast cancer or *Newsweek* reported that a new study had found women less inclined than men to move from plant to plant, the articles came complete with images of women, wearing the requisite bandanna, diligently at their posts—drilling in *Time*; inspecting artillery cartridges in *Newsweek*. In articles about African-American women moving into new industrial fields, *Opportunity* proudly showed black women working side by side with white women inspecting fuse closing plugs and making the patterns used in constructing battleships. The *New York Times* dotted its pages with close-up photos of dozens of modified Rosie the Riveters as well, showing women intently welding, tuning engines, and operating grinders on the assembly line.[32]

Changing the Social Order

World War II revolutionized women's role in American society. When the international conflict created a desperate demand for American workers, women responded with impressive quantities of enthusiasm, wherewithal, and—above all—ability. Between 1940 and 1944, the number of women in the workforce increased by more than half, with seven million women proving, both to themselves and to the public at large, that they were fully capable of succeeding in the workplace. What's more, they simultaneously shattered the conventional stereotypes of *women's work* and made major strides toward destroying sex labels.

The social revolution that began during the war did not end with the armistice. Even though at war's end a huge number of working women gave up their jobs—many against their will—and returned to full-time domesticity, many others remained in the workplace. In late 1946, one million more women were working in factories than had been there in 1940, and almost all the two million women who worked in offices during the war stayed there during peacetime. The change was most noticeable among married women, with the percentage of American couples in which both husband and wife worked leaping from 11 percent before the war to 20 percent after it. The idea of women working outside the home clearly was becoming an accepted part of middle-class life.

Numerous scholars have concluded that the media and their powerful influence over public opinion were central to bringing about this radical change in the social order. "None of the changes in women's work could have occurred without the active approval and encouragement of the principal instruments of public opinion," wrote historian William H. Chafe. "Newspapers and magazines did their part in the publicity build-up by depicting Rosie the Riveter as a national heroine and exhorting others to join her." Other scholars have expressed similar sentiments. In her study of World War II women, Leila J. Rupp wrote, "For the first time, the working woman dominated the public image. Women were riveting housewives in slacks, not mothers, domestic beings, or civilizers." In another study, Susan M. Hartmann concluded, "Media images of women were expansive, widening the range of acceptable behavior, providing positive examples of unconventional women, and blurring traditional gender distinctions."[33]

By sending out the call for working women and then praising the accomplishments of the highly resourceful women who responded to that call, the news media of the World War II era—through both their words and images—contributed immeasurably to the progress of American women. Even though the Fourth Estate's primary motive for this proactive effort was to help the United States win the war, as a byproduct of that campaign it also unwittingly nudged women toward developing a broader and more fulfilling role in American society. In the decades that followed, conservative forces attempting to maintain the status quo would find it no easier to turn back the emerging sense of worth and potential among American women than to turn back the hands of time. Social movements advance along a continuum, with each step forward leading to the next. The working women of the 1940s, with the news media's assistance, laid the psychological groundwork—creating the mindset, arousing the consciousness—of the next generation, ultimately paving the way for the women's liberation initiatives that erupted in the 1960s.

10

Exposing Joe McCarthy: Television's Finest Hour

SENATOR JOSEPH R. MCCARTHY'S political career was like a Roman candle. In early 1950, he was an obscure first-term senator. But by 1952, his star had risen to national prominence as his anticommunist witch hunt helped propel the Republican Party into the White House for the first time in twenty years. Then in late 1953, McCarthy's downward spiral began, careening out of control toward the ultimate nadir that today makes the very mention of his name send a chill down the spine of any fair-minded American.

McCarthyism was a reckless political gamble to convince voters that the Democratic Party had presided over the country through two decades not merely of bad timing or unfortunate accidents or errors or blunders—but treason. Through an endless barrage of charges and countercharges, McCarthy insisted that the government was riddled with subversives working to destroy American values. Exploiting the country's Cold War fears, he decimated the lives of thousands of innocent men and women.

The hand behind his bluff was printer's ink. Newspapers turned McCarthy's unsubstantiated charges into sensational stories that shrieked from page one. When accusations came from a United States senator who was leading a righteous campaign to save his country from evil forces, the Fourth Estate automatically accepted those allegations as newsworthy fact.

Ironically, the Fourth Estate also played a key role in bringing McCarthy down. For the force that, more than any other, brought the shameful era of McCarthyism to an end was television news. As other journalists shuddered at McCarthy's fierce power, Edward R. Murrow, destined to become the most revered figure in the history of broadcast journalism, stood tall. Murrow's *See It Now* on CBS first aired the story of an exemplary Air Force lieutenant who had fallen victim to McCarthy's witch hunt. Five months later came "A Report on Senator Joseph R. McCarthy," the legendary journalistic triumph that exposed the demagogue while earning laurels as the most important television program in history.

ABC then moved into the spotlight, providing gavel-to-gavel coverage of the most explosive congressional hearings in American history. For more than a month, ABC held eighty million viewers riveted to their televisions as the unforgiving camera revealed McCarthy to be a rude and sadistic bully. By the time the hearings ended, McCarthyism had been relegated to the history books.

Murrow and ABC were by no means the only journalistic forces that challenged McCarthy. By employing the unique characteristics of television news to their advantage, however, they clearly were the most effective in hastening the end of this bleak chapter in American history while at the same time creating what has come to be known as the finest hour in the history of television news.

The Nightmare Decade

McCarthyism did not develop in a vacuum. The American self-assurance won so dearly during World War II began to fade from the nation's consciousness at the end of the 1940s, with fear and uncertainty taking its place. The Cold War mentality crept into the American mind as communism consolidated its grip on Eastern Europe, as well as the Middle and Far East, to create a mood that was grim and unsettling.

The Soviet Union became perceived as the Evil Empire, a sinister enemy that threatened to annihilate the United States. In 1949, the Soviets flexed their muscles by detonating an atomic bomb. Even more shocking was China's fall to communism. For despite infusions of American aid, the Nationalist Chinese forces of Chiang Kai-shek withdrew to the island of Taiwan, sacrificing mainland China to communist leader Mao Tse-tung. A few months later, an American public still weary from World War II saw American men once again engaged in battle on foreign soil, this time in an effort to contain the spread of communism. The fighting in Korea continued for three years, claiming the lives of 54,000 American soldiers.

The pall of fear spreading across the country also caused many Americans to sense danger within their borders, as a long series of events shocked the nation. The State Department blamed internal sabotage for the failure of its China policy. American diplomat Alger Hiss was found guilty of perjury for denying that he had passed secrets to a communist agent. On Capitol Hill, the House Un-American Activities Committee investigated allegedly subversive activities by writers, actors, and directors in the entertainment industry. After scientists Ethel and Julius Rosenberg were convicted of wartime espionage for giving the Russians information about the atomic bomb, they were both executed. It became an era when to be accused was to be assumed guilty, a time when who a person associated with could destroy that person's entire life.

The Meteoric Rise of Joseph R. McCarthy

Joe McCarthy began his campaign in February 1950 by waving a sheet of paper in front of a woman's club in Wheeling, West Virginia, and bellowing, "While I cannot take the time to name all of the men in the State Department who have been members of the Communist Party and a spy ring, I have here in my hand a list of 205 that were known to the Secretary of State and, nevertheless, are still working and shaping the policy in the State Department." Neither the audience nor the nation that read the claim in the next day's newspapers knew that the letter contained not a single name.[1]

When McCarthy repeated his charges in Salt Lake City, Denver, and Reno during the next week, the specific number of communists changed each time, going from 205 to 207 to 81 to 57. Despite the inconsistencies, by the time he took his accusations to the Senate floor in late February, McCarthy had emerged as chief spokesman for a raging communism-in-government crusade that many Republicans recognized as the issue that could sweep them into the White House.

McCarthy's flair for drama forced the Senate Foreign Relations Committee to investigate his charges. For five months he used his position as witness to accuse various government officials of working day and night to advance the communist cause. The committee's official action, voted by the Democratic majority, was to denounce McCarthy's crusade as "a fraud and a hoax," chastising the senator for perpetrating deliberate and willful falsehoods.

Proof of the popularity of McCarthy's cause, however, came in the fall of 1950. By delivering thirty major addresses in fifteen states, he

In the sport of intimidation, Senator Joseph R. McCarthy was aided by his young and energetic chief counsel, Roy Cohn. Reprinted by permission of the Library of Congress.

propelled his anticommunist witch hunt into a major campaign issue. And after the ballots were counted, political observers credited McCarthy with Republican victories in a dozen Senate races. Most notable was the stinging defeat of Millard E. Tydings, chairman of the committee that had denounced McCarthy.

The anticommunist pitbull next set his sights on the 1952 national elections. He debased, demeaned, and vilified government workers and elected officials without pause, publicly calling President Harry Truman a "son of a bitch" and labeling Secretary of State Dean Acheson the "Red Dean." Republican presidential candidate Dwight Eisenhower privately opposed McCarthy, but Eisenhower also feared McCarthy's power. The former general bowed to political expediency and supported all Republicans—McCarthy included. During the 1952 campaign, the country's architect of anxiety again was highly sought after, stumping on behalf of candidates in sixteen states and earning a rousing ovation as a featured speaker at the Republican National Convention.

The results of the historic election reconfirmed McCarthy's power. He was cited as a major factor in helping the Republican Party take control of the White House in one of the most significant elections in American political history. Observers estimated that at least eight Republican senators owed their victories to McCarthy's support.

In the new Congress, McCarthy became chairman of the Permanent Subcommittee on Investigations, having wide discretionary authority to investigate government activities. What's more, he controlled a subcommittee staff, hiring as chief counsel the abrasive Roy Cohn. As subcommittee chairman, McCarthy earned a reputation as a savage inquisitor. In 1953, he initiated preliminary inquiries of an incredible 445 individuals. Of these, 157 became the subjects of full-scale investigations and seventeen were central figures in hearings—with McCarthy always chief interrogator.

"Joe" Exploits the Press

Although the climate of the times and Republican strategy contributed to McCarthy's rise, the single most important factor was his uncanny ability to manipulate the press. Journalists and scholars alike have acknowledged his media savvy. Two United Press wire service reporters spoke for their craft. George Reedy said of McCarthy, "He really had the press figured out," and John Steele admitted, "We bear a terrible scar because of that period." In his book *Joe McCarthy and the Press*, Edwin R. Bayley concluded that "He was able to generate massive publicity because he understood the press, its practices and its values; he knew what made news."[2]

In particular, McCarthy was a master at manipulating the wire services—the Associated Press, United Press, and International News Service. Because only a handful of newspapers had their own reporters in Washington, the wire services had major influence at the time. The wire services also had broad impact through radio, with virtually all radio news coming directly from the wires.

One of McCarthy's most successful media techniques involved the timing of accusations. He calculated the exact hour of the day he could make an accusation and be sure the wire services would not have time to track down a response from the accused person before stories were filed. So the journalists, driven by strident competition, had little option but to distribute the one-sided stories. Allen Alexander of the Associated Press recalled, "AP member newspapers also subscribing to competing UP and INS services would message frantically: 'Opposition reports that McCarthy said XXX. Where's ours?' What do you tell your superiors when they see a message like that?"[3]

McCarthy's tactics enabled him to manipulate newspapers into publishing dozens of lies. Reedy recalled the morning McCarthy waited until 10:50 to announce he had a letter proving that Owen Lattimore, a Johns Hopkins University professor, was a spy. Reedy knew the competing news services would report the charge for the 11 A.M. deadline. "We all wanted to see the letter, but he wouldn't give it up," Reedy recalled. "So I had to go down and write the story. At 11:45 A.M., Joe let go of the letter. There wasn't a thing in it to back up what he'd said." When the papers printed clarifications, they received far less prominence than the original accusations.[4]

Another of McCarthy's techniques exploited the concept of objectivity. News accounts in the 1950s barred all interpretation, as the journalistic convention of the day was that news stories should provide a bare-bones recitation of the facts—only. So McCarthy knew that journalists would report, without comment, any charge he made. Reporters were so fearful of allowing subjectivity to slip into their work that they would not, for example, include in a story the fact that a particular accusation was the fifth or tenth or fiftieth unsubstantiated accusation McCarthy had made that week. William Theis of International News Service lamented, "We let Joe get away with murder, reporting it as he said it, not doing the kind of critical analysis we'd do today. All three wire services were so God damned objective that McCarthy got away with everything, bamboozling the editors and the public." Theis said editors refused to believe a United States senator would make charges without having the evidence to back them up. "Joe saw what a bonanza he had, and he rode it," Theis said. "It was the most difficult story we ever covered, especially emotionally. I'd go home literally sick, seeing what that guy was getting away with."[5]

Many reporters came to regret how McCarthy had manipulated them into being mere recording devices for him. Reedy, who left journalism to become President Lyndon Johnson's press secretary, said, "We had to take what McCarthy said at face value. Joe couldn't find a communist in Red Square, but he was a United States senator. So we reported whatever he said."[6]

Edward R. Murrow Redefines Television News

At the same time that print journalism was committing acts that it would later rue, television news was developing the program that was fated to become the beau ideal of electronic journalism.

The Columbia Broadcasting System introduced *See It Now* in 1951. The narrator of the thirty-minute news program was the man who ultimately would wear the mantle "patron saint of the broadcasting profession" and "a figure of Olympian stature." Edward R. Murrow first won his place in journalism history while reporting for CBS radio during World War II. Speaking from the rooftops of London during bombing raids, from the trenches all over Europe, and from the Buchenwald concentration camp on the day it was liberated, Murrow became the most trusted voice of the war. His masterful abilities as a reporter were coupled with a superb delivery as well as a sense of humanity that created a prose style that sounded like poetry. Indeed, poet Archibald MacLeish spoke for millions of listeners when he wrote, "Ed Murrow burned the city of London in our houses, and we felt that flame."[7]

Murrow's behind-the-scenes collaborator was Fred W. Friendly, a young producer whose vision and technical wizardry enhanced Murrow's on-air strengths. The Murrow-Friendly partnership began in 1950 with *Hear It Now*, a magazine program on CBS radio. When television emerged as the electronic medium of choice, the two men transformed the program into a visual phenomenon.

Broadcast on Tuesdays at 10:30 P.M. Eastern time, *See It Now* offered audiences a conceit that was entirely new to the infant medium. For Murrow and Friendly created the first television news program to grapple with controversial issues, crafting programs about such provocative subjects as the quality and cost of health care, and the relationship between smoking and lung cancer. Media scholars have praised the duo for "endowing TV news with a sense of substance" and producing "the prototype of the in-depth quality television documentary." *See It Now*'s rise to legendary status was aided by the explosive growth of television. In 1947, only 1 percent of American homes had a television; by 1953, that percentage had jumped to 80.[8]

Defending the Little Guy: "The Case of Milo Radulovich, A0589839"

In 1953, Murrow and Friendly decided the time had come for a program to show that the paranoia gripping the country had gone too far. They began searching for an example of an upstanding citizen whose rights had been violated by the government's obsession with national security. They found him in Milo Radulovich, a twenty-six-year-old meteorologist who had served eight years in the Air Force and received a commendation for his work on a secret weather station. Radulovich had continued to serve as a reserve officer while attending the University of Michigan. Under McCarthyism, however, he had been classified as a security risk because he associated with people believed to be subversives—his father and sister. A military board of inquiry recommended that Radulovich be ousted from the reserves because his two family members subscribed to Serbian-language newspapers.

After developing the Radulovich program, Murrow and Friendly found the case so compelling that they asked CBS management for money to promote the segment. CBS refused. Then they asked *See It Now* sponsor Aluminum Company of America (ALCOA) to help publicize the broadcast. ALCOA also refused. Murrow and Friendly then took the unprecedented step of paying for an ad in the *New York Times* out of their own pockets. The ad, which cost them $1,500, contained no reference whatsoever to CBS but was signed simply "Ed Murrow and Fred Friendly."[9]

"The Case of Milo Radulovich, A0589839" aired on October 20. It began with Murrow's simple introduction, "This is the story of Milo Radulovich—no special hero, no martyr." Murrow then described the young man's impeccable military record, his efforts to secure an education, and the high regard his neighbors in Dexter, Michigan, had for him. Murrow was sketching the American Everyman, "His wife works nights at the telephone company. They live at 7867 Ann Arbor Street."[10]

Viewers next heard John Radulovich, Milo's father, say he subscribed to the Serbian-language newspaper because "I like their Christmas calendars" and read a poignant letter he had written to President Eisenhower asking for "justice for my boy." Margaret Radulovich then appeared, saying her choice of newspapers had nothing to do with her brother, "My political beliefs are my own private affair." Lieutenant Radulovich made the same point, speaking quietly but with conviction, "What my sister does, what political opinions or activities she engages in, are her own affair. They certainly do not influence me."[11]

The program included interviews with a cross-section of the good citizens of Dexter, a small town pulled from a Norman Rockwell canvas. To a person—from the mayor to the commander of the American Legion post—they said they would not want to be held responsible for the views of *their* relatives and that if this could happen to Radulovich, it could happen to anyone.

One of the program's most stunning revelations was that the "subversive" newspaper Radulovich's father and sister read was not, in fact, pro-communism. Murrow reported that the paper consistently supported Marshal Tito, the Yugoslavian leader who five years earlier had broken with the Soviet Union and since that time had been receiving aid from the United States.

Murrow ended the broadcast with a dramatic statement delivered directly into the television camera: "We believe that 'the son shall not bear the iniquity of the father,' even though that iniquity be proved. And in this case, it was not."[12]

Reaction was swift. Of 8,000 letters and telegrams CBS and ALCOA received, 7,200 supported Radulovich. Media reviews were overwhelmingly positive as well. *Newsweek* said the segment marked a "week of triumph" for *See It Now,* and *Variety* called it "easily the most important single contribution made to television in the year." The *New York Times* dubbed the broadcast "superb" and "a long step forward in television journalism," lauding the segment as the first program in television history to take "a vigorous editorial stand in a matter of national importance."[13]

The most potent praise came five weeks after the broadcast when the secretary of the Air Force appeared on *See It Now* to announce that Milo Radulovich would be allowed to continue to serve as an officer in the Air Force reserves. As Friendly later wrote, that statement "established for the first time the enormous impact of television reporting."[14]

Attacking the Big Guy: "A Report on Senator Joseph R. McCarthy"

The success of the Radulovich program encouraged Murrow and Friendly, in the colorful words of one observer, "to lunge for the heart of the beast." They decided to deliver a body blow to McCarthy by *showing*—not *telling*—viewers exactly the kind of unscrupulous methods McCarthy used.[15]

Neither the success of the Radulovich program nor the need to stop McCarthy, however, was enough to persuade CBS to advertise Murrow and Friendly's daring segment. As they had done for the Radulovich show, the two men had to use their own money to pay for a *New York Times* ad. Like the earlier one, the ad did not mention CBS.[16]

The bulk of the March 9, 1954, *See It Now* consisted of filmed speeches by McCarthy. The audience heard McCarthy contradict himself by first denouncing criticism of either major political party for fear such attacks would cause the decline of democracy, but then breaking his own rule by condemning the opposing party: "Those who wear the label 'Democrat' wear it with the stain of a historic betrayal—twenty years of treason." The audience also was given a taste of McCarthy's malice, seeing him badger witnesses and hearing his feigned slip of the tongue in referring to the 1952 Democratic presidential nominee not as Adlai Stevenson but as *Alger*—a mean-spirited allusion to convicted spy Alger Hiss.[17]

"A Report on Senator Joseph R. McCarthy" contained incisive statements by Murrow as well. He accused McCarthy of terrorizing innocent people, demoralizing the State Department, and continually lying to the American public. As the program neared its end, Murrow spoke directly to the viewers, "The line between investigation and persecution is a very fine one, and the junior senator from Wisconsin has stepped over it repeatedly." Murrow's voice became stern as he continued, "This is no time for men who oppose Senator McCarthy's methods to keep silent."[18]

For his final statement, Murrow continued speaking directly into the camera, in his trademark fashion, as he quoted from Shakespeare, "The fault, dear Brutus, is not in our stars, but in ourselves." As the face of the trusted newsman filled the screen, Murrow pressed his point. "We will not be driven by fear into an age of unreason," he said, "if we dig deep in our history and our doctrine and remember that we are not descended from fearful men—not from men who feared to write, to speak, to associate and to defend causes that were, for the moment, unpopular."[19]

Murrow's eloquent prose, however, took a back seat to the compelling visual images that he and Friendly had carefully chosen to depict McCarthy. Many observers who have viewed the program have attempted to transform those images into words. One characterized the clips as portraying the senator in "his full, foul glory," "as a villain and a bully," and "revealing his shoddy practices and demeanor." Another said McCarthy was exposed as "a giggling psychopath," and a third wrote of the senator, "Sneering, truculent and wholly evil, he rumbled his evasions and hesitations and lies. He was caught huffing and chuckling in a way that sounded as if he was just a little nutty." Another said the telecast showed McCarthy "in such vulgarian lapses as belching, picking his nose, ignoring witnesses before his committee, and otherwise displaying crudities of manner."[20]

The instant the program ended, network switchboards lit up with the largest flood of responses in television history. CBS received a phenomenal 12,000 phone calls and telegrams, with positive reactions outnumbering negative ones fifteen to one. The network also received 22,000 letters, with nine out of ten commending Murrow. Even after

After challenging McCarthyism, Edward R. Murrow became the most revered television newsman in history—one historian called him the "patron saint of the broadcasting profession." Reprinted by permission of the Library of Congress.

McCarthy took advantage of *See It Now*'s offer to broadcast a half-hour rebuttal—in which he, predictably, accused Murrow of being a communist—the mail continued to run overwhelmingly in Murrow's favor.[21]

The press response was equally enthusiastic. The *New Yorker* dubbed the program "an extraordinary feat of journalism," *Newsweek* announced that "no political show so damning [has] ever been done before," and *Variety* crowned Murrow a "national hero." *Broadcasting* magazine called the telecast "the greatest feat of journalistic enterprise in modern times."[22]

Press appraisals highlighted the program's political impact as well. The *New York Herald Tribune* praised Murrow and Friendly for their "frank and responsible approach. By refusing to be bullied, the broadcasters will assure their own future and help guarantee America's." And the *St. Louis Post-Dispatch* headlined an editorial "When Television Came of Age" and rhapsodized, "No one needs to fear television and radio so long as demagogues are matched—and more—by honest men who care about the fate of their country."[23]

The *New York Times*'s Jack Gould began his tribute, "Last week may be remembered as the week that broadcasting recaptured its soul." The dean of media critics said the program represented "crusading journalism of high responsibility and genuine courage. For TV, so often plagued by timidity and hesitation, the program was a milestone." Writing about McCarthy's actions in black-and-white newsprint, Gould said, could not possibly have had the impact of seeing them "on television."[24]

As time has passed, *See It Now*'s program on McCarthy has assumed monumental status, with many scholars calling it the single most important broadcast in television history. In particular, historians have praised the program's impact on McCarthy. The assessments have been legion, including, "The program was the decisive moment at which opinion turned against McCarthy," "Thereafter, McCarthy's fortunes went steadily down," and "It is no small tribute to the producers of *See It Now* that their efforts signalled the demise of Senator McCarthy." The author of one history of the mass media wrote unequivocally, "The man mainly responsible for silencing McCarthy was Edward R. Murrow."[25]

Televised Hearings Strike the Final Blow

The climactic moment in the downfall of McCarthy came two months later when the nation, in one communal experience, watched live as McCarthy reinforced what Murrow and Friendly had shown on tape: that he was a sadistic bully. Thanks to television, the drama unfolded before one of the largest audiences that would ever witness a major event in American history—a staggering eighty million viewers.

The Army-McCarthy hearings evolved out of the senator's charges that subversives had infiltrated the United States Army. Military officials then countercharged that McCarthy and counsel Roy Cohn had sought preferential treatment for Private G. David Schine, a young man who had worked for McCarthy's committee before being drafted. The two warring sides then met during Senate hearings.

In April 1954, the ABC and NBC television networks both broadcast the opening salvos, and CBS offered a nightly film summary. ABC aired continuous coverage all thirty-six days of the hearings—an aggregate of 180 hours. NBC suspended live coverage after three days, joining CBS in airing a summary each night. Evidence of the public appetite for the hearings evolved after NBC's decision to abandon live coverage led fifteen of its local affiliate stations to switch to ABC.[26]

Observers recognized that the hearings were journalism history in the making. Calling ABC's televising of the hearings an act of enormous public service, Jack Gould wrote in the *New York Times*: "No viewer sitting in front of his screen can be unaware of television's tremendous role in the hearings—politically, educationally and socially. The television audience constitutes the real jury. Whatever the viewer's personal political predilections, he is his own eye-witness, reporter and judge."[27]

During the hearings, thirty witnesses marched to the microphone and described how Cohn, with McCarthy's support, tried to secure special treatment for Schine, the handsome young heir to a hotel fortune who had developed an unusually close relationship with Cohn. According to testimony, Cohn repeatedly demanded that the secretary of the Army appoint Schine to a post near Cohn in New York City, threatening to intensify the investigation of the Army if the demand was not met. After Schine was assigned to a base in Georgia, Cohn demanded that the young soldier be excused from Saturday duty and be granted extra passes so he could travel to New York every weekend.

One vivid confrontation during the hearings instantly became imbedded in the consciousness of the American public. It pitted McCarthy against Joseph Welch, the Army's special counsel. Welch was an avuncular Bostonian blessed with a keen legal mind and a gentle charm, but also a flair for courtroom drama. McCarthy grew to detest Welch because he had won, through the television camera, the nation's affection and admiration, feelings the senator craved for himself. Sensing that McCarthy was about to attack Welch, CBS and NBC had begun to broadcast the hearings live once more.

On the fateful day, Welch won point after point. Then McCarthy abruptly broke into the testimony and began the reckless accusation that history would never forget—or forgive. Sneering at Welch, McCarthy accused him of "treason" because one of the associates in Welch's Boston law firm had been a member of a communist-front organization.[28]

When McCarthy began the accusation, Welch lowered his head into his hands and stared at the table in front of him. After a few minutes of McCarthy's raging, Welch slowly raised his leonine head and formed the muted word: "Stop." Leaning toward the microphone, he asked Committee Chairman Karl Mundt for the right to speak. As Welch began, McCarthy turned away to talk to an aide. Welch asked for his attention. McCarthy responded, laughing, "I can listen with one ear." Welch said sternly, "This time, I want you to listen with both." When Welch tried to continue, McCarthy kept talking to his aide. Welch then unleashed the first of several dramatic statements he would utter that day: "Until this moment, Senator, I think I never really gauged your cruelty or your recklessness."[29]

The entire hearing room—and the nation—held its breath, silenced by the stone-cold emotion in Welch's voice. He explained that Frederick Fisher had participated in the communist-front organization when he was a student at Harvard long before joining Welch's law firm. Welch said he initially had wanted Fisher to be one of his assistants during the Army hearings in Washington but, upon learning of Fisher's activities in college, had decided the young lawyer should remain in Boston. Welch then turned to McCarthy: "Little did I dream you could be so reckless and so cruel as to do injury to that lad. He shall always bear a scar needlessly inflicted by you." In the tone of a compassionate minister being forced to chastise a wayward soul, Welch continued speaking to McCarthy: "If it were in my power to forgive you for your reckless cruelty, I would do so. I like to think I am a gentle man, but your forgiveness will have to come from someone other than me."[30]

In a horribly miscalculated effort to win the audience to his side, McCarthy then struck back at Welch by saying he had no right to speak of cruelty. Welch turned to McCarthy and said scornfully, "Let us not assassinate this lad further, Senator. You have done enough." Welch then released another of the verbal bullets that ultimately would prove fatal to McCarthy: "Have you no sense of decency, sir? At long last, have you left *no* sense of decency?"[31]

The hearing room was silent, as every occupant seemed to be quietly recalling Chairman Mundt's repeated warnings that anyone who applauded would be removed. Six uniformed police officers were stationed in the room to enforce the rule. But this time no one could stanch the flood of emotion. Suddenly, the entire audience exploded with spontaneous applause. Every man and woman who had observed the heart-stopping verbal exchange knew that Welch had triumphed—and wanted to shower their approval on him. Mundt did not raise his gavel, and the police officers did not move a muscle, thereby paying their own solemn tribute to Welch.

When Welch stood to walk from the room, reporters raced to the telephones to tell the nation of McCarthy's humiliating defeat. As the gentle lawyer—now the noble defender of civility—approached the hearing-room door, a woman laid her hand softly on his arm and, overcome with emotion, burst into tears.

While the room emptied, McCarthy remained seated in his chair, looking confused and deserted. He breathed heavily and reached out forlornly for someone to talk to, but not a single person would listen. He held out his arms and spread his palms upward as if to say in desperation: "What did I do?"[32]

The *New York Times* reported that McCarthy's televised performance "demonstrated with appalling clarity precisely what kind of man he is." Reporter James Reston continued: "One cannot remain indifferent to Joe McCarthy in one's living room. He is an abrasive man. And he is recklessly transparent. The country did not know him before, despite all the headlines. Now it has seen him." Reston concluded: "The things that have hurt him and cost him support are his manner and his manners. The Senator from Wisconsin is a bad-mannered man."[33]

Other observers expressed similar sentiments. The *Times*'s Jack Gould said, "The coverage did McCarthy in. People started to laugh at him. He became a joke, then a bore. He got tiresome." Scholars studying the legendary event echoed the same thoughts, writing, "The close-up exposure left a feeling of distaste for McCarthy" and "Joe came across as boorish, disruptive, and anarchic. It was brute soap opera." Even Cohn agreed, writing of the television coverage, "The blow was terribly damaging to Senator McCarthy. He was pictured before the nation as a cruel man who deliberately sought to wreck a fine young lawyer's life."[34]

The American people spoke as well. In January 1954, a Gallup Poll reported that 50 percent of the people surveyed had a favorable response to McCarthy. After the hearings ended in June, however, that favorable figure plummeted to 34 percent.[35]

Media critics lavished paeans on ABC for broadcasting the hearings, particularly because the action cost the network dearly. All the revenue that sponsors would have paid for the huge block of air time was lost, as no sponsors were willing to be associated with programming that could harm McCarthy. Airing the hearings cost ABC more than $500,000. The network ultimately benefited from televising the hearings, however, because the decision proved to be a turning point in its evolution. ABC previously had been considered third rate, trailing far behind CBS and NBC. But with the McCarthy hearings, ABC came of age as a serious competitor.[36]

The coverage led to action. Immediately after the hearings, senators began efforts, in earnest, to silence McCarthy. They ultimately censured him, marking only the fourth time in two centuries that the Senate had taken such severe action. In December 1954, the Senate voted 67–22 to strip McCarthy of his power, subjecting him to public disgrace. McCarthy's life came to an abrupt end three years after the Senate action. A heavy drinker, he died of liver disease associated with alcoholism. He had not yet reached his fiftieth birthday.

Regrettably, *See It Now* did not enjoy a long life either. Neither CBS nor ALCOA was nearly as enamored with the program as were the public and the critics. The company continued sponsoring the program for only one year after the McCarthy segment. The network then pushed the program to a less-desirable Sunday afternoon slot and then, in 1958, canceled it. CBS replaced *See It Now* on Tuesday night with a far different program: *The $64,000 Question.*

Trial by Television

Beginning in 1950 and continuing for three years, Senator Joseph R. McCarthy became a fierce and putrid presence in America. Stopping him required a power of great might. That valiant savior of the democratic way of life began to emerge when Edward R. Murrow committed *See It Now* to attacking the anticommunist demagogue, first in the fall of 1953 with the Radulovich segment and then in the spring of 1954 with a riveting program crafted to reveal McCarthy as a malicious thug. That same spring, ABC joined the campaign by airing an unparalleled 180 hours of live coverage of the Army-McCarthy hearings—including Joseph Welch's gripping verbal assault that, thanks to the television camera, unfolded in the living rooms of eighty million Americans.

McCarthy and McCarthyism had gained such enormous power that no single entity was strong enough to defeat them, requiring various political and social institutions to coalesce to end his tirade of fear and hatred. Ultimately, the United States Senate, White House, and American public all found it increasingly difficult to abide the senator's unfair tactics. And yet, the frustration that drove each of these constituencies was informed by the medium of television. For this new medium—fast becoming the most powerful in communication history—clearly was pivotal to exposing exactly how McCarthy operated.

Many scholars have acknowledged the central role that television played in ending McCarthyism. One labeled the *See It Now* programs followed by the televising of the hearings "the decisive blow to Senator McCarthy," and another stated those words and then went on to add that because of television, "A whole nation watched him in murderous close-up—and recoiled." Another called the Murrow programs followed by ABC's gavel-to-gavel coverage of the hearings "the most courageous instance of broadcast journalism in the history of television."[37]

It took a force of immense potential and proportion to tame a power as diabolical as the Roman candle known as Joe McCarthy. But in the early 1950s, the infant institution of television news distinguished itself—in its finest hour—by demonstrating that it was fully equal to such a formidable task.

11

Pushing the Civil Rights Movement onto the National Agenda

BY THE 1950s, slavery had been outlawed in the United States for nearly a century, but southern racists had devised other forms of tyranny to keep black Americans in their "place." Poll taxes, grandfather clauses, unfairly administered literacy tests, and various acts of intimidation denied African Americans their right to vote, and the fallacious concept of "separate but equal" deprived black men and women of public facilities and decent educations, forcing them to remain on the bottom rung of the nation's economic ladder.

In 1954, the United States Supreme Court pronounced six words that forever altered the legal status of black Americans: "Separate educational facilities are inherently unequal." The *Brown vs. Board of Education of Topeka* decision prompted blacks to challenge unjust laws and discriminatory practices, spawning the Civil Rights Movement. The initial challenges largely failed, though, because of the wall of bigotry that segregationists had constructed—they ruled the American South like kings ruled feudal estates.[1]

And then came television. By covering the movement's various events, television news awakened people throughout the nation to the realities of black oppression in the South. By pushing those realities into the face of the American people, television news propelled the Civil Rights Movement into the American consciousness and onto the national agenda. Northern newspapers such as the *New York*

Times and *Boston Globe* also covered the movement with courage and commitment, but television news had decidedly more impact.

Journalists and scholars alike have praised the vital role that television played in advancing American race relations during the late 1950s and early 1960s. Venerable CBS commentator Eric Sevareid said, "Television was a critical prod to America's conscience and the spur to congressional action," and CBS producer William Peters put it even more boldly when he said, "The Negro revolution of the 1960s could not have occurred without television coverage." Among the scholars who have lauded television's role in mobilizing the nation to end segregation was Bayard Rustin. In the book *Strategies For Freedom*, Rustin wrote, "With the coming of television, the violence of the South was no longer tucked away from the nation's attention. As the TV viewer saw it, the South was not holding a dialogue with black people; it was attempting to crush them. Television was clearly a boon to the civil rights struggle." And in *Electronic Journalism*, broadcast historian William A. Wood wrote, "The on-the-scene coverage of intimidation and bestiality in the old South made indelible impressions on many who had been oblivious to or indifferent over home-grown, American brutality and injustice. Suddenly men and women all over the country were as close as across the street to the crucible of revolution. Whites everywhere were awakened."[2]

As the television camera followed the movement's trail of tears from Little Rock to Anniston to Birmingham to Selma, people all over the country were able to witness the South's inhumanity—black men, women, and children being cursed, spit upon, attacked by police dogs, and blasted with firehoses merely because they were trying to exercise the rights that had been guaranteed to them, and to every American, by the United States Constitution. When those images became imbedded into the nation's consciousness, public opinion suddenly galvanized in support of the Civil Rights Movement. The camera continued to track the revolution as it moved to the nation's capital, spotlighting the gentle Baptist minister who stood in front of the Lincoln Memorial and spoke not only for his people but for the entire country when he said, with simple eloquence: "I have a dream."[3]

The First Great Television News Story

By the late 1950s, the technology had been developed to allow television to compete with newspapers on a daily basis, and the Civil Rights Movement was the first great television news story. NBC newsman Bill Monroe wrote that "Television conveyed the emotional values of a basically emotional contest with a richness and fidelity never before achieved in mass communications." Monroe said, "When you *see* and *hear* a wildly angry man talking, whether he is a segregationist or integrationist, you can understand the man's anger, you can feel it—the depth of it, the power of it. But if you *read* a description of what the man said, you find that, by comparison, the words are dried-up little symbols through which only a fraction of the story comes."[4]

Television newsmen also recognized that black America's struggle for equal rights was the most important story of the day. NBC correspondent Herbert Kaplan put it bluntly, "Anyone who was a journalist at the time wanted to get a piece of the story."[5]

The fact that reporters wanted to cover the movement did not, however, mean the South wanted them there. The stability of African-American oppression rested on local control of information, with many southern newspapers refusing to publish news that might disturb the existing racial pattern. As segregationists began to realize that network television was disrupting the system, they viewed reporters as outside agitators—and enemies. CBS correspondent Dan Rather recalled looking for a motel to stay at when covering a story in Mississippi and being greeted by a sign in the window that read: "NO DOGS, NIGGERS OR REPORTERS ALLOWED." Charles Quinn of NBC recalled that many southerners developed nicknames for ABC, CBS, and NBC—*Afro* Broadcasting Company, *Colored* Broadcasting System, and *Nigger* Broadcasting Company.[6]

Segregationists did not stop with name calling, for dozens of correspondents were injured while covering the movement. When NBC's Richard Valeriani was reporting from Alabama in 1965, he was struck from the back with a wooden club, sustaining a severe head wound that kept him in the hospital for several days. Valeriani recalled how law enforcement officials responded: "A state trooper saw the whole thing. He took the ax handle away from the guy, telling him, 'You've done enough damage for one night.' But that was it. The trooper didn't even arrest the guy."[7]

Although network correspondents were sympathetic to the goals of the movement, they bristled at the suggestion, which segregationists often made, that television initiated the revolution. John Chancellor, who covered the movement for NBC, said, "History was the initiator of the movement. Journalism does not *initiate* social change, but journalism can *amplify* social change. We worked as an amplifier."[8]

Correspondents for African-American news organizations, in contrast, had no intention of remaining detached observers. *Chicago Defender* reporter Ethel Payne covered every major event in the Civil Rights Movement—often not only writing about protests but also participating in them. Payne, known as the First Lady of the Black Press, said, "We could not stand aside and be so-called *objective* witnesses. I could not divorce myself from the heart of the problem, because I was *part* of the problem. So I had to learn how to give the essence of the story and to somehow or other transmit my own views into that total picture."[9]

Knocking Down Walls in Little Rock

Observers point to a neo-Gothic high school in Arkansas as the backdrop for the first chapter in television's epic coverage of the Civil Rights Movement. CBS correspondent Robert Schakne said, "Little Rock was the first case where people really got their impression of an event from television. It was the event that nationalized a news story that would have remained a local story if it had just been a print story."[10]

During the summer of 1957, African-American leaders in the city decided to challenge the segregated school policy by enrolling nine black students, each with a flawless record of behavior and academic performance, in the city's most highly regarded—and all-white—public high school. In early September, network cameras were on hand to show the nation the students walking gravely toward Central High School—the girls in crinolines and penny loafers, the boys in white shirts and pressed trousers—and then being turned away, blocked by Arkansas National Guardsmen. Governor Orval Faubus had ordered the soldiers to stop the students from entering the school.[11]

Every image that day was gripping, but one stood out from all the rest. Daisy Bates, the leader of the local National Association for the Advancement of Colored People (NAACP), had arranged for the youngsters to be brought to the school in a police car for protection. But one student, Elizabeth Eckford, did not have a telephone. So the petite fifteen-year-old, in bobby socks and starched white blouse, arrived at the school alone. Confronted by an impenetrable wall of redneck segregationists and without the protection of the police, the tiny figure was captured on film as the crowd screamed "Lynch her! Lynch the nigger bitch!" Clutching her school books and trying desperately not to cry, the girl was shown surrounded by thousands of sneering white men towering over her. But from somewhere, deep within her soul, Elizabeth was able to find the stamina to remain poised and dignified. The camera continued to focus on the lone girl—an indelible symbol of the strength of the human spirit—until a middle-aged white woman finally helped her escape onto a city bus.[12]

Television cameras captured in vivid images the curses and hateful venom that became part of Elizabeth Eckford's daily life as one of the Little Rock Nine. Reprinted by permission of the National Archives.

The cameras remained in Arkansas throughout the month, as President Eisenhower struggled with how to respond to Faubus. No crusader for racial equality, Eisenhower preferred that local citizens resolve local issues. But this time Faubus had gone too far. By refusing to allow the students to attend the school, the Arkansas governor was openly defying the Supreme Court's desegregation ruling—in front of the entire country, thanks to television. After three weeks of indecision, the president finally placed the Arkansas National Guardsmen under federal control, ordering the soldiers to protect the Little Rock Nine.

The cameras were in front of Central High School the next morning as the students again attempted to enter the building. But this time the black youngsters were dwarfed by thousands of angry segregationists who covered the school grounds chanting, "Two-Four-Six-Eight! We don't wanna integrate!" The soldiers—with their bayonets drawn and pointed toward the mob—surrounded the frightened African-American students and inched their way through the angry sea. The faces were contorted as the white crowd jeered and screamed "Hey, boy!" and "Go home, nigger!"[13]

Daily coverage continued. The cameras documented uniformed soldiers marching through the streets of Little Rock and the barrage of curses and threats spewed onto the tiny band of black students as they walked across the school grounds. Each morning viewers around the country saw the caravan of military jeeps in front of and behind the Army station wagon escorting the black students from their homes to the school; each afternoon, the cameras recorded the return trip taking the students home again.[14]

Breaking Barriers at the University of Georgia

By early 1961, the country had a youthful new president, and civil rights leaders savored new hope that John F. Kennedy's Democratic administration would bring more positive reaction to their march toward racial equality.

Testimony to the new optimism came the same month as Kennedy's inauguration, when a federal court ruled that the venerable University of Georgia, for the first time in its 175-year history, had to admit African-American students. The two young people were Hamilton Holmes and Charlayne Hunter, who later would make her mark on journalism as *New York Times* and Public Broadcasting Service correspondent Charlayne Hunter-Gault. Their admission unleashed a maelstrom of hatred, and the networks rushed to Athens, Georgia, to document it.[15]

The attention centered on Hunter because she, as a female student, was required to live on campus, but Holmes, as a male student, was allowed to move off campus. Then a frightened eighteen-year-old, Hunter appeared nightly on the television screen for days on end, looking toward the ground as white students screamed and spit at her. One piece showed the world how students taunted Hunter as well as other black student pioneers; the film showed a female student walking up to Hunter, tossing a quarter on the floor and sneering, "Here, nigger. Here's a quarter. Go change my sheets."[16]

On another occasion, the cameras focused on the thousand students who gathered outside Hunter's dormitory, holding a banner scrawled with the angry words, "Nigger, go home!" Other footage showed students lighting firecrackers and hurling bricks through Hunter's dormitory window. Viewers witnessed the police trying to disperse the crowd by using tear gas and then saw how the tactics merely enraged the mob even more—finally to the point that events surged out of control. Film showed hundreds of segregationists roaming the campus, committing random acts of vandalism and burning effigies of African Americans.[17]

Although the contempt that the students demonstrated toward Hunter initially must have seemed beyond belief to many northern viewers, similar images would become commonplace in the next few years. The same scenes unfolded time and time again as other educational institutions in the South—including the University of Mississippi later in 1961 and the University of Alabama in 1963—gradually and fitfully became desegregated.

Riding Buses for Freedom

The next phase of television coverage evolved from a Supreme Court decision banning segregation in interstate travel. To test the new law, in May 1961 a racially mixed group of college students purchased bus tickets to take them from Washington, D.C., to New Orleans. When the students were dubbed "freedom riders," the television networks had their next story.[18]

NBC cameraman Moe Levy boarded one of the buses with the students, capturing their images on film. The young, attractive men and women who climbed aboard the first two buses in Washington were well dressed and well groomed. One slender young African-American woman wore a tailored traveling suit and carried a white patent leather purse. The young man beside her wore a dark suit and club tie, a carefully folded handkerchief protruding from his breast pocket.[19]

As the freedom riders traveled south through Virginia and the Carolinas, segregationists occasionally taunted them, but those acts were quickly eclipsed once the buses crossed the Alabama state line. When one bus stopped in Anniston to refuel, Ku Klux Klansmen punctured the tires. The riders were unaware of the damage until the bus had traveled a few miles out of town and the tires went flat. Klansmen then surrounded the Greyhound bus and set it on fire. News coverage of the incident showed young men and women rushing from the burning bus and then being struck by stones thrown by the klansmen, as clouds of black smoke billowed into the sky. If a highway patrolman had not been aboard to protect the riders, they very well may have been killed.[20]

Riders on the second bus, the one carrying Moe Levy, fared far worse. The thirty vehicles that the Alabama State Police had promised would escort the bus from Birmingham to Montgomery vanished at some point along the way. When the bus pulled into the Montgomery station, a mob of 2,000—armed with bricks, chains, baseball bats, and lead pipes—attacked the students. Although no images of the bloodbath were filmed because the mob smashed Levy's camera, the networks broadcast images of the bruised and blood-soaked students—including a white seminarian—in their hospital beds. The young men and women lost teeth and suffered black eyes and multiple broken bones, many of them beaten so severely that they were disfigured for the rest of their lives. Levy was clubbed and beaten; one of his legs was permanently injured.[21]

Defying the Power Structure in Birmingham

In the early 1960s, Birmingham was the most segregated city in America, and it also was home to a hot-tempered police commissioner who epitomized racism at its most vile: "Bull" Connor. City officials not only denied blacks a voice in city government but even refused to hear their complaints. So the largest city in Alabama was fated to become a notorious battlefield in the civil rights struggle, a city where an extraordinary 3,000 black men, women, and children would be arrested in one seething spring, many of them injured by a shocking display of police brutality. Cameras were in place to spread the images throughout the country, and viewers who saw the images would never forget them.[22]

In 1963, the Reverend Martin Luther King, Jr., and other civil rights leaders targeted Birmingham for a series of nonviolent protests aimed at overturning the city's white power structure. They saw Birmingham as pivotal to the civil rights crusade; if progress could be made here, other cities would follow. The campaign began in early April with demonstrators picketing in front of stores and conducting sit-ins at lunch counters. In week two, the campaign expanded to marches. As the arrests climbed to triple digits, demonstrators from other cities streamed into Birmingham.[23]

Television broadcast the peaceful protests across the nation, showing that some participants were in their twenties but others were middle-aged women in dresses, hats, and white gloves. The only violence portrayed on film was by whites. Footage would begin with blacks walking quietly up to a lunch counter and sitting on the stools. As the waitresses ignored them, the blacks continued to gaze forward, some of them lost in prayer. But then the serenity of the scene would be shattered by a white approaching one of the peaceful protesters from the rear and pouring a bottle of ketchup over the person's hair. The blacks remained poised as the whites pointed their fingers and laughed at the ketchup dripping onto the protester's shirt or blouse. In some scenes, the whites became enraged by the victim's lack of reaction and pulled at the person's clothes and pushed him or her off the stool. Then a white police officer would enter the picture, arresting the black while allowing the white to go free.

During the next several weeks as the daily dramas continued to play out on the evening news, the eyes of the nation turned to Birmingham. Every day the arrest total, already in the hundreds, grew ever larger. The black community's ability to unite and willingness to be arrested increasingly frustrated and angered Connor and the other racist authorities. The protest had now continued for a full month, the city jail was overflowing, and the protesters were clearly succeeding in their efforts to shine the spotlight on Birmingham. Tension was high.

In early May, protest organizers introduced a daring new strategy to win the nation's compassion: allowing school children to join the demonstrations. Thousands of African-American boys and girls, many still in elementary school, took to the streets for a massive march through downtown. The children celebrated the "Black and Glad" aspect of the movement, laughing and dancing while they sang simple but poignant freedom songs to a jazz tempo—creating dynamite television images.[24]

Connor was not amused. He arrested 700 youngsters and ordered his officers to become more *physical*. The adults as well as the children were stunned when officers began using high-pressure firehoses so powerful that even the strongest of men could not remain standing against them. The firemen manning the hoses pushed men, women, and children to the ground and pinned them against buildings as if they were animals.

More startling still was the other instrument of domination that Connor authorized: German shepherd police dogs. Trained to attack dangerous criminals, the ferocious animals snarled and pulled at the leather straps with which the officers held them. The dogs were so frightening that many of the school children became hysterical. As they did, some parents threw stones and bottles at the officers. Connor responded by ordering the dogs forward, yelling, "Look at those niggers run!"[25]

Television captured the terror. And that night on their television screens, the American people saw a level of police brutality far beyond what most of them had ever imagined. Viewers saw, for example, a middle-aged woman being held to the ground by five white police officers, one with a knee across her throat. A man wrapped his arms around his wife and child in a futile effort to shield them from the torrent. A dignified woman, dressed in high heels and a pearl necklace, kneeled in prayer amid the chaos on all sides of her.[26]

The specific scene from that day of infamy that produced the most reaction was of a German shepherd, with its fangs bared, tearing at the stomach of a black schoolboy. To make the scene complete, the police officer controlling the dog grasped the boy's sweater, keeping the victim in place so the dog could maul him. One historian went so far as to credit the success of the Birmingham campaign to that one image, writing, "If there was any single event at which the 1960s generation of 'new Negroes' turned into a major social force, the appearance of that photograph was it. Intense pressure upon President Kennedy to initiate federal action began to be applied the moment that image appeared."[27]

The country's leading newspaper reacted to the televised images, with a *New York Times* editorial stating, "The use of police dogs and high-pressure firehoses to subdue school children in Birmingham is a national disgrace." And Americans around the country demonstrated their solidarity with the Birmingham protesters when 250,000 people spontaneously organized public marches in forty cities.[28]

In Birmingham, negotiations that previously had failed now succeeded. The day after the images of the firehoses and police dogs were televised, President Kennedy sent a Justice Department official to Birmingham to act as a mediator between city officials and the demonstrators. And exactly one week after the American people saw those images, the leaders reached an agreement.[29]

The television images prompted action on the national level as well, prompting Kennedy to propose civil rights legislation of a scope and boldness that a few months earlier would have been impossible. He asked the networks for fifteen minutes during prime time and said what African Americans had been waiting generations to hear: "We preach freedom around the world, but are we to say to the world—and much more importantly, to each other—that this is the land of the free, except for the Negroes? The time has come for this nation to fulfill its promise."[30]

A Birmingham police officer held this young man in place so the attack dog could rip into his stomach—and the television networks saw to it that the whole world was watching. Reprinted by permission of the National Archives.

Marching on Washington

Building on the political momentum that the Birmingham images had created, civil rights leaders decided to expand their crusade to the power center of American government. What's more, the leaders recognized that the March on Washington had the potential of becoming a television spectacle—a potential that was fully realized.[31]

Network coverage of the August 1963 demonstration began early and continued late. NBC led its rivals with the network's popular *Today* morning program kicking off with a thirty-minute report, followed by updates throughout the day, a two-hour recap in the afternoon, and a final report at night. ABC hopped in and out of coverage throughout the day as well, and CBS carried the speeches live for three hours in the afternoon and ran an hour-long special during prime time. The networks received widespread praise for their coverage. The *Washington Post* story about television coverage began, "As a TV spectacular, the March on Washington was a program without parallel"; *Variety* awarded the networks a "Great Coverage of Great Event" citation.[32]

And a great event it was. With heads high and chests forward, 200,000 Americans marched, some spending their life savings to make the pilgrimage to the nation's capital. The marchers showed well on television, especially when the networks took their cameras high into the Washington Monument for panoramic shots and then cut away to marchers carrying signs that demanded "DECENT HOUSING NOW" and "JOBS AND FREEDOM NOW." One creative group hoisted a coffin marked "Jim Crow," and every marcher sang—hymns, anthems, spirituals, improvised chants of protest.

The main speaker of the day was a man that television loved—and had helped boost to his preeminent stature in the movement. Though he stood only five feet five inches tall, Martin Luther King, Jr., with his broad, sloping face and heavily-muscled neck and shoulders filled the television screen with a sense of physical as well as spiritual power. In his rich baritone voice, the thirty-four-year-old Baptist preacher spoke the moving words that generations of African-American boys and girls would commit to memory: "I have a dream that my four little children will one day live in a nation where they will not be judged by the color of their skin, but by the content of their character."[33]

Television took a step toward that dream a few days later when NBC produced *The American Revolution of '63*, a news special that has been described as a "magnum opus" of civil rights coverage. Jack Gould wrote in the *New York Times*: "*The American Revolution of '63* must stand as a turning point in TV's journalistic evolution. Never before has so much valuable prime time been accorded to a single domestic issue in one uninterrupted stretch."[34]

NBC airing the three-hour program was particularly courageous because sponsors refused to support it, fearing segregationists would boycott any products advertised during the show. The network stood firm, canceling its entire evening of commercial programming to show the special. By filling the commercial breaks with in-house ads for NBC rather than ads from paying sponsors, the network lost half a million dollars in revenue that night.[35]

The program profiled cities that had played critical roles in the movement up to that point, giving the network a chance to replay gripping images of terrified students in Little Rock and ferocious police dogs in Birmingham. Frank McGee's introduction was as stirring as the footage: "Did this American Revolution begin this year in Birmingham? Or did it begin in 1954 with a Supreme Court decision? Or in 1863 with a Presidential proclamation? Some of its roots reach back to 1776 to an independence declaration—even back to the year 52 when the Apostle Paul, preaching in Athens, said, 'God hath made of one blood all nations of men.'"[36]

NBC's president later spotlighted the program as a sterling example of how television news could shape history. Robert E. Kintner said, "Watching *The American Revolution of '63*, many people sensed for the first time the depth and continuity of what had previously seemed a spasmodic and puzzling protest. The program helped establish the national consensus which expressed itself in the Civil Rights Act of 1964."[37]

Some Americans, however, still did not support the civil rights revolution—or the medium that was covering it. Mississippi Governor Ross Barnett said, "Fellow Americans, you are witnessing one more chapter in what has been termed the 'Television Revolution.' The TV networks have publicized and dramatized the race issue far beyond its relative importance in today's world. The three-hour special program and the degree of coverage accorded to the August 28 March on Washington underlined the fact that the American public is being propagandized by overemphasis."[38]

Barnett was not the only segregationist who chastised television for supporting the movement. After NBC canceled its telecast of the Blue-Gray college football game because black players were not allowed to participate in it, Alabama Governor George Wallace denounced the decision as "irresponsible," and when CBS president Frank Stanton testified at a Senate communications hearing, South Carolina Senator Strom Thurmond attacked him for devoting too much coverage to civil rights, asking Stanton point blank: "Don't you care about white people?"[39]

Back to Birmingham

The fact that many racists continued to feel disdain for African Americans burst into the nation's consciousness two weeks after the March on Washington, when members of the Ku Klux Klan ignited a bomb at Birmingham's Sixteenth Street Baptist Church on a Sunday morning. The bomb killed four little girls, aged eleven to fourteen, and injured twenty other children. The incident was particularly poignant because the bomb exploded just as the children finished their Sunday school lesson and were changing into their choir robes, and because the victims had not participated in the movement—these were not marchers or freedom riders.[40]

Television crews rushed back to Birmingham to show American viewers images of the remains of the red brick church that now looked like something out of World War II Berlin. The cameras also captured the drama of the funerals with the huge bouquets of pink carnations covering the four caskets and the emotion-filled expressions on the faces of the mourners. Mothers and fathers sobbed quietly, lost in their private grief; young children looked forlorn, unable to comprehend that their innocent playmates had become the latest victims of racial hatred.[41]

Seeking Constitutional Rights in Selma

In 1964, civil rights leaders turned their attention toward blacks in the Deep South being denied the vote. In Selma, Alabama, Americans of African descent comprised 57 percent of the residents but less than 1 percent of the registered voters. King set out to change that statistic by emboldening Selma blacks while informing the nation of their grievances—such as the fact that most white registration examiners could not, themselves, even read the test they were administering to blacks. King ultimately drew some 6,000 workers to Selma to help him. He brought the media as well.[42]

Network correspondents came to Selma to capture the voter registration campaign on film. Typical of those images was one showing a tall, distinguished-looking black man in a suit and tie appearing at the registrar's office but being taunted by white hooligans. The teenage boys pushed the middle-aged man out of line and then chased him down the street, yelling obscenities at him. When one of the toughs knocked off the man's hat and he leaned over to pick it up, several of the boys kicked him and spit on him.[43]

King's most daring idea of how to bring attention to the voter registration drive was to organize a march from Selma to the state capitol in Montgomery fifty-four miles to the east, ending with the protesters delivering a petition to the governor. Governor Wallace publicly opposed the Sunday, March 7, 1965, event.[44]

The protesters were not deterred. Some 600 of them set out down U.S. Route 80. But after marching 300 yards, they found the highway blocked by fifty state troopers and 100 possemen, white men who had eagerly volunteered for the duty of chastening rebellious blacks. The men were led by James G. Clark, Selma's quick-tempered sheriff—a graduate of the "Bull" Connor school of police brutality. After the marchers refused to disperse, Clark and his men attacked them in full force.

The televised images of the event showed clubs flying in all directions as black men and women began screaming and falling to the ground while the officers continued forward, stomping on the people who lay on the pavement. Then the film showed officers targeting particular marchers, running after them and clubbing them without mercy. A middle-aged woman in a head scarf hunched down toward the ground, but an officer struck her on the head with his nightstick; when the woman collapsed on the ground, another officer ran into the picture and kicked her in the stomach and clubbed her again.[45]

Fifteen possemen were mounted on horses, and they added another gruesome dimension to the scene. Looking like Cossacks overpowering the peasants, the mounted men spurred their horses and charged into the crowd with nightsticks swinging and boots kicking at the protesters. Meanwhile, hundreds of whites stood on the edge of the highway whooping and cheering.[46]

The scene became even more horrifying when clouds of tear gas filled the screen. As the white officers and possemen covered their faces with their gas masks, African-American men and women fell sputtering and coughing to the ground. Officers then raced like savages from one bleeding body to another, striking them again and again with the nightsticks. The cameras moved in for closeups of some of the bloody figures lying motionless, and still the officers continued to beat and kick them. Other cameras followed possemen into the black sections of Selma where bullwhips were used to brutalize men and women who had been nowhere near the march. More than ninety people were injured.[47]

The incident—dubbed "Bloody Sunday"—ignited a powder keg of protest across the country. Members of Congress, governors, state legislators, clergymen, and labor union officials denounced the brutality. Michigan Governor George Romney led 10,000 marchers in a spontaneous demonstration in Detroit, 15,000 New Yorkers marched in Harlem, and thousands of other indignant Americans snarled traffic in Chicago, Los Angeles, and Washington. Episcopal Bishop James A. Pike called for the country's 400,000 ministers, priests, and rabbis to converge on Selma.

Like much of the nation, President Lyndon Johnson found the images appalling. After Wallace flew to Washington to meet with the president, Johnson announced, "I told the governor that the brutality in Selma last Sunday must not be repeated." Another Selma march was conducted two weeks after the first, the crowd swelling to more than 3,000 protesters from across the country. With President Johnson insisting that Wallace provide protection for the marchers, the event went smoothly.[48]

But L.B.J.'s more important activity that month was a televised address to a joint session of Congress. The speech, which Johnson delivered with visible emotion, was in preparation for a voting rights bill he submitted two days later—and which was enacted within four months. Johnson said, "Many of the issues of civil rights are complex and difficult. But about this there can be no argument: Every American citizen must have an equal right to vote. There is no reason which can excuse the denial of that right."[49]

Television Images Nourish a Social Revolution

Congress ultimately passed two pieces of legislation that became the most important tangible products of the Civil Rights Movement. The Civil Rights Act of 1964 established the Equal Employment Opportunity Commission and prohibited restaurants, hotels, theaters, and other facilities of public accommodation from turning away any person because of his or her race. The Voting Rights Act of 1965 banned all barriers to Americans exercising the right to vote.

In the same breath that journalists, historians, and activists speak of these landmark pieces of legislation, they describe the pivotal role television news played in gaining support for the measures. In particular, observers point to the televised images of police brutality in Birmingham and Selma. NBC commentator Edwin Newman said, "When the people around this country saw people being beaten by hoodlums while they were seeking the right to vote, there was a sense of righteous indignation. The effect of these scenes, brought into our homes via television, was one of shock. We saw civil rights marchers and children being bitten by police dogs. The Civil Rights Act suddenly had the support it needed. Those images changed history." NBC correspondent Bill Monroe agreed, saying unequivocally, "The Civil Rights Act of 1964 wouldn't have happened without TV." Ralph McGill, editor of the *Atlanta Constitution*, had similar praise for the broadcast medium, saying, "Had it not been for television showing us 'Bull' Connor and his dogs and the march on Selma, there would not have been the momentum to push the Civil Rights Acts through Congress. Television performed a magnificent service."[50]

From a historian's viewpoint, Gary Orfield wrote of the images from Birmingham, "Anyone watching TV could understand what it felt like to have a dog, capable of tearing a man apart, lunge at him during a peaceful march. One image of a woman held down by five policemen was worth a million pious words. Brutal use of powerful firehoses to knock down demonstrators made the crisis clear in homes across the country." And John Lewis, who in 1965 led the voting rights march in Selma and today is a member of Congress, said, "If it hadn't been for television on that day, we wouldn't have gotten the Voting Rights Act of 1965. The Civil Rights Movement in this country owes a great deal to television."[51]

Newspapers and magazines can communicate information about an event, but television news has the power to transmit the experience of actually *being part* of that event. For two centuries, a minority of American citizens committed to advancing the cause of black civil rights had struggled to convince the majority of the justness of their cause. During the late 1950s and early 1960s, television allowed that minority to succeed by bringing a simplicity and a moral clarity to the confrontation between the bigotry of segregationists and the determination of oppressed African Americans. The images that television news conveyed to its viewers moved the conscience of a nation and helped propel the people of the United States to take concrete steps toward leveling the racial playing field in this country.

12

Vietnam War: Bringing the Battlefield into the American Living Room

THE COMING OF AGE of television news not only coincided with the Civil Rights Movement but also emerged at virtually the same time as the United States military buildup in Vietnam. The nightly network evening news programs expanded from fifteen minutes to half an hour in 1963; the first American ground troops were sent to Indochina in 1965. The Vietnam War, therefore, became the first televised war. It also eventually evolved into the least successful foreign war in American history. These two facts may not be coincidental.

Many media and political experts have argued that by bringing grisly images of battle into the American living room, television news played a key role in turning the American public against the Vietnam War and, ultimately, in hastening the end of that prolonged conflict. Although those observers are widely divided on whether ending the war was the right or wrong decision, they agree that television news showed the raw horror of war in ways that print journalism could not. Violence, carnage, and human suffering were depicted in withering reality, but politics and strategy, which were not easily translated onto film, were largely ignored. So television viewers were left to conclude that the Vietnam War was senseless and immoral.

Numerous scholars as well as journalists have made this point. In the book *The Vietnam Legacy*, Edward Shils wrote, "Television gave the American people vivid images of certain aspects of the war in

Vietnam which they could never have gotten from reading newspapers and periodicals. It made them see the war as a meaningless destruction of lives and landscapes." Nationally syndicated columnist Bob Greene wrote, "Forget the words that the network correspondents spoke. It was that video, night after night, that turned Americans against the Vietnam adventure. It was one thing for a newspaperman to describe, even in the most graphic terms, carnage that he had seen; it was quite another for a television viewer to see the same carnage at dinnertime." And veteran NBC commentator Edwin Newman concluded, "Television brought the Vietnam War into our living rooms on a nightly basis. They produced close-up, sensational images of war. American viewers saw the real experience of war transformed into theatrics on the twenty-one-inch screen. And they recoiled."[1]

Although the observers range widely in their political perspectives on the war, they share the fundamental belief that television news caused the American people to question the morality of war and ultimately to lose what could be called the national *will to kill.* Many critics say this loss of resolve resulted in American forces being withdrawn from Southeast Asia prematurely; others praise the United States for finally ending a prolonged war it never should have entered in the first place. For better or worse, graphic televised images turned the American public against the war and helped bring an end to the fighting.

America's Longest War

President Truman initiated U.S. involvement in Vietnam in the early 1950s when he sent military aid to the French colony. Truman and the men who entered the White House after him hoped to stop Vietnam from following China, its neighbor to the north, into communism. In 1954, Vietnam was divided in half—Ho Chi Minh's communist government in the north was headquartered in Hanoi; the prodemocracy government in the south was centered in Saigon. American involvement continued under both Republican and Democratic administrations, with President Eisenhower dispatching military advisers to South Vietnam and then President Kennedy increasing the number of advisers. President Johnson took an even stronger hand against the communists, for the first time committing American troops to Indochina.

Vietnam first moved onto the radar screen in the lives of most Americans in 1964. American military personnel announced that North Vietnamese patrol boats had fired on American destroyers in the Gulf of Tonkin, prompting Johnson to order a retaliatory strike that destroyed twenty-five boats and an oil depot. At L.B.J.'s request, Congress passed the Gulf of Tonkin resolution assuring its support for "all necessary action" to defend United States forces in Southeast Asia.

In 1965, Johnson ordered offensive bombing raids and sent the first ground troops, with the number of GIs in Vietnam rising to 175,000 by year's end. Although the Americans were better equipped than the North Vietnamese, they were unfamiliar with the warfare practiced by the rebel Viet Cong guerrilla fighters. Time after time, the enemy evaded the Americans by *melting* into the jungle. Determined to defeat the communists, Johnson continued to escalate the American war effort. By 1967, troops exceeded 500,000.

Ultimately, the United States paid a high price for fighting in Vietnam, with more than 58,000 American men and women dying in the war. The number of Southeast Asians who died is not known; estimates generally range from one million to three million.

The Most Powerful Medium in History

Although television existed during the Korean War, it had not yet evolved into a major news medium. By the mid-1960s, however, more people were receiving their news from television than from newspapers. And as the Vietnam War continued, that balance increasingly shifted toward television. By 1972, two out of three persons surveyed named television as their major news source.[2]

By the height of the war, the network evening news programs were drawing huge numbers of viewers. CBS, NBC, and ABC attracted a combined audience of thirty-five million per night. One of the most committed of those viewers was President Johnson, who became so obsessed by television news that he had three TV sets in the Oval Office—one for each network.

Television correspondents in Vietnam, as well as their print counterparts, were free to go where they pleased and report what they wished. For this was the first—and last—American war with no military censorship. During the early years of fighting, journalists were such committed cheerleaders for the government that officials felt voluntary guidelines were fully adequate. Those rules identified fifteen categories of information, such as troop movements and casualty figures, that were off limits until they were officially announced in Saigon. Violation of the rules meant a reporter would lose his or her accreditation, but that happened only four times during the entire war.

Television coverage brought the reality of the battlefield—such as this young private enduring his own suffering while trying to care for his wounded buddies—into the American living room. Reprinted by permission of the National Archives.

Through 1967, television coverage was overwhelmingly favorable to American policy, although many of the images from the war certainly offended human sensibilities. After the Tet Offensive in early 1968, television's portrayal of the war became more critical.

Technological advances in the 1960s boosted the capabilities of television news. New, lightweight cameras combined with jet air transportation and communication satellites meant that for the first time, film from the front became a regular part of daily news coverage. Further advances meant that black-and-white images were transformed into color ones—blood could be seen in all its horrific brilliance.

Exposing the Horrors of War

From the moment ground troops arrived in Vietnam in 1965, television presented viewers with the most realistic battlefront images possible. TV defined the reality of war as, in a word, *blood*.

Mike Wallace of CBS recalled that he and other correspondents, eager to get their stories on the air, did their best to find the gory combat footage their bosses in New York wanted. Wallace said, "Correspondents kept a kind of scorecard as to which pieces were and were not used, and an inordinate number of *combat* pieces were used, compared with some first-rate pieces in the political area or non-bloody stories."[3]

Typical was a 1967 piece in which NBC's Greg Harris joined a platoon of GIs. Harris reported, "In the first twenty-six days of the present operation, this particular unit killed 270 VC while suffering only three wounded Americans." Film then showed American soldiers charging boldly into a village, bayonets drawn. Harris continued, "Cong Phu was burned and blasted to death." As footage showed the huts burning, Harris began his summation, "The war in First Corps is changing for the enemy"—but then he stopped. He remained silent for several seconds so the image of a Vietnamese body being pulled out of a hole, by the hair, could have its full, gruesome impact. His final words added more drama still, "Today the Viet Cong lost the use of Cong Phu. Tomorrow they will lose the use of another village, then another." As Harris wrapped up, the film showed the huts in the village continuing to burn.[4]

Hundreds of such reports aired day after day, week after week. Each told of a unit burning a village, with film often showing dead bodies—many of them charred. NBC correspondent Jack Perkins said matter-of-factly during one report about a village being burned, "There was no discriminating one house from another. There did not need to be. The whole village was destroyed."[5]

Although lurid images of dead and wounded Vietnamese soldiers and civilians often filled the screen, the most sought-after film was of blood flowing from the veins of American GIs. An NBC News vice president said at the time, "It's not a Vietnamese war; it's an *American* war in Asia. And that's the only story the American audience is interested in." He told his correspondents to concentrate on providing graphic images of American soldiers engaged in combat—preferably mortal.[6]

The bloody scenes were often featured as dramatic close-ups with flames engulfing thatched roofs and black smoke billowing into the sky serving as backdrops. Typical was a heart-rending NBC sequence that showed, in the distance, women and children fleeing from their burning homes while, in the foreground, a young GI screamed in anguish "It hurts! It hurts!" as medics rushed him past the eye of the camera, his right leg reduced to a bloody stump.[7]

A Zippo Cigarette Lighter Ignites a Firestorm

The most controversial story of the early years of the war was by Morley Safer of CBS. One day in 1965, Safer was having coffee with some marine officers when one of them asked if he would like to join them on a field operation the next day. Safer did not hesitate a moment. After an amphibious carrier took them to Cam Ne, the men marched single file into the village and, in very orderly fashion, burned every hut to the ground. The film was riveting. As the huts burst into flames, the marines could be seen warning the Vietnamese peasants to run; but the film also showed that the warnings were useless because they were in English, while the confused looks on the women's and children's faces communicated that they understood only Vietnamese. But the most poignant detail on the film evolved from the equipment the marines used to ignite the thatched roofs: Zippo cigarette lighters.

When the film arrived in New York, network executives recognized the explosive nature of a report that depicted American soldiers cavalierly destroying a Vietnamese village. Fred Friendly, the producer who had piloted Edward R. Murrow through his battles with Joseph McCarthy ten years earlier, was awakened in the middle of the night. Friendly agreed to run the footage only after talking with Safer personally over the telephone to be sure the story was accurate.

Safer's narrative for the story began with a recitation of facts—"The day's operation burned down 150 houses, wounded three women, killed one baby, and netted these four prisoners"—as Safer pointed to four elderly men. The intrepid correspondent, clearly shocked by the horror he had witnessed, then added his own highly critical comments, "Today's operation is the frustration of Vietnam in miniature."[8]

Friendly did not go home after the "Zippo segment" aired. Instead, he went knowingly to his office and began answering the phone calls from hundreds of angry Americans who cursed CBS for portraying American GIs as heartless killers and America's effort to stop communism as a senseless exercise in inhumanity.

Among the callers was President Johnson. The leader of the free world called Frank Stanton, president of CBS News. Johnson's first question was as vivid as the film itself—"Frank, are you trying to *fuck* me?" Letting loose with the full fury of his monumental temper, Johnson continued, "Your boys just shat on the American flag." L.B.J. denounced Safer as a communist and accused him of having bribed the marine officer. The president later had Safer investigated. When the reporter's record was found to be flawless, Johnson took solace in learning that Safer had been born in Canada. The president said petulantly, "I knew he wasn't an American."[9]

Tet Stuns a Nation

The single most significant military action in the war erupted in late January 1968 when the North Vietnamese orchestrated the Tet Offensive. Named for the Lunar New Year holiday that coincided with it, this ambitious attack included simultaneous assaults on more than 100 sites—virtually every city, town, and military base in South Vietnam. The most dramatic assault was by a Viet Cong suicide squad on the supposedly impregnable new United States Embassy in Saigon, killing five American soldiers. That action ended after a few hours, but heavy fighting continued throughout the south for another ten days. Battles raged even longer at the marine base in Khe Sanh and the holy city of Hue.

Tet's repercussions were far-reaching. On the communist side, following an initial advantage gained from the surprise factor, the ground taken was lost again. In addition, the Viet Cong, by abandoning the jungle and exposing themselves to American firepower in conventional combat, suffered enormous casualties. The offensive was, in short, a military failure. Because of the reaction in the United States, however, the Viet Cong could claim a major psychological victory. Tet shocked the American public, which had believed that success in Vietnam was imminent. The offensive seriously damaged the credibility of the Johnson administration; the American people were suddenly impatient with this inconclusive war. And in a presidential election year, the public had a direct means of expressing its dissatisfaction.

The role television news played in the Tet Offensive was momentous. Just as Vietnam was America's first television war, Tet was America's first television superbattle. The story had drama, suspense, and enormous public interest. With the communists acting offensively and taking the United States military by surprise, the very future of democracy seemed to be on the line. Television news pulled out all the stops.

The epicenter of the offensive was the very symbol of the United States presence in Vietnam: the American Embassy. In the chaos of the surprise attack and the haste to report the news as quickly as possible, inaccurate information was broadcast. NBC's Chet Huntley told anxious viewers, "The Viet Cong seized part of the United States Embassy in Saigon early Wednesday. Snipers are in buildings and on rooftops near the embassy and are firing on American personnel inside the compound. Twenty suicide commandos are reported to be holding the first floor of the embassy." Huntley was wrong. The Viet Cong entered and held the embassy compound for six hours but never penetrated the embassy building itself.[10]

The embassy remained the focal point of coverage for three days, as an ongoing gun battle on the grounds provided a live-action bonanza for TV crews. Barrages of automatic weapon fire, scenes of men running for cover behind trees, and the lifeless bodies of two fallen GIs made for some of the most eye-popping news images in American military history—as exciting as a Hollywood Western. On the network evening news shows, CBS aired a full minute of the gun battle, NBC let its film run for two minutes, and ABC continued its film uninterrupted for three minutes—including footage of the network's Vietnamese sound man being wounded on camera by a stray bullet.[11]

CBS and NBC quickly produced half-hour special news programs on Tet that aired that third night. Alarmist in tone, the programs portrayed the offensive as a brutal bloodbath, with lengthy footage that was unmatched in its sheer volume of gore and carnage. The prime-time spectacles strongly reinforced the message that Tet was a devastating defeat for the United States. CBS called its special *Saigon Under Fire*; NBC opted for *Viet Cong Terror: A Guerrilla Offensive*.

At the same time the networks filled the TV screens with portraits of havoc and an American military run amok, they also filled the ears of the public with words of pessimism. Jeff Gralnick of CBS told his audience, "The Viet Cong proved they could take and hold almost any area they chose." And ABC's Joseph Harsch expressed a similar skepticism toward American forces when he reported, "Best estimates here are that the enemy has not yet, and probably never will, run out of the manpower to keep his effort going. It is the exact opposite of what American leaders have, for months, been leading us to expect."[12]

In the midst of the crisis, it was understandable that the networks had initially reported incomplete and inaccurate information. Impossible to excuse, however, was the fact that CBS, NBC, and ABC all continued to portray Tet as a Viet Cong victory even after the fog had lifted and the Americans were providing indisputable evidence that the offensive had failed. Despite that evidence, the networks failed to set the record straight, allowing their hasty judgments to stand.

Later in 1968, field producer Jack Fern proposed that NBC undertake a three-part series showing that Tet had, in fact, been a military failure for the Viet Cong. Network executives rejected the proposal, saying such a series would only confuse viewers. The executives told Fern, "Tet was already established in the public's mind as a defeat, and, therefore, it *was* an American defeat."[13]

The Shot Felt 'Round the World

The single television image that, more than any other, burnt the brutalities of war into the consciousness of the American people was the filmed execution of a Vietnamese man on a Saigon street a few days after the Tet Offensive began.

NBC correspondent Howard Tuckner and his two Vietnamese cameramen were standing on a street near the Buddhist An Quang Pagoda, a center of government opposition, on the fateful morning. At the far end of the block, they saw several South Vietnamese soldiers with a prisoner wearing casual civilian clothes—plaid shirt, black shorts, no shoes. The soldiers walked toward the newsmen to present the prisoner to General Nguyen Ngoc Loan. The cameramen began filming the prisoner, clearly showing that his hands were tied behind his back and he had been beaten.

The prisoner was marched down the street toward Loan, who then drew his snub-nosed .38 revolver and waved away the soldiers. The prisoner stood three feet away, his eyes downcast. Without speaking to the man, Loan lifted his right arm and stretched it out straight as his index finger squeezed the trigger. There was the crack of a shot and a grimace on the prisoner's face as the bullet slammed into his brain. The dead man's legs folded beneath him. As he fell to the ground, blood spurt grotesquely from his head. General Loan calmly returned the revolver to its holster.[14]

Tuckner knew what he had. He cabled NBC in New York: "THIS STORY IS COMPETITIVE. CBS AND ABC WERE THERE BUT WE ARE THE ONLY ONES WHO HAVE FILM OF THE EXECUTION."

The American public was shocked by the image of a South Vietnamese general—a man supported by the United States—assassinating a Viet Cong officer on a Saigon street. Reprinted by permission of the National Archives.

Tuckner ended the cable by flagging the fact that there could be "BLOOD SPRAYING OUT" of the prisoner's head and then referring to the cameraman: "IF HE HAS IT ALL, IT'S STARTLING STUFF."[15]

He had it all. He also had a huge audience. Because of the excitement that the Tet Offensive had created, the NBC audience watching that night's program had jumped from the standard fifteen million to a staggering twenty million. And the full-color images of the street-corner execution made history: the world's first televised death.

Robert Northshield, executive producer of the *NBC Huntley-Brinkley Report*, never considered not running the film, but he cut it immediately after the gunshot in order to spare viewers from the spurting blood. Northshield "went to black" as soon as the man hit the ground and kept the screen empty for three seconds to provide a buffer between the stomach-wrenching image and the commercial that followed. Even so, the producer acknowledged, "It was the strongest stuff American viewers had ever seen."[16]

Tuckner's narration was terse. He merely said who the men in the images were—although the victim was not identified by name, then or since—and let the film roll: "Government troops had captured the commander of the Viet Cong commando unit. He was roughed up badly but refused to talk. A South Vietnamese officer held the pistol taken from the enemy officer. The Chief of South Vietnam's National Police Force, Brigadier General Nguyen Ngoc Loan, was waiting for him."[17]

Viewers were horrified. More than a thousand of them called NBC to complain that the film was in bad taste, particularly because it was aired during the early evening when children might be watching. Tuckner defended airing the chilling scene, saying, "The film showed, at a time when all eyes were on Saigon, that although the United States went over there ostensibly to keep South Vietnam free from communism and the communists were accused of atrocities, that a leading figure of the Saigon government killed a man in the street without a trial."[18]

Observers have described the film as having a seminal effect on the American public. *Washington Post* Vietnam reporter Don Oberdorfer labeled the film "the picture that shocked the world," saying the grotesque scene "seemed to many people to confirm the suspicion that this was a 'wrong war.'" The Associated Press wrote that there was a "worldwide reaction" to the film, and *Time* magazine said, "That picture is lodged in people's memories" because it showed a South Vietnamese government official "cold-bloodedly executing" a thin, frightened man by "remorselessly blowing the suspect's brains out." In his study of the impact of television on American society, NBC's Edwin Newman said, "This film revolted the nation. 'What was this war turning us into? What kind of people allowed such things to happen?' Television pictures were disturbing. Public opinion was moving. Television caused the change."[19]

Post-Tet: Exposing the War as Horrible . . . and Unwinnable

The man who set the tone for television coverage after the cataclysmic Tet Offensive was Walter Cronkite. The avuncular CBS anchor, with his kind and gentle manner, had shepherded the nation through many momentous events—from presidential elections and space launchings to the Kennedy assassination. The anchor of the country's most-watched news program, Cronkite had been, in the early and mid-1960s, a committed supporter of the American military's effort in Vietnam. President Johnson, fully aware of Cronkite's prestige and power, called him to the White House three times during 1966 and 1967 for private meetings.

And then came Tet. Like other Americans, Cronkite was shocked by the first news reports of the communist offensive. On that fateful night, he was in the CBS newsroom in New York. As the news flashes from Saigon came clattering across the teletype, Cronkite ripped a page from the machine and screamed incredulously, "What the hell is going on?" Reading on to discover that communist forces had penetrated the sanctity of the American Embassy compound, he cried out the same refrain that people all across American would soon echo: "I thought we were *winning* this war!"[20]

Cronkite decided that he owed it to the people who watched him every night to find out what, indeed, was going on in Vietnam. It was a risky step, as it meant shedding his mantle of impartiality and sharing his personal impressions about the most important story of the era. But at this moment when the entire nation was utterly confused, Cronkite concluded, it was his duty as the signature figure in the country's oldest and largest network news operation—Edward R. Murrow's network—to clarify the situation for his viewers.

By the third week of the offensive, Cronkite was in Southeast Asia interviewing soldiers and visiting battle sites. Two weeks later, Cronkite—the man polls identified as the most trusted man in America—was poised to broadcast the most influential program of his life. Footage on *Report from Vietnam by Walter Cronkite* showed him wearing a steel helmet and flak jacket as he walked through the rubble of warfare.

In the assessment that the whole country was waiting for, Cronkite began, "Who won and who lost in the great Tet Offensive against the cities? I'm not sure. The Viet Cong did not win by a knockout, but neither did we." He went on to predict other standoffs in the fighting: "It seems now more certain than ever that the bloody experience of Vietnam is to end in a stalemate."[21]

With no trace of the reassuring smile that had become his trademark, the usually benevolent Cronkite spoke somberly. Every word and subtle change in his facial expression communicated one emotion: grave concern. America's revered uncle was worried about the future of his nation: "To say that we are closer to victory today is to believe, in the face of the evidence, the optimists who have been wrong in the past. To suggest we are on the edge of defeat is to yield to unreasonable pessimism. To say that we are mired in stalemate seems the only realistic conclusion."[22]

Cronkite then told America exactly where he, personally, stood on the future of the war: "It is increasingly clear to this reporter that the only rational way out, then, will be to negotiate—not as victors, but as an honorable people who lived up to their pledge to defend democracy, and did the best they could." His final expression that lingered on the screen combined pained acceptance with solid resolve.[23]

The country's most influential newscaster had determined that for the first time in 200 years, the United States was unable to win a foreign war. Rather than continue to sacrifice human lives, he posited, American officials should negotiate a peace settlement and leave Vietnam.

Cronkite's assessment had unprecedented impact. For among the millions of rapt Americans who were glued to their television sets that night was Lyndon Johnson. And when the program ended, Johnson said sadly, "If I've lost Cronkite, I've lost the war." Opinion polls confirmed Johnson's fear. In one of the most dramatic shifts of public opinion in history, within six weeks after the Tet Offensive began, one American in five switched from supporting the Vietnam War to *not* supporting it. So for the first time in fifteen years of involvement, a majority of Americans opposed the war.[24]

A month after Cronkite's special, Johnson shocked the nation with a double-barreled announcement: He would not run for reelection, and he would begin reducing America's participation in the war. The public clearly agreed with Johnson's decision; his approval rating jumped up sharply, as did support for bringing the GIs home.[25]

Observers have lauded Cronkite's program and Johnson's subsequent decision to downscale the war as a clear example of the news media's mighty power in shaping history. David Halberstam of the *New York Times* wrote, "Cronkite's reporting changed the balance; it was the first time in American history a war had been declared over by an anchorman." Frank Stanton, president of CBS News, agreed, "It [Cronkite's special] had a lot to do with Lyndon Johnson deciding he wasn't going to run for re-election. He thought that Walter's broadcast had really cut the ground right out from under him."[26]

Because Cronkite's assessment coincided with the news media's portrayal of the Tet Offensive as a Viet Cong victory, the impact of the two events cannot be separated. What is clear, though, is that coverage changed radically. War began being portrayed not merely as Hell but as *senseless* Hell. Before January 1968, editorial comments by television journalists had run four to one in favor of American government policy; after that point, comments ran two to one against government policy.[27]

Typical of the new tone was Frank McGee's gloomy special report, *Vietnam: A New Year, A New War*. While showing action film of gunfire, destruction, wounded American soldiers, and the street-execution, the NBC newsman said gravely, "It is a new war in Vietnam. The enemy now has the initiative." McGee ended with the bleak summation, "The war, as the administration has defined it, is being lost."[28]

The new skepticism infected nightly news stories as well. One way the tone changed was that the networks paid more attention to the human cost of the war. When reporting weekly casualty figures, NBC's David Brinkley commented morosely, "Today in Saigon they announced the casualty figures for the week, and though they came out in the form of numbers, each one of them was a man, most of them quite young, each with hopes he will never realize, each with family and friends who will never see him again."[29]

Contributing to the increasingly negative tone of the coverage were two high-profile revelations related to Vietnam. In November 1969, freelance journalist Seymour Hersh reported the My Lai massacre. During that event that had occurred a year and a half earlier, American soldiers had destroyed an entire Vietnamese village, killing between 200 and 500 civilians. My Lai dealt a devastating blow to the American military, with Lieutenant William Calley ultimately being convicted, in 1971, of mass murder. The second revelation exposed the shocking realities of what forces had driven American policy toward Vietnam. In June 1971, the *New York Times* and *Washington Post* began reporting on secret government documents, known as the Pentagon Papers, that showed American military action often had been guided not by humanitarian concern but by political benefit. Although the government attempted to block publication of the material, the United States Supreme Court sided with the newspapers, saying the material did not endanger national security—it merely embarrassed the government.

As more and more troops were withdrawn from Vietnam and the war ground toward its eventual end, the critical comments by television correspondents became both more frequent and more direct. In 1972, a piece by ABC's Jim Bennett included film of an officer struggling to motivate his reluctant troops to go on a mission by assuring them that the operation was not an offensive one but was necessary to protect other soldiers. Bennett's commentary: "The average American soldier no longer wants any part of this war—even in a defensive posture."[30]

Anti-War Protesters Fight for the Spotlight

Protests against United States involvement in Vietnam began as soon as the first troops were sent to Indochina, and their number swelled as the war escalated. Seeing the new medium of television as a potential avenue for changing the social order, the protesters played to the cameras. And because the anti-war movement's colorful marches and vociferous leaders translated into novel images, TV news accommodated and helped the protesters succeed in grabbing the media spotlight—prompting military brass to refer to CBS as the *Communist* Broadcasting System.

By no means, however, did securing air time guarantee positive—or even fair—coverage. As a forum for social and political debate, television remained the province of established, and establish*ment*, institutions. In the heady days early in the war when American correspondents doubled as government handmaidens, they openly condemned anti-war protesters as traitors—unwashed traitors, at that. Typical was Peter Jennings's choice of words in introducing a 1965 ABC report on one anti-war group. "While Americans fight and die in Vietnam, there are those in this country who sympathize with the Viet Cong." In fact, most such groups opposed the war but did not sympathize with the enemy.[31]

Journalists also took proactive steps to solicit negative reaction to the protesters. The day before the first nationwide anti-draft rallies, CBS aired a piece from Vietnam in which Morley Safer showed a group of GIs a draft-resistance film produced by an anti-war organization and then asked for reaction. Safer said to one soldier, "You're getting shot at. Five of your buddies were killed down the road the other day. How did you feel watching that film?" The leading question netted Safer precisely the kind of emotional outburst he was hoping for, with the young GI saying he wished the protesters in the movie, not his buddies, had been going down that road.[32]

Anti-war coverage changed radically by mid-1968. In addition to the Tet Offensive and Cronkite's pessimistic assessment of the war, both of which made journalists more skeptical of government policies, the anti-war stances of presidential hopefuls Robert F. Kennedy and Eugene McCarthy moved the protests onto the mainstream political stage. Police brutally clubbing protesters at the Democratic National Convention in Chicago—in front of television cameras—also made journalists more sympathetic to the dissidents.

By the mammoth Anti-War Moratorium in the fall of 1969, protesters were no longer treated with total disdain. Cronkite said, "The Moratorium demonstration was historic in scope. Never before had so many demonstrated their hope for peace. The Moratorium was a dignified, responsible protest that appealed to the conscience of the American people."[33]

Six months later when the American people learned that President Richard Nixon had, despite his pledge not to expand the war beyond Vietnam, sent troops into Cambodia, the protests exploded. In May 1970, National Guardsmen opened fire on the Kent State University campus in Ohio, killing four students and transforming one and a half million more students into angry *dissidents*. When half the college campuses in the country became protest sites, television news rushed to capture the bedlam.

Television News Helps End a War

The many journalists and scholars who argue that grisly television images were a major force in turning the American people against the war in Vietnam are on solid ground. The process began in the mid-1960s when the blood of dead and wounded American GIs, as well as Vietnamese soldiers and civilians, first began to flow across the television screen—night after night, week after week, month after month, year after year. As they sat in the comfort of their living rooms, viewers also were repelled by the inhumanity of American soldiers as depicted, for example, in marines casually pulling Zippo cigarette lighters out of their pockets to torch a Vietnamese village and kill innocent civilians.

Then came Tet. Television images of Viet Cong penetrating the American Embassy compound, with bodies of American soldiers lying in the streets, showed the American people that—regardless of what the politicians and military brass had been saying and despite the many years of human suffering America had condoned—the United States was *not* winning the war. And then the American people witnessed, in living color, a South Vietnamese officer—one of the men who was fighting on *our* side—shoot an untried prisoner in cold blood on a Saigon street. The American people, including Walter Cronkite, realized that perhaps those crowds of long-haired young people who had been protesting the war actually made some sense after all. The hearts and minds of the American public had shifted. People were finally willing to say out loud that they had been supporting a hideous and inhuman war for too many years. And they refused to continue.

For a book whose goal is to document the impact that the news media have had on American history, it should be sufficient to establish that television coverage of the Vietnam War played a key role in bringing that war to an end. When the discussion includes not only the most divisive war in the nation's history but also the role of the news media in covering future armed conflicts, however, that discussion seems incomplete without going the final precarious step of suggesting whether television hastening the end of the Vietnam War was a positive or a negative contribution to history.

Journalists and government officials have both identified the central issue. Nationally syndicated columnist Bob Greene wrote, "The argument can be made that any war—even World War II—shown in the gory, close-up way in which television showed Vietnam is destined to lose the public's support; that once they have seen the videotape, all they will want is out." Dean Rusk, who served as Secretary of State in the 1960s, made the same point, saying that war is the principal obscenity on the face of the Earth, and the impact of Vietnam battle scenes on the ordinary citizen every day was powerful. Rusk said, "One can reflect upon what might have happened in World War II if Dunkirk had been on television and the other side was not using it. So I think we need to do a good deal of thinking about whether or not an armed conflict can be sustained for very long if the worst aspects of it are going to be reflected on television every day. There may have to be certain kinds of censorship."[34]

When television news brought the *worst aspects* of the Vietnam War into the American living room, it was doing its job—and doing it well. As long as a free press remains fundamental to the democratic form of government, the news media's accurate depiction of reality—no matter how vivid or horrifying that reality may be—is a *positive* contribution to that country. Television news showed the American people exactly what their military forces were doing halfway around the world, and, armed with that information, the people chose not to continue.

Until the loathsome day that the men and women elected to positions of national leadership in this country succeed—as Rusk suggested may be necessary—in limiting what freedom of the press means, there can be no question that reporting the realities of war is both the duty and the responsibility of the American news media. If the people of the United States are willing to send their young men and women into battle, they also must be willing to acknowledge that death, destruction, and human suffering are byproducts of that decision.

13

Watergate Forces the President to His Knees

AT 2:30 ON THE morning of Saturday, June 17, 1972, three Washington, D.C., police officers caught five men attempting to place listening devices inside the Democratic National Committee offices on the sixth floor of the plush Watergate office complex in the nation's capital. The men wore business suits and rubber surgical gloves.

That event opened Pandora's box on a scandal that ultimately revealed that the Richard Nixon White House was at the center of the most widespread system of political corruption ever revealed to the American people. The break-in led to revelations about misuse of campaign contributions, laundered money, political sabotage, deception, immorality, and any number of illegal activities—all by an administration elected on a law-and-order platform. After two years of unprecedented actions by the judicial, legislative, and executive branches of the United States government, President Nixon was forced to resign from office.

The stunning abuses of power did not expose themselves through their own volition. They were propelled by the persistence of two hungry young reporters and the might of the newspaper—the *Washington Post*—that stood behind them despite condemnations from their fellow journalists and bitter denunciations by the most powerful political and governmental institutions in the country. The reporters and the courageous newspaper they worked for demonstrated, perhaps more clearly than at any other time in history, the value of the Fourth

Estate joining the official branches of the government to serve the American people.

More Than a Third-Rate Burglary

By sheer instinct, the *Washington Post* placed the burglary story on page one—Washington is a political town, it was an election year. That initial story did not speculate on the larger significance of the Democratic National Committee break-in, but, by noting the bizarre details, the story hinted that perhaps this was more than an average burglary: "The men had with them at least two sophisticated devices capable of picking up and transmitting all talk, including telephone conversations. In addition, police found lock picks and door jimmies, almost $2,300 in cash, most of it in $100 bills with the serial numbers in sequence." The story also reported that the men carried a walkie-talkie, a shortwave receiver that could pick up police calls, forty rolls of unexposed film, two cameras, and three pen-sized tear gas guns.[1]

Two days later, White House Press Secretary Ronald L. Ziegler refused to comment on what he dismissed as a "third-rate burglary" and groused that "certain elements may try to stretch this beyond what it is." Ziegler's comments prompted the *Post* to editorialize—with what ultimately proved to be remarkable prescience—that though it was possible to suppose that the break-in was the work of a foreign government, "the finger naturally points, in a time of intense and developing political combat, to the Democrats' principal and natural antagonist; that is to say, it points to somebody associated with or at least sympathetic to—we may as well be blunt about it—the Republicans".[2]

The *Post* assigned two reporters to the Watergate story. Bob Woodward, 29, graduated from Yale and spent five years in the Navy before focusing on a career in journalism. *Post* editors farmed him out to a suburban weekly until the persistent reporter started calling the *Post* editor at work, at home, on vacation. The *Post* hired Woodward as a local reporter in 1971. Carl Bernstein, 28, worked as a copy boy at the *Washington Star* and then dropped out of the University of Maryland to come to the *Post* in 1966, assigned to suburban Virginia.

Woodward was sent to the arraignment of the Watergate burglars and sat in the front row of the courtroom when the judge asked James W. McCord Jr., one of the defendants, what he did for a living. When McCord whispered "CIA," Woodward's antennae began to quiver. And from that moment on, the reporting duo never let up. Bernstein later recalled, "We just very logically, through many hours, did the kind of reporting they teach in J-school, the kind that when I

Because of their coverage of the Watergate scandal, Carl Bernstein (left) and Bob Woodward were propelled to the status of journalistic icons. Reprinted by permission of the National Archives.

was a copy boy I watched other reporters do—that is, not to let anything fall through the cracks." Woodward added, "It was like putting together a puzzle. You'd get a piece here and a piece there, and you'd try to fit them together and see what kind of picture they made." Despite an impenetrable White House bureaucracy, the dogged reporters held on tight to the biggest story of the era—a story that not only made them journalistic legends but also changed the course of American history.[3]

Flushing Out the Evidence

Woodward and Bernstein got their first break when the address books of two of the burglars contained the name E. Howard Hunt. In one book, the letters "W. H." came after Hunt's name; in the other, "W. House" followed the name. With some fancy telephoning, Woodward connected the burglary to the White House. His *Post* story gave readers a glimpse of how the resourceful reporter's detective work had caught the White House consultant off guard: "When Hunt was asked by a reporter yesterday why two of the suspects had his phone number, he said, 'Good God!' He then paused and said, 'In view that the matter is under adjudication, I have no comment.' He then hung up the telephone.'"[4]

It was the first of a series of page-one broadsides the *Post* published, beginning two days after the break-in and reaching a climax in late October, only a few weeks before the presidential election.

- In early August, Woodward and Bernstein reported that the burglars were paid with Nixon campaign funds: "A $25,000 cashier's check, apparently earmarked for President Nixon's reelection campaign, was deposited in April in a bank account of one of the five men arrested in the break-in."[5]
- By mid-September, the intrepid reporters had implicated the former United States Attorney General, the country's top law enforcement official, who had by then become Nixon's campaign manager: "Funds for the Watergate espionage operation were controlled by several principal assistants of John N. Mitchell and were kept in a special account of the Committee for the Re-election of the President."[6]
- In early October, Woodward and Bernstein exploded their story into something far larger than merely one burglary. For they reported that Nixon's entire reelection strategy was based on playing "dirty tricks" on the major Democratic presidential contenders—thereby subverting the entire process of presidential politics. The blockbuster story read: "The Watergate bugging incident stemmed from a massive campaign of political spying and sabotage conducted on behalf of President Nixon's re-election and directed by officials of the White House."[7]
- By the middle of that same month, the tenacious reporters connected White House aide Dwight L. Chapin, who met daily with the president, to the political espionage: "President Nixon's appointments secretary served as a 'contact' in the spying and sabotage operation against the Democrats."[8]
- And, finally, by late October, Woodward and Bernstein showed that both the Watergate burglary and the campaign of political sabotage were financed by a secret fund controlled by the president's closest aide. In short, they had succeeded in tracing the trail of political corruption to the very doors of the Oval Office. They wrote: "H. R. Haldeman, President Nixon's White House chief of staff, was one of five high-ranking presidential associates authorized to approve payments from a secret Nixon campaign cash fund."[9]

After four months of nonstop investigation, the tireless newsmen had uncovered solid evidence that what the White House had dubbed a "third-rate burglary" was, in fact, the tip of the iceberg in the most astonishing abuse of power in the history of the American presidency.

While Woodward and Bernstein worked day and night, seven days a week, pursuing leads on the Watergate story, others at the *Washington Post* added kindling to the fire. Sanford J. Ungar, another hard-charging young reporter, documented that a California court had found that Nixon and Haldeman had approved a campaign to sabotage Nixon's opponent during his 1962 gubernatorial race. Support came from the *Post* editorial page as well, with Roger Wilkins writing many of the strongest verbal indictments and Pulitzer Prize winner Herbert A. Block—Herblock—translating the accusations into compelling editorial cartoons.[10]

Pushing the Limits of Investigative Reporting

None of the bombshells came easy. Observers who have studied Woodward and Bernstein's reporting have praised their remarkable quantities of initiative, energy, creativity, and tenacity.

When *Post* editors initially forced the independent young reporters to become a team, neither danced on the city desk. They were, indeed, a journalistic odd couple. Woodward was a registered Republican who drove a Karmann-Ghia and shopped at Brooks Brothers; Bernstein was as close to the counterculture as a reporter could get and still keep his job at a somewhat stodgy newspaper—shoulder-length hair, rumpled clothes, loose tie.

Post management clearly favored the cautious Woodward. Executive Editor Ben Bradlee later recalled, "Woodward had developed a knack for getting into the paper. You'd send him into the most remote corner of some damned suburb, and Woodward would still somehow come back with a front-page story." Bernstein, in comparison, was a newsman's newsman who displayed the grit of a streetwise reporter; besides being brash and always eager to take a chance, he was a polished writer and cunning interviewer.[11]

The Woodward-Bernstein collaboration initially faltered, with each reporter keeping his own list of phone numbers and fighting ferociously over points in their stories. Ultimately, though, the personalities and talents of the two young men fit together like a lock and a key. They fell into a rhythm that produced results far superior to what either man could have achieved on his own.

The techniques they used were those of all good journalism. Bernstein said, "You knock on a lot of doors; you make a lot of telephone calls." One of their key steps was obtaining, by twisting the arm of a

Post researcher, a list of the names and home addresses of the 300 men and women who worked for the Committee for the Re-election of the President (CREEP). The reporters then visited some fifty CREEP staff members at their homes. "The big factor is going out and talking to people," Woodward said. "If you call somebody at the White House on the telephone and ask for an appointment, they'll tell you no. But if you're standing out there on their front porch, facing them, they may let you in."[12]

Potential sources, most of them committed members of the Republican Party, resisted talking to the reporters. One pleaded, "Please leave before they see you." Another said, "I know you're only trying to do your job, but you don't realize the pressure we're under. Please go." The persistent reporters often returned half a dozen times before they finally gained the trust of reluctant sources. Indeed, Bernstein said he had so many doors slammed in his face that he felt like a door-to-door magazine salesman—"For every sale, you had 50 rejects." On one occasion they approached a house and saw that a dinner party was in progress. Woodward recalled, "We went down to McDonald's and ate hamburgers and waited for two and a half hours until we figured the party was over. Then we went back"—and got their interview.[13]

Despite the vigor the two reporters brought to the Watergate investigation, several months passed before they realized the dimensions of the corruption. "The one thought that kept haunting us in the beginning," Woodward said, "was that when you have five men with sophisticated photographic and electronic equipment breaking into the Democratic National Headquarters, you cannot accept it as merely a 'petty crime.'"[14]

The aggressive reporters begged, lied, badgered sources, and, on occasion, broke the law. While a grand jury was hearing charges against White House officials, for example, Woodward went to the court clerk's office and asked to see the names of the jurors. He was legally permitted to read the names but not to take notes. So Woodward memorized the names and then went to a men's room and wrote them down. The reporters called one of the jurors at home, which was against the law. The juror refused to discuss the case with them, but Federal Judge John J. Sirica later wrote, "Had they actually obtained information from that grand juror, they would have gone to jail."[15]

Although the reporters never depended on a whistle blower for insider information, they relied heavily on the most famous anonymous source in the history of American journalism: Deep Throat. A good friend of Woodward's before the Watergate break-in, he was described as an executive branch official with "extremely sensitive" antennae that picked up every murmur of conspiracy at the country's political nerve center. Deep Throat, named after a pornographic film popular at the time, never gave the reporters any new information, but he confirmed dozens of facts that Woodward and Bernstein had heard elsewhere but needed to verify with a second source before printing. The source extraordinaire also steered the reporters away from various false leads.

Woodward and his mysterious source—Bernstein never met Deep Throat, although he knew his identity—met dozens of times, often in the wee hours of the morning to avoid detection. They developed an elaborate system of signals right out of a spy novel. When the reporter wanted to initiate a meeting, he moved a flowerpot with a red flag in it to the rear of his apartment balcony, meaning the two men would meet at 2 A.M. in a specific underground parking garage; when Deep Throat wanted to set up a meeting, he drew clock hands indicating the rendezvous time on page 20 of Woodward's morning copy of the *New York Times*.

Even though Deep Throat could make a fortune by publishing his memoirs, he still continues to hide his identity today. Bernstein said, "It's the one great secret in the world. We knew everything about the Russians; they knew everything about us. This is a *real* secret." Woodward and Bernstein have made arrangements to name Deep Throat upon his death.[16]

Going It Alone

The *Washington Post* played a key role in exposing the Watergate scandal, and the journalistic triumph was, essentially, a solo performance. For throughout the first six months after the break-in, the *Post* was virtually the only news organization that committed its investigative might to uncovering the details of the story. Indeed, many of the nation's leading newspapers, news magazines, and television networks not only did not follow the story themselves but accused the *Post* of *overplaying* the story.

"For months we were out there alone on this story," said *Post* Managing Editor Howard Simons. "We used to ask ourselves: 'Where are the AP, the UPI, the *New York Times, Newsweek*?' It was months of loneliness."[17]

Why didn't other news organizations pick up on the burglary's implications earlier? Most Washington reporters were playing what critics call "mouthpiece journalism"—writing stories based on the official statements from the government's army of public relations flacks. In a scathing indictment of the Washington press corps, Charles Peters of *Washington Monthly* wrote that White House reporters were too lazy to do anything but attend the daily press briefings. "The correspondents are like a herd of seals," Peters sniped, "waiting for the fish that are reliably tossed their way instead of looking elsewhere for sustenance." Bill Moyers, President Johnson's press secretary, also was critical: "The White House press corps is more stenographic than entrepreneurial in its approach to news gathering. Too many of them are sheep."[18]

Television news did a particularly abysmal job of covering Watergate. Unlike the Civil Rights Movement and Vietnam War, this story did not translate easily into visual images. Most elements of the Watergate story involved backroom strategizing that lent itself only to headshots of the various presidential aides involved—not good television. "It's not the kind of story we do best," said Frank Jordan, NBC's Washington bureau chief. "It's not visual, and it's also very complicated."[19]

Although none of the networks provided extensive coverage of the scandal, CBS performed better than the others. Walter Cronkite hosted two special reports on Watergate—one fifteen minutes and the other eight—that CBS executives later criticized as including too much editorializing. During the first report, Cronkite said pointedly, "At first it was called the Watergate *caper*, but the episode grew steadily more sinister." One of the network's longest regular news stories was a three-minute piece in October 1972 reporting that the House Banking Committee had voted not to investigate Watergate. Correspondent Lesley Stahl ended her story with an accusatory summary: "The debate itself focused on the questions of infringement of civil liberties and the right of the voters to know the truth before the election."[20]

Critics pointed out that the most serious repercussion of the news media downplaying Watergate was that it did not become a major issue in the 1972 presidential election, which Nixon won by a landslide. A Gallup Poll taken a month before the election showed that only 52 percent of Americans even recognized the word "Watergate."

Standing Firm

From June 1972 until January 1973, the only journalists committed to the Watergate story seemed to be working inside a beige brick building on 15th Street in Washington, D.C. That commitment extended far beyond Woodward and Bernstein. Indeed, the two persons who ultimately bore the hefty burden of responsibility for the *Washington*

Post's relentless pursuit of Watergate were Bradlee and publisher Katharine Graham.

Bradlee, buoyant and personable, had built the *Post* into one of the best newspapers in the world; Graham, soft-spoken and genteel, was the stereotypical iron butterfly—she never flinched. The executive editor and publisher formed their own mutual-admiration society. Bradlee said of his boss, "She's got the guts of a burglar." Graham said of her top editor, "Ben Bradlee had never let me down. I had no reason not to have confidence in him."[21]

Continuing to support the Watergate investigation became increasingly difficult, however, because throughout the months immediately after the break-in, the White House admitted nothing, denied everything, and lashed back—first with verbal attacks and then by calculated efforts to punish the *Post*. Nixon aides cut off access to administration sources and threatened to cancel the licenses for two Florida television stations the *Post* owned.

Graham was shocked at the vehemence of Nixon's attack. "The most astonishing thing was the vindictiveness in the government—sometimes at the personal level—to me or Ben. You know, 'We're going to get you!'—it really got rough." A graphic image illustrating that roughness came in a telephone conversation between Bernstein and Mitchell on the night before the *Post* was to publish the story implicating the former attorney general in the burglary. Bernstein called Mitchell at home to ask him if he wanted to make any statement for the story. Mitchell responded angrily, "Are you going to run this? If you are, Katy Graham's *tit* is going to get caught in a wringer."[22]

The first verbal attacks uttered in public came in response to the *Post* accusing the Nixon reelection campaign of sabotaging Democratic candidates—such as fabricating slanderous letters about both heterosexual and homosexual peccadilloes. Ziegler said haughtily, "I will not dignify with comment stories based on hearsay, character assassination, innuendo, or guilt by association." Senator Robert J. Dole, chairman of the Republican National Committee, joined the bitter chorus, charging, "The *Post*'s reputation for objectivity and credibility has sunk so low that they have almost disappeared from the Big Board altogether."[23]

The attacks intensified after the *Post* reported that Chief of Staff Haldeman participated in the political corruption—the story that came closer than any other to implicating Nixon himself. Vice President Spiro T. Agnew, a fierce media critic, lambasted the *Post*'s Watergate reporting as "journalistically reprehensible" and stated, "I deny that there is any secret fund."[24]

This was the point at which Bradlee's and Graham's trust was tested most gravely because Woodward and Bernstein had, in fact, made a mistake. In the lead sentence of the Haldeman story, they said he was authorized to approve payments from a secret fund, according to "sworn testimony before the Watergate grand jury."[25]

Wrong.

The reporters were right in stating that Haldeman was authorized to approve payments from the fund, but the allegation had not been made before the grand jury. "It was a mistake," Woodward later admitted. "It was the worst moment in all of this." The error had evolved from a hasty conversation with Hugh Sloan, the treasurer of CREEP who had resigned when he learned of the committee's sordid political antics; Sloan's information was accurate, but he had not given it as testimony because the grand jury had not asked him to. Five days after publishing the erroneous detail, the *Post* corrected its mistake in a page-one story.[26]

It was, however, a crippling error because fellow journalists who had not been keeping up with the Watergate story now used the mistake to accuse the *Post* of overplaying it. Referring to "sensational disclosures" and Republican denials of the existence of any secret fund, the *New York Times* grouched, "There has been no public indication that either the President or any of his close advisers played roles in or had advance knowledge of an illegal assault upon the opposition party."[27]

Such statements unnerved Woodward and Bernstein. Woodward said, "We were hurting. We had written all these stories. Lots of people didn't believe them. We were out on one long limb, and there were lots of saws working on that limb."[28]

The White House began the punishment phase of its anti-*Post* campaign immediately after the election. Reporter Dorothy McCardle was excluded from important White House social functions, and *Post* reporters on various national beats found once-cooperative sources no longer willing to talk to them. Nixon administration officials also began to feed stories to the *Post*'s competition, the *Washington Star*, including granting the *Star* exclusive interviews with the president. Fearful of White House retribution, even Woodward and Bernstein's closest sources began to avoid them.[29]

Meanwhile, behind the scenes Nixon was using—actually *mis*using—the power of his office to retaliate against the *Post*. His target was the two Florida television stations the Washington Post Company owned, and his vehicle was the Federal Communication Commission, the organization that licenses television stations.

According to tape recordings that later became public, the president instructed his aides, three months after the *Washington Post* began its Watergate investigation, to have political supporters in Jacksonville and Miami challenge the license renewals of the stations, claiming they were not providing the community-service programming that was required for stations to have their licenses renewed. Nixon told Haldeman, "The *Post* is going to have damnable—*damnable*—problems out of this one. They have television stations, and they're going to have to get them renewed." The president continued, "It's going to be goddam active here. The game has to be played awfully rough."[30]

Three and a half months after that conversation, Nixon supporters formally challenged the two stations' license renewal applications—the first time either station's applications had ever been questioned. George Champion Jr., Florida finance chairman for Nixon's 1972 campaign, filed the challenge against WJXT-TV in Jacksonville; partners of Sen. George A. Smathers, a close friend of Nixon's best friend, Bebe Rebozo, filed the challenge against WPLG-TV in Miami. Both stations overcame the challenges only after they documented that they had, in fact, fully fulfilled the community service requirements.[31]

In the taped Oval Office conversation, Nixon also directed his aides to use his presidential powers to retaliate against *Post* lawyer Edward Bennett Williams. Nixon told Haldeman, "I would not want to be in Edward Bennett Williams's position after this one. We are going to fix that son of a bitch." Nixon went on to say he was willing to use all of the $5 million left in his campaign treasury "to take the *Washington Post* down a notch." Clearly agitated and speaking in a loud voice, Nixon continued, "We're going to stop it. I don't care how much it costs." Nixon's contempt for the press was recorded in other venues as well. In his personal diary, Haldeman quoted the president as saying, "The press and TV don't change their attitude and approach unless you hurt them."[32]

By the first of the year, the *Post* began feeling the impact of the White House campaign—in its pocketbook. The value of a share of *Post* stock dropped from $38 in December to $21 by May. Graham could not prove that the White House was putting pressure on Wall Street, but she suspected exactly that. She pointed out that *Post* stock dropped more than that of any other major publisher, despite the fact that "We'd just had our best year." Meanwhile, Bradlee became so sure of a White House conspiracy against the *Post* that he had the newspaper's telephones swept for wiretaps, at a cost of $6,000. No taps were found.[33]

As the evidence against Nixon mounted, the president himself lashed out at the *Post*. In an extraordinary press conference in October 1973, Nixon said bitterly, "I have never heard or seen such outrageous, vicious, distorted reporting in twenty-seven years of public life." When reporters asked him to identify the specific acts that angered him, he responded with pure disdain. "Don't get the impression that you've aroused my *anger*," Nixon told the reporters. "One can only be *angry* with those he *respects*."[34]

The Press Joins Forces with the Other Estates

Though the *Washington Post* deserves enormous praise for its efforts, the Fourth Estate alone did not expose the Watergate scandal. The political corruption was of such monumental proportions that it demanded the joint effort of all four arms of government—unofficial as well as official.

The judicial branch entered the fray early and stayed long. The opening salvo came in September 1972 when the five burglars plus their two bosses—Hunt and G. Gordon Liddy—were indicted. Judge Sirica played a seminal role in the unfolding of events in January 1973, after Woodward and Bernstein had completed their string of revelations and had no other promising leads, when he publicly announced that he was "not satisfied" that the seven indictments told the full story. McCord then broke ranks with his fellow burglars and told Sirica he wanted to talk, in exchange for a lighter sentence. Most important for the Fourth Estate, McCord's testimony confirmed much of Woodward and Bernstein's reporting.

Other crucial activities by judicial officials included a federal grand jury indicting Nixon's closest aides—Mitchell, Haldeman, and Chief Domestic Affairs Adviser John D. Ehrlichman—while naming Nixon a "co-conspirator," followed by Sirica demanding that he be allowed to listen to Nixon's secret Oval Office tape recordings, and then the United States Supreme Court supporting Sirica.

The legislative branch's role in exposing Watergate first rose to prominence in February 1973 when the United States Senate voted to establish a committee to investigate charges of corruption in the 1972 election. The Senate's role in the revelations dominated the country from May to August 1973 as the colorful Sam Ervin led the high-profile televised hearings for thirty-seven memorable days. Those hearings were credited with shifting public opinion against the White House.

The legislative branch brought Watergate to a climax when the House of Representatives Judiciary Committee voted three articles of impeachment in July 1974, charging Nixon with obstruction of justice, abuse of power, and contempt of Congress for defying committee subpoenas.

Although the executive branch was the last to become actively involved in the Watergate exposé, its participation was the most dramatic because the president himself stood at the head of executive departments and agencies. In May 1973, Attorney General Elliot Richardson appointed a special prosecutor, Harvard law professor Archibald Cox, to investigate Watergate. The executive branch then soared into the eye of the Watergate hurricane in October 1973 with what was later dubbed the Saturday Night Massacre. Judge Sirica wanted to hear the White House tapes, but Nixon refused to release them. When an appeals court ruled in Sirica's favor and Cox indicated he would continue to seek the tapes, Nixon told Attorney General Richardson to fire Cox. Richardson refused and resigned from office. When Nixon next ordered Deputy Attorney General William Ruckelshaus to fire Cox, Ruckelshaus also resigned. Nixon then named Solicitor General Robert H. Bork acting attorney general, and Bork fired Cox.

The executive branch in the state of Maryland also played a role in the historic events when the federal attorney in Maryland informed Vice President Agnew in August 1973 that he was being investigated on charges of committing bribery, extortion, and tax fraud while he had been governor. Agnew eventually resigned, admitting that he had falsified his income taxes, and House Minority Leader Gerald R. Ford was appointed vice president.

The White House Collapses

In early 1974, the dam broke. A panel of experts appointed by Sirica said eighteen and one-half minutes in one of the tape recordings had been erased manually. The gap occurred on June 20, three days after the break-in, prompting critics to accuse Nixon of erasing evidence that would have proven that he had known about the break-in before it had occurred.

As the sordid stain of Watergate crept steadily toward the Oval Office, Nixon began a desperate attempt at damage control that included Haldeman and Ehrlichman resigning in April. When Nixon was finally forced to release the tapes, the American people heard that their president was a mean-spirited, lying, foul-mouthed bigot. Although the tapes did not prove conclusively that Nixon knew about the break-in in advance, they left no doubt that he helped plan the cover-up. This was the "smoking gun" that stilled all doubts that Nixon had broken the law. Before the impeachment process could be completed, Nixon, on August 9, 1974, became the only U.S. president in history to resign from office.

Reporters as All-American Heroes

Watergate was a disturbing tale of political corruption in which President Nixon and the men around him orchestrated a massive effort to subvert both the election process and the presidency. Nixon and his aides were revealed as amoral villains who, to feed their hunger for power, came dangerously close to destroying the democratic form of government.

The American people, however, prefer happy endings to sad ones. So as the nation struggled to put the dark days of Watergate behind it, the resilient human spirit that has sustained the United States for more than two centuries searched among the rubble for heroes. The people ultimately found their white knights in the form of two youthful reporters.

Newsweek dubbed Woodward and Bernstein the "Dynamic Duo," and *Time* coined "Woodstein" as its term of endearment; the media criticism journal *Columbia Journalism Review* praised two of its own as the "Davids who slew Goliath." Adoration of the All-American heroes soon spread far beyond the journalistic sphere, with such unlikely publications as *American Psychologist* and *Senior Scholastic* singing their paeans. Indeed, Woodward and Bernstein became such a national sensation that even *Vogue*—the arbiter of American glamor—paid homage.[35]

The Dynamic Duo's rise to fame clearly produced dividends for the news media. Opinion polls found that the American public felt new respect for reporters; schools of journalism around the country began bursting at the seams with aspiring Woodsteins. More than at any other time in American history, journalists were lauded as the saviors of democracy.

Fame is often accompanied by wealth, and Woodward and Bernstein quickly realized that tradition. Before Watergate, the annual salaries of the pair of local reporters totaled less than $30,000. Two years later, their combined incomes had soared beyond the $1 million mark. Their first money-making venture was writing *All the President's Men*, the best-selling book about their Watergate experiences. Even more profits—and more fame—followed when heartthrob Robert Redford, one of the most popular film stars of the day, read the book and dubbed it "the greatest true detective story of all time!" Redford, a Democrat known for supporting liberal causes, urged Warner Brothers to transform the book into a major motion picture. In the 1974 box office hit, Redford starred as Woodward while Academy Award winner Dustin Hoffman portrayed Bernstein.[36]

The reporters and the *Washington Post* both carried their awards home in wheelbarrows—the Drew Pearson Investigative Reporting Award, George Polk Memorial Award, American Newspaper Guild's Heywood Broun Award, Sigma Delta Chi National Reporting Award, Worth Bingham Award for Investigative Reporting. . . . The most prestigious was the Pulitzer Prize gold medal for meritorious service. According to the citation, "The *Washington Post* from the outset refused to dismiss the Watergate incident as a bad political joke, a mere caper. It mobilized its total resources for a major investigation, spearheaded by two first-rate investigative reporters, Carl Bernstein and Robert Woodward."[37]

The new status enjoyed by the news media provided a venue for leading advocates of a free press to remind the country of the key role the Fourth Estate plays in a democracy. Katharine Graham was the most eloquent of those voices. When accepting the Elijah Parish Lovejoy Award for her contributions to American journalism, Graham noted that the Constitution singled out the press as an institution whose freedom could not be abridged. Graham said that no limits were placed on the membership, methods, or reach of the press. She continued, "Nothing illustrates better that the Founding Fathers sought to keep the forces of inquiry—the transmitters of information, the instruments of free debate—as varied, numerous, and independent as possible. Freedom of speech and of the press was the essential counterweight to government, the basic check against abuses of official power."[38]

At no time in American history had the importance of such a free press been more dramatically illustrated than during the bleak chapter that was symbolized by the early morning in 1972 when five men wearing surgical gloves and carrying $100 bills broke into the Watergate office complex—and the country would never be the same.

14

Rush Limbaugh: Leading the Republican Revolution

THE 1994 ELECTIONS ended four decades of Democratic domination in the United States Congress, placing both the Senate and House under Republican control for the first time since 1954. By throwing dozens of liberals out of office, American voters established a new political paradigm by overwhelmingly endorsing the downsizing of the government's role in their lives—with social and cultural programs among the first targets of the conservative revolution. When pundits searched for a single figure to credit for the sea change in American politics and governance, they turned not to an elected official or party stalwart but to a man that many observers previously had dismissed as an inconsequential blowhard.

Rush Limbaugh had risen, in half a decade, from failed disc jockey to one of the country's most influential figures, the man at the center of the history-making "talk-radio election." Among political commentators, he had no peer. Each week twenty-five million Americans were tuning in to his bombastic banter carried fifteen hours a week on 660 radio stations nationwide. His unique blend of conservative ideology and vaudevillian humor also translated to television, with 250 stations airing his half-hour program nightly. Limbaugh had conquered the print media as well, with his first book selling more copies than any other nonfiction title in the history of American publishing and his *Limbaugh Letter* becoming the most widely read political publication in the country. Limbaugh had successfully tapped in to a festering anger and frustration among the American electorate to emerge as a loud and pervasive political voice. At the same time, he had revolutionized the medium of radio and led a sweeping move toward combining news and show business into a new amalgamation: "infotainment."

Despite the establishment news media's widespread hostility toward the conservative icon, millions of voters saw him as their messiah—a courageous man willing to speak out against what many people viewed as a failed political and social liberalism that had prevailed for decades and, if allowed to continue, threatened to destroy the greatest democracy of all time. A month after the 1992 election, former president Ronald Reagan anointed Limbaugh his spiritual son. "Now that I've retired from active politics," Reagan told the commentator, "you have become the Number One voice for conservatism in our country. Keep up the good work."[1]

By no means, however, were all assessments of Limbaugh positive. He inspired passion from detractors as well as devotees, with members of both camps seeing him as a central figure in a cultural and political war not only for the future of America but for the country's very soul. Critics lambasted Limbaugh as an avatar of hatred who spread lies with reckless abandon. President Bill Clinton called him a racist and assailed his "unremitting drumbeat of negativism and cynicism." News organizations labeled Limbaugh a bigot, demagogue, zealot, buffoon, rabble rouser, and anarchist, comparing him to Father Coughlin and Adolf Hitler. Limbaugh thrived on the controversy, mockingly boasting that he was, indeed, "the most dangerous man in America."[2]

Early Years of Failure

Rush Hudson Limbaugh III was born in 1951 in Cape Girardeau, Missouri, into a Republican family—his grandfather held a seat in the Missouri legislature and served as President Eisenhower's ambassador to India. By sixteen, young Rush was infatuated with radio, working as a deejay at the local station.[3]

A mediocre student who failed Speech 101, he broke with three generations of Limbaughs and opted *not* to pursue a law career. Instead, after a year at Southeast Missouri State, he dropped out of college and took a job in McKeesport, Pennsylvania. Though hired to flip records, Limbaugh couldn't resist tossing in personal comments as well. The habit got him fired two years later.[4]

Throughout the 1970s, Limbaugh lived the gypsy life of small-time radio, working at four stations in Pennsylvania and Missouri. In each

After the historic election of 1994, dozens of new members of Congress thanked radio talk-show king Rush Limbaugh for pushing them to victory. Photo courtesy of EFM Media Management.

case, Limbaugh was fired because he refused to accommodate to station management.[5]

After a decade of failure, he abandoned radio to work as a public relations assistant for the Kansas City Royals. His responsibilities ranged from putting together pocket schedules to arranging tickets for children's birthday parties at the baseball park. Despite the routine nature of the work, he stuck with it for five years—far longer than with any of his radio jobs.

When Limbaugh returned to the air in Kansas City in 1983, he initially read the news but later won the chance to prove himself as a commentator and talk-show host. As he experimented with outrageous on-air insults, his remarks presaged the unique shtick that ultimately would make him a household name. Most memorable was his mock trepidation about what might happen to the country every twenty-eight days if Democratic vice-presidential nominee Geraldine Ferraro ever became president. Limbaugh's tenure at the station lasted ten months.[6]

First Taste of Success

In 1984, Sacramento station KFBK, desperate to pull itself out of the red, took a gamble and hired Limbaugh to host its three-hour morning program, giving him free rein to pump as much high octane into the show as he wanted. Geronimo! It was as if someone had told Pablo Picasso he could start coloring outside the lines. Within months, Limbaugh became the hottest act in the city—and American radio has not been the same since.

Limbaugh's unique quality was an uncanny ability to find humor in every issue. He made heinously offensive remarks with such razor-sharp wit that even listeners who were repulsed by his comments caught themselves laughing reflexively.

The provocateur's favorite target was women. The patron saint of white male chauvinists denigrated one of the most important social movements of modern times by saying, "I love the women's movement—especially when I am walking behind it." He called the National Organization for Women a "terrorist organization" and referred to feminists as "femi-Nazis." He belittled female professionals by referring to them as "reporter-ettes" and "professor-ettes," and he adopted the grossly sexist policy of requiring female listeners to send him photos of themselves before he would take their calls on the air.[7]

Racial minorities received their share of insults as well. When Limbaugh had trouble understanding an African-American caller, he told the man, "Take that bone out of your nose and call me back," and he insulted one of the most high-profile blacks in the country by asking his listeners, "Have you ever noticed how all newspaper composite pictures of wanted criminals resemble Jesse Jackson?" When a Mexican national won the New York Marathon, Limbaugh said the man had run at breakneck speed because an immigration agent had been chasing him.[8]

Limbaugh routinely referred to gays as "faggots" and "perverts" and in his "Gerbil Update" described gay men jamming rodents into their rectums to achieve sexual pleasure—a practice that sounded as alien to gay men as to other listeners. Limbaugh's homophobic attitude was particularly ironic because the man who had championed and groomed him for the Sacramento job was radio executive Norm Woodruff, a gay man who later died of AIDS.

Despite the offensive nature of much of Limbaugh's material, the station's profits soared. When he arrived at KFBK, 5 percent of the people tuned to a Sacramento radio station chose his program. Limbaugh tripled that figure, allowing the station to raise ad rates for his time slot from $50 to $150 a minute.

Mr. Bombast clearly was destined for a larger arena. Edward F. McLaughlin, a former president of the ABC Radio Network who had recently gone into the syndication business for himself, recognized Limbaugh's potential as a national star.

Bursting into the National Spotlight

In 1988, McLaughlin created the Excellence in Broadcasting Network. It initially included fifty stations that aired Limbaugh's call-in show two hours a day, five days a week. The grandiloquent commentator then moved to New York and made his debut broadcasting to America.

A taste of Limbaugh's extraordinary appeal came a few weeks later when a Pennsylvania caller registered her complete agreement with every word Limbaugh had ever uttered when she said simply: "Ditto." The term instantly became enshrined in the gospel of St. Rush, as disciples eagerly labeled themselves "dittoheads" and greeted him with exuberant "megadittos."

In speaking to his national audience, Limbaugh expanded the caustic concepts he had developed in Sacramento. His "Animal Rights Update" raged against "idiots" seeking to protect animals: "If the spotted owl can't adapt to the superiority of humans, screw it." The mood for that particular shtick was set by Andy Williams crooning "Born Free" until the music was interrupted by screeching animals being mowed down by automatic gunfire and exploding mortars. The "Sexual Harassment Update" featured "My Eyes Adored You" as background music and ridiculing comments from Limbaugh: "We're in bad shape in this country when you can't look at a couple of huge knockers."

The "AIDS Update" was set against Dionne Warwick singing "I'll Never Love This Way Again" and Limbaugh ridiculing the life-saving concept of safe sex by placing a condom over his microphone to create "safe talk."[9]

Many Limbaugh critics believed their nemesis dipped to his lowest point in 1989 with "caller abortions." The offensive gimmick reinforced Limbaugh's antiabortion stand while providing him with a way of getting annoying callers off the line. Whenever the czar of political *in*correctness wanted to end a call, he played a recording of the sucking sound of a vacuum cleaner followed by a blood-curdling scream.

In spite of the bruising nature of Limbaugh's humor, his entry into the national spotlight was a triumph. After four years, he was the most listened-to radio commentator in the country. Advertising rates skyrocketed as well. When Limbaugh went national in 1988, he sold commercial time for $600 a minute; five years later, that figure had jumped twenty-fold to a daunting $12,000. Major companies did not hesitate to pay the heavy freight, with AT&T, Snapple soft drinks, and Motel 6 among those lining up to sign long-term contracts.[10]

The president of the United States got in line, too. For as George Bush's political future dimmed, he set out to woo the influential radio commentator. The feat was a challenge, as Limbaugh's far right-wing stripe was more in keeping with that of reactionary Pat Buchanan, who was vying with Bush for the Republican nomination. So in June 1992, Bush played his trump card by inviting the titan of talk to the White House—even carrying his guest's suitcase. Bush's obsequious behavior initially paid off, as Limbaugh endorsed the president. But, alas, the egomaniac's power was not yet strong enough to save his president-cum-bell boy from political failure.

In 1992, "Rush Limbaugh: The Television Show" debuted with Roger Ailes, who had orchestrated the media campaigns that had propelled Reagan and Bush into the White House, as executive producer. The TV show competed well against major network offerings such as "Nightline" and "The Tonight Show." *Time* magazine gushed, "Rush has taken to the medium in no time flat. He guffaws, he blusters, he bats his eyes, he makes kissy-face. He will do anything to keep you watching."[11]

A month after launching his TV show, Limbaugh pioneered in the print media by creating the *Limbaugh Letter*. Circulation of the monthly newsletter soared to 500,000, far surpassing such veteran conservative voices as *Human Events* and *National Review*. The *Limbaugh Letter* got a big boost from the master of self-promotion's on-air sales pitch: "Every month you receive my keenest insights to help you see through the dense liberal fog."[12]

Readers eager to absorb Limbaugh's every fulmination soon made him a megastar of book publishing as well. His first book, *The Way Things Ought To Be*, sold more than three million copies to surpass *Iacocca* as the best-selling nonfiction book in publishing history. That success was followed by *See, I Told You So*, which sent dittoheads scurrying back to bookstores for a second purchase.[13]

By this point in Limbaugh's multimedia success story, observers analyzing the reasons for his popularity pointed to the showman's joie de vivre. Pre-Limbaugh conservatives tended to be somber, sounding like stern college professors chastising the American public for overspending. Limbaugh, however, packaged the familiar conservative ideology—free-market solutions instead of government programs, self-reliance rather than entitlements—in a comedic song-and-dance routine punctuated with giggles and squeaky dolphin voices, impromptu warbling of "Blue Moon," goofy bathroom humor such as calling the *Atlanta Journal and Constitution* the "Urinal and Constipation," and contortions of his 300-pound bulk into comical positions by imitating an environmentalist skipping daintily through the woods. His blend of bedrock conservatism with a sledgehammer sense of humor created what previously amounted to an oxymoron: a funny conservative.

The political tilt-a-whirl also displayed a masterful sense of when to add comic relief. Immediately after firing off a cruel remark about First Daughter Chelsea Clinton being so ugly she was the unofficial White House dog, he zapped his audience with a mockingly grandiose monologue: "Greetings across the fruited plain, this is Rush Limbaugh, the most dangerous man in America, with the largest hypo*thal*amus in North America, serving humanity simply by opening my mouth," he continued without taking a breath, "destined for my own wing in the Museum of Broadcasting, executing everything I do flawlessly with zero mistakes, with half my brain tied behind my back just to make it fair because I have talent on loan from . . . God. Rush Limbaugh. A man. A legend. A way of life."[14]

Defining a 1990s Populism

Describing Limbaugh as the hottest property in talk radio only hinted at the popularity of his convulsively entertaining style. His core constituency was white lower- and middle-class men, but his appeal stretched far beyond that demographic band. Edward K. Capano, publisher of the right-wing public affairs magazine *National Review*, laughingly dubbed Limbaugh the "first rock star of the conservative movement."[15]

Mainstream news outlets helped fuel the Limbaugh populism that had grown too large for even liberal publications to ignore. Although the profiles uniformly carried a sarcastic tone—the *Chicago Tribune* used the headline "Motormouth"; the *Washington Post* wrapped its profile around an image of a rotund court jester with the snout of a pig—they nevertheless swelled his army of admirers even more. Appearances as a guest on ABC's "Nightline" and NBC's "Meet the Press" also helped.[16]

True to his rule-breaking style, though, Limbaugh was not willing to limit his venues of communication to the traditional media. Limbaugh was hard-wired and uplinked to the future, a pioneer in a trend that was rapidly reducing the importance of newspapers and television networks. In 1991, the CompuServe computer bulletin board created the Rush Limbaugh Forum, giving the dittoheads among its two million subscribers an electronic "Rush Room" where they could converse with each other, trade information, and mobilize for political action. The forum also gave fans a chance to contact Limbaugh directly, as he spent his free time grazing the 600 E-mail messages sent to him each day.

By 1995, Limbaugh's wealth had soared. He was merchandising coffee mugs, T-shirts, calendars, neckties, and video cassettes, making personal appearances at $25,000 a pop, earning a hefty salary from his radio and TV shows, and pulling in book royalties—for a decidedly capitalistic total income of $20 million a year.[17]

Reign of Error

Among journalists, the most serious problem with Limbaugh was that his commentaries were riddled with factual errors resulting from what the *New Republic* labeled a proclivity for "repeating rumors with abandon and twisting facts at whim." Limbaugh described his radio program as "the turnpike of truth," and assured his trusting flock, "You need never read a newspaper again. I'll read them for you and tell you what to think." He also insisted all the information he presented was absolutely true, saying, "I do not lie." Nevertheless, anyone with access to a library could document numerous errors in Limbaugh's antiliberal tirades.[18]

In defending President Reagan—"Ronaldus Magnus," in Rush-speak—Limbaugh called the Iran-Contra investigation an example of the Democrats wasting time and money. "We just spent seven years and $40 million looking for any criminal activity on the part of anybody in the Reagan administration, and guess what? We couldn't find any," Limbaugh told his audience. "There is not one indictment. There is not one charge." In reality, fourteen people—including Secretary of Defense Caspar Weinberger and National Security Advisers Robert McFarlane and John Poindexter—were indicted, and eleven were ultimately convicted of criminal charges related to selling arms to Iran, diverting the profits to Nicaraguan rebels, and lying to Congress about the operation.

Although the self-proclaimed "poster boy of free speech" constantly castigated the news media—"The press doesn't care about truth. Journalists are lying, dishonest thieves"—many of Limbaugh's criticisms were, themselves, inaccurate. When discussing the Clintons' investment in the Whitewater land development deal, Limbaugh told his followers, "I don't think the *New York Times* has run a story on this yet. I mean, we haven't done a thorough search, but I—there has not been a big one, front-page story, about this one that we can recall." The *New York Times*, in fact, *broke* the Whitewater story, with a 1,700-word piece on page one.[19]

Limbaugh apologists might argue that such inaccuracies were bound to occur in the pressure-cooker atmosphere when the microphone was on or the television camera was rolling. But myriad examples of Limbaugh's cavalier attitude toward truth also can be found in his published works. He wrote in his first book, "Feminists don't put pro-abortion initiatives on state ballots, because they have lost more times than they have won," but pro-choice forces actually had won all three times they had taken the expensive route of statewide ballot initiatives. The book also said of Democrats, "They relished blaming Reagan administration policies, including the mythical reductions in HUD's [Housing and Urban Development's] budget for public housing, for creating all of the homeless! Budget cuts? There were no budget cuts! The budget figures show that actual construction of public housing *increased* during the Reagan years." In reality, HUD's public housing construction budget in 1988 was only 15 percent of what it had been in 1980, dropping from $3.7 billion to $573 million.[20]

In one news media denunciation of Limbaugh's ongoing record of errors, the *Los Angeles Times* wrote, "Truthman appears to be factually right at least as often as he's wrong. Hitting 50% or 60% of your shots makes you a star in basketball. However, that's unacceptable for a self-defined oracle whose trustworthiness is taken for granted by a hefty number of Americans."[21]

Impact of the "Most Dangerous Man in America"

As Limbaugh's following swelled, he demonstrated enormous power in shaping both the medium of radio and the world of public policy. Limbaugh's impact on radio was astonishing. Between 1985 and 1995, the number of American talk-radio programs jumped from 200 to 1,000, and network radio revenue leaped from $565 million to $1.2 billion. The interest in radio that the dittomaster spawned was so enormous that some observers credited him with single-handedly saving the medium from extinction. After such Limbaugh wannabes as Buchanan, Watergate conspirator G. Gordon Liddy, and Iran-Contra operative Ollie North took to the airwaves, a Times-Mirror Center for the People and the Press poll indicated that talk radio had become the primary source of political information for a staggering 44 percent of the American people.[22]

An early sample of Limbaugh's impact on public policy involved the 1992 House of Representatives check-bouncing scandal. After the story broke, Limbaugh was enraged that Democratic Speaker of the House Tom Foley refused to reveal the names of the accused scofflaws. So Limbaugh gave out Foley's phone number on the air, urging listeners to demand that the names be disclosed. The House telephone switchboard was immediately inundated with calls from all over the country, and the next day Foley folded to public pressure and made the names public.[23]

That was merely the pregame warm-up. Conservative activists and members of Congress were soon crediting Limbaugh with a daunting list of successes in impeding the Democrats—blocking Clinton's job stimulus package, stopping an effort to require home-schooling teachers to be certified by the federal government, forcing Clinton to moderate his budget request, and decimating an effort to reinstate the Fairness Doctrine to stifle talk radio.[24]

By 1993, right-wing lawmakers were lobbying Limbaugh to champion their legislative proposals. Republican strategist Mary Matalin observed, "Senators and congressmen all across the board on the Republican side call him all morning long before he goes on the air." House Minority Leader Newt Gingrich faxed Limbaugh regular briefings from the Republican leadership. Gingrich, the man destined to lead his party in the conservative revolution, said of Limbaugh, "Every day he educates millions of people around the country who then become centers of communication."[25]

In early 1994, Limbaugh used the radio to trumpet hot and spicy—though totally unfounded—rumors about the death of Deputy White House Counsel Vince Foster. Initial reports were that Foster had committed suicide. The day Limbaugh told his radio audience that Foster actually had been murdered and the crime covered up by Clinton, the Dow Jones Stock Index fell sharply.[26]

Political observers recognized Limbaugh's growing power. In a 1993 cover story, *National Review* anointed Limbaugh "The Leader of the

Opposition." Senate Minority Leader Bob Dole praised Limbaugh's broadcast charisma: "He's a powerhouse antidote to the liberal cheerleading you hear all the time from the national media." Ted Koppel, host of ABC's "Nightline," warned Democrats: "You ignore him at your own peril." CBS, the oldest of the television networks, did more than praise Limbaugh; in 1994 it tried unsuccessfully to hire him as a political commentator.[27]

But the most important Rushophile was former President Reagan. After the 1992 election carried a Democrat into the White House for the first time in a dozen years, Reagan passed his mantle as the country's most influential conservative not to Bush or Dole, but to the broadcasting behemoth. In a "Dear Rush" letter that was widely printed in right-wing publications, Reagan wrote, "I know the liberals call you 'the most dangerous man in America,' but don't worry about it, they used to say the same thing about me." Reagan ended the letter with a full endorsement, "America needs to hear 'the way things ought to be.'"[28]

According to Limbaugh, there ought to be new leaders in Washington. After Clinton's election, Limbaugh dedicated his daily radio and television rhetoric almost exclusively to destroying the administration. Day after day for seventeen and a half hours a week, he pummeled the Democrats with a barrage of hazy innuendo mixed with hardcore criticism of "Slick Willie's" alleged marital infidelity, support of the "gay agenda" and "environmental wackos," opposition to gun- and property-owner rights, improprieties in the Whitewater land development deal, advocacy of sex education and condom distribution, and central role in a "liberal conspiracy to destroy everything that is sacred" in America. When Clinton was the subject, Limbaugh took no prisoners.

By mid-1994, the Democrats were hurting. When Limbaugh did fund-raisers for Republican candidates, crowds were large and enthusiastic. Realizing his party's forty-year hold on Congress was in jeopardy, the president complained that Limbaugh had too much influence and blamed the Democratic Party's drop in the polls on the commentator's unrelenting attacks. "You've got Rush Limbaugh and all this right-wing extremist media," Clinton said, "just pouring venom at us every day and nothing to counter that rhetoric." The most powerful politician in the world grousing about a radio host having too much influence did not, however, play well with the American people. Clinton's whining was ineffective; Limbaugh's winning was guaranteed. The day before the November 1994 election, Limbaugh issued a dramatic call to action, urging his dittohead foot soldiers to "be ready at dawn tomorrow" to gain Republican control of Congress.[29]

The Republican avalanche was extraordinary. Voters blasted dozens of liberal Democrats out of Congress, relegating Democratic dominance to the history books. The landslide extended to gubernatorial mansions as well. In New Jersey, Limbaugh's last-minute campaign—he told listeners to vote for incumbent Democrat Jim Florio only if they held a "perverted desire to bend over, grab your ankles and beg for new taxes"—was hailed as the deciding factor in Christine Todd Whitman's surprise victory.[30]

In postmortems after the historic election and with the launch of the so-called Republican Revolution, even the most liberal cynics had to acknowledge that Limbaugh was a political kingmaker who had played a singular role in the Republican rout. The *Washington Post* wrote, "The talk radio election—a campaign in which anger and alienation have echoed across the airwaves—came full circle yesterday as conservative hosts did rhetorical high-fives." The article detailed how Limbaugh had celebrated his victory. "To the strains of James Brown's 'I Feel Good,' Rush Limbaugh switched on his 'gloat-o-meter' and proceeded, well, to gloat," the *Post* wrote. "The bombastic conservative hailed 'one of the most massive shifts to the right in *any* country in *any* year since the *history of civilization*. This was a personal, political and ideological refutation and repudiation of the most amazing attempt to move this country to the left we've seen in 50 years.'"[31]

Other news organizations joined in reporting Limbaugh's pivotal role in the historic election. The *San Francisco Chronicle* called him a "central force in forging the Republican juggernaut that seized control of Congress" and dubbed the newly elected Republicans the Dittohead Caucus. The *Detroit News* said it had searched long and hard for why voters had turned to conservatism and finally had settled on the impact of the bellicose talk-show host as the paramount reason. "We ascribe the turnabout to Mr. Limbaugh's phenomenal hold over the minds of men (and, yes, women too)," the newspaper said. "Voters turned the political world upside down by delivering Congress to the Republicans. And not just any Republican, but Rush Limbaugh." The *News* went on to honor Limbaugh as its man of the year: "Here's to Rush, the man who has done more to turn a sad-sack Republican remnant into a congressional majority than Newt Gingrich himself."[32]

The next hallelujah chorus came from members of the new majority. In early December, they held a victory dinner with Limbaugh as the main speaker. After chowing down on red meat and apple pie, the seventy-three new Republican members of Congress turned the event into a Limbaugh love feast. "The freshman class," according to the *New York Times*, "whooped and applauded, proving itself one big fan club of the man it believes was primarily responsible for the Republican avalanche in November."[33]

Heady with victory, the euphoric lawmakers declared themselves the Limbaugh Congress and jubilantly made the commentator an honorary member of their elite group by giving him a specially crafted pin reserved exclusively for them—plus Limbaugh. It read "Majority Maker" and served as the emblem of the newcomers who had earned their party majority status for the first time in modern history. Six Republican women fashioned their own special tribute by presenting Limbaugh with a plaque reading: "Rush Was Right." At the presentation, the new congresswomen proudly announced, "There's not a femi-Nazi among us."[34]

Individual lawmakers then heaped more praise on the Pillsbury Doughboy of right-wing politics. Barbara Cubin from Wyoming told Limbaugh that because 74 percent of the country's newspapers had endorsed Democratic candidates, "Talk radio, with you in the lead, is what turned the tide." Dick Chrysler from Michigan said of Limbaugh, "He helped make us the majority." In his effusive comments, Jon Christensen of Nebraska credited Limbaugh with fueling his interest in politics and then described a poignant element of his winning campaign strategy, "Wherever there was a 'Rush is right' bumper sticker on a car, we would put a brochure underneath their windshield [wipers] that began 'Dear Rush fan.'" Turning more serious, Christensen looked Limbaugh in the eye and said, "Tonight it is a real opportunity for me to say thank you."[35]

Vin Weber, cochairman of the Empower America conservative think tank, capped the evening. Citing a poll taken after the election, Weber said people who listened to ten or more hours of talk radio each week voted Republican three-to-one. Weber concluded, "Those are the people who elected the new Congress." Weber summed up the sentiments of his fellow Republicans by saying, "Rush Limbaugh is as responsible for what has happened as any individual in America."[36]

After the Republican landslide, Limbaugh continued his relentless attack on the Clinton administration and Democratic Party, pointing out that the mid-term conservative rout had been effected by thirty-eight million voters—and that he reached more than half that number every week. Limbaugh promised to deliver twenty million votes to the presidential candidate of his choice in the next election.[37]

"Let me entertain you . . . "

Rush Hudson Limbaugh III had, by any number of standards, achieved remarkable success in the field of political journalism. His meteoric rise from failed disc jockey to wealthy commentator, author, and entrepreneur earning $20 million a year had lifted him to national prominence and influence. His ability to attract an audience of twenty-five million loyal listeners suggested that his boastful claim of possessing "a talent on loan from God" was not so far off the mark. His mastery at developing an engaging style that relied on his own talent, creativity, and verve had proven him to be a media innovator without peer. While triumphing in the volatile field of talk radio, he simultaneously had transformed the field into a white-hot media enterprise soaring in size, profits, and influence. When House Speaker Newt Gingrich made plans to announce and promote the Contract With America, he bypassed television as well as newspapers and chose radio as his medium of choice, lining up 300 talk-radio interviews to broadcast the details of his conservative manifesto.[38]

In the context of this book, Limbaugh most certainly had shaped history. Not only blocking numerous public policy measures, he also played a singular role in the historic Republican Revolution that redefined the political, social, and economic landscape during the final decade of the twentieth century—and he was only in his mid-forties.

From a news media perspective, Limbaugh's ascendancy to the apex of influence was profoundly important in two ways. The first involved the Fourth Estate's most sacred possession: accuracy. Journalism must be factual. It must strive, above all else, to report the truth. And on the occasions when reporters or commentators make mistakes, they must admit and correct their errors. Limbaugh defied this convention. Whatever the venue, he was unapologetically biased, unbalanced, and partisan. His broadcasts, as well as his books and newsletter, were littered with errors. What's more, he refused to correct mistakes even after they had been pointed out to him. After Limbaugh told millions of listeners that Vince Foster had been murdered and that the White House had covered up the crime, the independent counsel examining Whitewater, Robert B. Fiske Jr., stated unequivocally that Foster had, as originally reported, committed suicide. Limbaugh neither apologized nor corrected his erroneous statements. Such disregard for accuracy by the most listened-to commentator in the country is severely damaging to the American news media's credibility.

The second media-based concern about Limbaugh was that he was on the vanguard of a shift from journalism as distributor of information to journalism as purveyor of entertainment. Limbaugh helped create and champion "infotainment," with his unique style of commentary joining tabloid television programs such as "Hard Copy" and "A Current Affair" to make it virtually impossible for media consumers to determine exactly where to draw the line between fact and fiction. In particular, Limbaugh's juxtaposing humorous hyperbole with political and social criticism—at a rapid-fire pace and clouded with supercilious sneers and cackles of dismissive laughter—left listeners and viewers drowning in a sea where fantasy could not be distinguished from fabrication. And yet, "pseudonews" appeared to be the trend of the future. Even after dozens of Limbaugh's errors had been exposed, CBS—the first citizen of the most powerful medium in the history of humankind—attempted to hire him as a political commentator. What stronger endorsement could there be for news being redefined as pseudonews?

15

How the News Media Have Shaped History: Focusing on the *How*

THE NEWS MEDIA have shaped American history. Absolutely. Boldly. Proudly. Fervently. Profoundly.

From the 1760s when patriot editors created the "Journal of Occurrences" to propel their countrymen toward the American Revolution through the 1990s when a radio tilt-a-whirl mixed humor with political commentary to lead the Republican Revolution, the Fourth Estate has been a central force in how this nation has evolved. Between those two revolutions, a legion of journalists and news organizations stayed the course, serving as catalysts for social movements as well as landmark events that have defined this country's past. The news media have generally used their might as a positive force—but sometimes not.

Now that I have piloted the reader through two centuries of discrete episodes in which American journalism has influenced the nation's history, in this concluding chapter I want to focus on one final and fundamental question: *How?* To answer this question, I have looked closely at the individual journalists and news organizations that have been the major players in the fourteen episodes I have focused on in this book. More specifically, I have examined that collection of newspeople and news outlets with an eye toward identifying the common characteristics that they have shared. The following list of recurring traits, then, suggests some of the precise methods that the American news media have used while helping to shape this country.

The news organizations that have influenced important events have not been afraid to set the agenda. They have approached the news media as an institution that *leads* the news, not as an institution that merely *reports* the news. Not one of the news organizations profiled in the previous fourteen chapters defined its role so narrowly that it blithely recorded the news without comment or interpretation. None of them, in short, was willing to function as a stenographic service.

Examples abound. *McClure's* magazine did not produce its brilliant exposé of Standard Oil Company by asking Ida Minerva Tarbell merely to record the prepared statements mouthed by John D. Rockefeller; Tarbell pored over court documents, wooed inside sources, and listened to disgruntled competitors until she understood the inner workings of the largest and most ruthless monopoly in American history. Half a century later, network correspondents were not handed press releases or feted to media receptions when they went into the segregated South to cover the Civil Rights Movement; the correspondents faced signs reading "NO DOGS, NIGGERS OR REPORTERS ALLOWED" and heard racists belittle them for working for the *Nigger* Broadcasting Corporation. Likewise, Bob Woodward and Carl Bernstein did not uncover the Watergate scandal by becoming two more sheep in the White House press corps that "covered" the president by rewriting the handouts produced by his army of public relations flacks; Woodstein assiduously avoided—indeed, felt the wrath of—the official presidential spokesman.

Not for a moment did these fearless journalists waver in their commitment to excellence in news coverage—or to setting the nation's agenda.

For many of the journalists and their news organizations, standing tall meant standing alone. They spurned the concept that today is known as "pack journalism"—in which dozens of reporters swarm like honey bees onto the hot story of the moment and then buzz off, in unison, to search for the next communal hot spot. The journalists who have helped build this country into what it is today did so partly by consciously and fearlessly breaking from the pack, despite what were often severe consequences.

William Lloyd Garrison founded the *Liberator* to advocate the end of slavery; other editors castigated him as a "pitiful scoundrel" and a "toad eater," with pro-slavery groups offering as much as $20,000 to the bounty hunter who could capture him. A century later, a troika of courageous newspapers spoke out against the Ku Klux Klan even though the vast majority of the nation's news voices maintained a deafening silence on the subject. In the early 1950s, wire services and newspapers were one of the major forces that propelled Joe McCarthy onto the national stage, until Edward R. Murrow took American history's most famous demagogue to task. Twenty years later, Walter Cronkite followed Murrow's example when he broke away from the pack of pro-Vietnam correspondents to urge the nation to bring its soldiers home. And a few years after that, the *Washington Post* was the only news organization in the country committed to uncovering Watergate; the *Post* refused to let loose of the story even after the former U.S. attorney general hurled one of the more colorful epithets in the history of American journalism at the newspaper's publisher, threatening, "Katy Graham's *tit* is going to get caught in a wringer."

Journalists who have stood up to the various demons in American society have been willing to expose themselves to more than mere name calling. Dozens of the courageous newsmen and newswomen have been threatened with bodily harm—much of it ultimately delivered.

When Thomas Nast of *Harper's Weekly* refused to stop publishing bruising cartoons against "Boss" Tweed in the late 1860s, the death threats became so frequent that Nast had to relocate his wife and children to ensure their safety. During the Civil Rights Movement, television correspondents were cursed, spat upon, clubbed, and kicked right along with the black men, women, and children whose protests they were filming—NBC cameraman Moe Levy was among those disabled for the rest of their lives.

But the most dramatic acts of physical violence were against nineteenth-century abolitionist editors and writers. William Lloyd Garrison was stoned, pelted with rotten eggs, and taken within a hairsbreadth of being lynched; Maria Stewart's fiery discourse netted her a barrage of insults—as well as rotten tomatoes. Abolitionist editor Elijah Lovejoy lost four printing presses to pro-slavery mobs before he finally paid the supreme price by giving his very life to the cause, becoming America's first martyr to freedom of the press.

The news organizations that have shaped American history have placed journalistic principle above financial gain. Time and time again, these courageous publications and broadcast voices have—in order to preserve the integrity of their chosen value system—accepted serious economic setbacks that have threatened their survival.

When *Harper's Weekly* refused to end its crusade against New York's nefarious Tweed Ring, city officials canceled the Harper Brothers Publishing Company contract to provide textbooks for the school system. When *Collier's* announced that its new editorial campaign meant that it would no longer accept ads from patent medicine companies, the magazine's revenues dropped $80,000 in a single year.

When the *Washington Post* refused to allow the Watergate story to die, in six months the value of a share of *Post* stock plunged from $38 to $21—thanks to President Nixon's friends on Wall Street.

Television journalists have endured financial strains as well. When CBS would not pay to advertise *See It Now*'s legendary programs attacking Joe McCarthy, newsman Edward R. Murrow and producer Fred Friendly dipped into their own pockets to pay for the ads; when NBC could not find sponsors for its prime-time *American Revolution of '63* news special about the Civil Rights Movement, the network lost half a million dollars in revenue in a single night.

Perhaps the least admirable characteristic of the news organizations that have shaped American history has been their tendency to ignore or to malign minorities. The Fourth Estate has traditionally been a bastion of white, Anglo-Saxon, protestant men who have been less than eager to crusade on behalf of the disenfranchised.

Opponents of chattel slavery became so frustrated with establishment newspapers' support of the peculiar institution that they created their own journalistic genre; without abolitionist newspapers such as the *St. Louis Observer* and *Freedom's Journal*, slavery most assuredly would have continued far longer than it did. Nor have American women been served well by the news media. *Ladies Magazine* and other eighteenth-century periodicals communicated that women did not possess the ability to function beyond the domestic sphere, and the Brahmans of nineteenth-century journalism pulled out all the stops to block women's march toward equality—the *New York Herald* called the Seneca Falls meeting the "Woman's Wrong Convention," and the *New York World* denigrated Susan B. Anthony as "lean, cadaverous; with the proportions of a file and the voice of a hurdy-gurdy." In a similar way, Father Charles E. Coughlin modulated his golden radio voice to attack Jews.

Later landmark events indicated, however, that by the middle of this century the news media had begun to treat the powerless more fairly. Newspapers, magazines, and radio stations of the 1940s helped expand the limits of the American woman by helping to impel her into the workforce—though they undertook the crusade for the benefit of the war effort, not the women. A decade later, television news chose African Americans to be the beneficiaries of its first major crusade, with televised images of the Civil Rights Movement pushing that social revolution onto the nation's agenda.

Another important characteristic of the various news organizations that have influenced American history has been an eagerness to harness the phenomenal power of visual images. Nineteenth-century magazines and newspapers found that editorial cartoons could be a remarkably effective weapon in their journalistic crusades, and in more recent years television news has lifted the power of visual images to unparalleled heights.

Harper's Weekly pioneered this theme by publishing Nast's devastating cartoons to loosen the Tweed Ring's stranglehold on the citizens of New York City during the late 1860s. At the end of the century, the *New York World* employed Frederic Remington's artistic talents in its campaign to shove the United States into war with Spain, including front-page drawings of a naked young woman being depicted as the object of the lustful leers of Spanish officials and of the U.S.S. *Maine* being destroyed by a Spanish mine—both images as misleading as they were effective. In the 1920s, the Memphis *Commercial Appeal* published searing anti–Ku Klux Klan cartoons as the centerpiece of its courageous campaign against the most powerful nativist movement in American history.

During the second half of this century, the compelling nature of visual images has been central to making television the most potent medium of communication in the history of humankind. In an impressive series of events beginning in the 1950s, television news repeatedly demonstrated that its images could move the entire nation. In what has been called television's finest hour, Murrow and Friendly exposed McCarthy as a mean-spirited bully. And then the three major networks combined forces, first to propel the Civil Rights Movement onto the nation's front burner and then to hasten the end of the Vietnam War. In fact, the good that television has accomplished has emerged as one of the major themes in this book.

As the title of this book suggests, the news organizations that have taken leading roles in shaping this country have consistently recognized that the pen, as well as the visual image, can be mightier than the sword—and mightier than tyranny or bigotry or demagoguery or political corruption. The instrument of communication has varied from a quill pen in the eighteenth century to electronic mail in the twentieth, but the communicators highlighted in this book have proven that the combination of writing talent and driving passion can be potent. The episodes described in the previous pages repeatedly have shown that this combination can stir the emotions of the American people at crucial moments.

During the 1770s, Thomas Paine's muscular prose helped transform lukewarm patriots into fiery revolutionaries. Half a century later, the suffering that defined the early lives of Maria Stewart and Frederick Douglass inspired them to write with a depth of feeling that helped turn the nation's conscience against slavery. Very different emotions—including feelings of scorn and outrage—erupted in nineteenth-century newspaper readers when male wordsmiths labeled women's rights activists "hermaphrodite spirits" and "*Amazons*" who were "*bolting* with a vengeance," while compressing the philosophy of the American press into two appalling sentences: "A woman is nobody. A wife is everything." American industry's abusive treatment of women and children served as the genesis for more powerful prose—thanks to the talent and commitment of muckrakers such as Rheta Childe Dorr. And in contemporary America, Rush Limbaugh has emerged as a highly influential political commentator/entertainer who draws laughter even from listeners who totally disagree with what he says.

Ultimately, perhaps the most important characteristic that has allowed news organizations to shape American history has been an acceptance not of the power of the news media but of the limitations of that institution. Although the journalists and news organizations profiled in this book cherished the Fourth Estate's role as watchdog over the official branches of government, none of the historic events described here was brought about solely by the news media. News articles or broadcasts often served as catalysts, but not in a single instance did the news media function in a vacuum. Journalists may have placed a particular topic on the agenda, but the support and commitment of other institutions was always essential for meaningful change to occur.

Examples abound. *Harper's Weekly* and the *New York Times* exposed Tweed's wrongdoing, but the citizens of New York had to band together before the political corruption was finally ended and the wayward city officials wore prison stripes. The muckrakers fearlessly shined the bright light of truth into the dark corners of America, but it took other institutions to enact reform measures—the Supreme Court to dissolve the Standard Oil monopoly, Congress to pass the Pure Food and Drug Act, the American public to vote corrupt senators out of office. Television brought the grisly images of battle into the American living room, but President Johnson, responding to the pressure of public opinion, ultimately had to bring the troops home from Southeast Asia.

Watergate is the paramount example of the limited role that the Fourth Estate can play. The *Washington Post* revealed the dimensions of the immorality of the Nixon White House, but then the Justice Department investigated the charges, the Supreme Court demanded the White House tapes, and Congress voted the articles of impeachment that toppled a president.

Although the previous fourteen chapters—as well as this list of eight characteristics describing how the news media have shaped American history—are all products of the past, I feel compelled to end this book with a few brief comments on the present and the future.

For as a former journalist and now an educator of aspiring journalists, I am concerned about the Fourth Estate's current status—or lack of it.

The news media are on trial today as never before. In the eyes of the American public, reporters are rude, arrogant, self-righteous, cynical, irresponsible, unpatriotic, and amoral. They seek out the most negative angle of a story and twist the facts to suit their liberal agenda. They meddle in politics, invade people's privacy, and sensationalize the news. Broadcast journalists are more interested in entertaining than informing, and their print counterparts are guided by one principle above all others: Sell newspapers. Public respect for journalism has plummeted, threatening the very foundation of one of the pillars of our democratic system of governance. Journalism is struggling to retain the public trust, but it is not succeeding in that effort. In the euphoric days following the *Washington Post*'s Watergate revelations, 68 percent of the people polled expressed "trust and confidence" in the American news media; by 1995, that figure had dropped to a mere 21 percent.[1]

As a historian, I believe that looking back is essential in charting a course for the future. And as a *journalism* historian, I believe that the news media of the 1990s should be guided by the episodes described in this book as well as by the news media traits listed in this concluding chapter. For a number of those characteristics suggest principles of behavior that could help the American news media both survive and thrive in the new millennium. Therefore, I say to the citizens of the Fourth Estate:

Be willing to set the agenda.

Be willing to break from the pack.

Be willing, when an important issue is at stake, to sacrifice financial gain.

Be willing to reach out to the politically or socially disenfranchised, including women as well as racial and sexual minorities.

Strive to harness—but also respect—the tremendous power of visual images.

Let compelling writers write compellingly.

Do not be so arrogant as to think that journalism is the country's only institution of consequence.

Some wags and virtually all bean counters will criticize these suggestions, saying such a call for news organizations to travel the journalistic high road ignores the economic realities facing the industry today. It is true that these suggestions are based on an idealistic premise that not everyone shares: Journalism that is substantive in content and strong in backbone ultimately will succeed, prosper, and serve a democratic people well. Yes, I believe in this lofty principle. Indeed, if this premise is no longer worth defending, I question—with considerable despair—if the Fourth Estate is still an institution worthy of salvaging.

Notes

Introduction

1. Thomas Jefferson, letter to Thomas Paine, 19 June 1792, in Paul Leicester Ford, ed., *The Works of Thomas Jefferson* (New York: Putnam, 1904), vol. VII, 122.

Chapter 1

1. Samuel Adams, "Instructions of the Town of Boston to Its Representatives in the General Court," May 1764, in Harry A. Cushing, *The Writings of Samuel Adams* (New York: Octagon, 1968), vol. I, 5.
2. Samuel Adams letter to James Warren, 9 December 1772, in W. C. Ford, ed., *Collections of the Massachusetts Historical Society* (Boston: Samuel Hall, 1795).
3. *New York Journal*, 13 October 1768, 2.
4. Oliver M. Dickerson, comp., *Boston Under Military Rule, 1768–1769* (Boston: Chapman & Grimes, 1936), ix.
5. *Boston Evening Post*, 1 May 1769, 1; *New York Journal:* 8 December 1768, 1; 29 December 1768, 1; 19 January 1769, 1; 13 April 1769, 1.
6. *New York Journal:* 10 November 1768, 1; 22 December 1768, 1.
7. *New York Journal* (*Supplement*): 29 June 1769, 1; 1 June 1769, 1.
8. *Boston Evening Post*, 26 June 1769, 1; *New York Journal* (*Supplement*): 29 June 1769, 1; 27 July 1769, 1.
9. *New York Journal*, 3 November 1768, 2; *New York Journal* (*Supplement*), 29 June 1769, 1; *Boston Evening Post:* 26 June 1769, 1; 24 July 1769, 1; 31 July 1769, 1.
10. *New York Journal:* 10 November 1768, 1; 24 November 1768, 2; 29 December 1768, 1.
11. Francis Bernard letter to Lord Hillsborough, 25 February 1769, in Sir Francis Bernard Papers, New York Public Library, New York; Thomas Hutchinson letter to Israel Williams, 26 January 1769, in Israel Williams Papers, Massachusetts Historical Society Library, Boston.
12. Thomas Hutchinson letter to Israel Williams, 26 January 1769, in Israel Williams Papers, Massachusetts Historical Society Library, Boston.

13. *Boston Evening Post*, 26 June 1769, 1.

14. *Boston Gazette*, 28 May 1770.

15. Samuel Adams, *Boston Gazette:* "Article," 31 December 1770, 1; "Article Signed Vindex," 28 January 1771, 1.

16. "A Monumental Inscription on the Fifth of March," 1772, reprinted in Philip Davidson, *Propaganda and the American Revolution* (Chapel Hill: University of North Carolina Press, 1941), 222.

17. David Ramsay, *The History of the American Revolution* (Philadelphia, 1789; reprinted New York: Russell & Russell, 1968), vol. I, 91.

18. Thomas Paine: *Pennsylvania Magazine*, 24 January 1775; *Postscript to the Pennsylvania Journal and the Weekly Advertiser*, 8 March 1775.

19. Benjamin Rush to James Cheetham, in Lyman H. Butterfield, ed., *The Letters of Benjamin Rush* (Princeton, N.J.: Princeton University Press, 1951), vol. II, 1007.

20. Thomas Paine, *Common Sense*, in Moncure D. Conway, *The Writings of Thomas Paine* (New York: AMS, 1967), 68, 84–85.

21. Paine, *Common Sense*, in Conway, *Paine*, 72, 84, 99.

22. Paine, *Common Sense*, in Conway, *Paine*, 118–19.

23. Paine, *Common Sense*, in Conway, *Paine*, 100–01.

24. Philip S. Foner, *The Complete Writings of Thomas Paine* (New York: Citadel, 1945), ix.

25. George Washington letter to Joseph Reed, 1 April 1776, in John C. Fitzpatrick, ed., *The Writings of George Washington from the Original Manuscript Sources, 1745–1799* (Washington, D.C.: U.S. Government Printing Office, 1931–44), vol. IV, 455; Abigail Adams letter to John Adams, 21 February 1776, in Lyman H. Butterfield, ed., *Adams Family Correspondence* (Cambridge, Mass.: Harvard University, 1909), vol. I, 350; Thomas Jefferson letter to Francis Eppes, 19 January 1821, in Paul Leicester Ford, ed., *The Works of Thomas Jefferson* (New York: Putnam, 1904), vol. XII, 195.

26. *Connecticut Gazette*, 22 March 1776; *Pennsylvania Packet*, 12 February 1776.

27. Ramsay, *History*, vol. I, 338–39.

28. Eric Foner, *Tom Paine and Revolutionary America* (New York: Oxford University Press, 1976), 87.

29. Paine, *Crisis*, in Conway, *Paine*, 170.

30. Paine, *Crisis*, in Conway, *Paine*, 176.

31. Silas Bent, *Newspaper Crusaders: A Neglected Story* (Freeport, N.Y.: Books for Libraries, 1939), 19.

Chapter 2

1. Elijah P. Lovejoy, *St. Louis Observer*, 16 April 1835.

2. Lovejoy, *St. Louis Observer:* 30 April 1835; 11 February 1836.

3. *Missouri Republican:* 17 July 1837; 28 August 1837.

4. *Alton Observer*, 8 September 1836.

5. Elijah P. Lovejoy speech delivered 30 October 1837 in Alton, Ill., in Edward Beecher, *Narrative of Riots at Alton: In Connection with the Death of*

Rev. Elijah P. Lovejoy (Alton, Ill.: George Holton, 1838; reprint Miami: Mnemosyne, 1969), 91.

6. William Lloyd Garrison, "A Martyr for Liberty," *Liberator*, 24 November 1837.

7. John Quincy Adams diary, 20 November 1837, in Charles F. Francis, ed., *Memoirs of John Quincy Adams, Comprising Portions of His Dairy from 1795 to 1848* (Freeport, N.Y.: Books for Libraries, 1969), vol. IX, 432; Edward Beecher letter to Owen Lovejoy, 14 November 1837, Owen Lovejoy Papers, William L. Clements Library, University of Michigan; William Ellery Channing, "Channing's Letter to the Citizens of Boston," *Liberator*, 15 December 1837.

8. Minutes of the Executive Committee of the American Anti-Slavery Society, Boston Public Library, December 1837.

9. William Lloyd Garrison, "Black List," *Genius of Universal Emancipation*, 20 November 1829, 2.

10. William Lloyd Garrison, "To the Public," *Liberator*, 1 January 1831, 1.

11. William Lloyd Garrison, "Editors," *Liberator*, 29 January 1831, 2.

12. William Lloyd Garrison, "Incendiary Publications," *Liberator*, 8 October 1831, 1.

13. *Liberator*, "Threats to Assassinate," 10 September 1831, 1.

14. William Lloyd Garrison, "The Insurrection," *Liberator*, 3 September 1831, 3.

15. William Lloyd Garrison, "Address to the Friends of Freedom and Emancipation in the United States," *Liberator*, 31 May 1844, 2.

16. "The Meeting at Framingham," *Liberator*, 7 July 1854, 2.

17. William Lloyd Garrison, "Speech of Wm. Lloyd Garrison," *Liberator*, 16 December 1859, 2.

18. *Nation*, "The 'Liberator' Released," 4 January 1866, 7.

19. Frederick Douglass, in John W. Blassingame and John R. McKivigan, eds., *The Frederick Douglass Papers* (New Haven, Conn.: Yale University Press, 1992), vol. 5, 369.

20. Samuel Cornish and John B. Russwurm, "To Our Patrons," *Freedom's Journal*, 16 March 1827, 1.

21. Maria Stewart, "An Address, Delivered at the African Masonic Hall, in Boston," *Liberator*, 4 May 1833, 4.

22. Frederick Douglass, "Prospectus," *North Star*, 5 November 1847, 4.

23. Frederick Douglass, "Colored People Must Command Respect," *North Star*, 24 March 1848, 2.

24. Frederick Douglass, "The Slaves' Right to Revolt," *North Star*, 16 June 1848, 2.

25. Frederick Douglass, *Life and Times of Frederick Douglass* (Hartford, Conn.: Park, 1881), 326; untitled article, *North Star*, 21 January 1848, 2.

Chapter 3

1. Elizabeth Cady Stanton, Susan B. Anthony, and Matilda Joslyn Gage, eds., *History of Woman Suffrage* (New York: Fowler & Wells, 1881), 70.

2. "Thoughts on Women," *Ladies Magazine*, August 1792, 112; "To the Editors of the Ladies Magazine," *Ladies Magazine*, August 1792, 122; "On the Happy Influence of Female Society," *American Museum*, January 1787, 63.

3. "The Cultivation of the Mind Recommended," *Ladies Magazine*, April 1793, 220; "On Female Society," *The Dessert to the True American*, 2 February 1799, 3.

4. "Letter from a Brother to a Sister at a Boarding School," *Ladies Magazine*, November 1792, 260.

5. "On Fashionable Female Amusements," *Ladies Magazine*, February 1793, 125–26; "On Matrimonial Happiness," *Weekly Magazine*, 10 March 1798, 153; "On Conversation," *Weekly Magazine*, February 1798, 122–23.

6. "Woman's Rights Convention," *Seneca County Courier*, 14 July 1848, 1.

7. Stanton, Anthony, and Gage, *History*, 70; Aileen S. Kraditor, *Up from the Pedestal* (Chicago: Quadrangle, 1968), 186–88.

8. Kraditor, *Up*, 188.

9. Stanton, Anthony, and Gage, *History*, 71.

10. "Women Out of Their Latitude," *Mechanic's Advocate*, reprinted in Stanton, Anthony, and Gage, *History*, 802–03; "Insurrection Among the Women," *Worcester Telegraph*, reprinted in Stanton, Anthony, and Gage, *History*, 803; *Rochester Daily Democrat*, reprinted in Stanton, Anthony, and Gage, *History*, 804; "The Reign of Petticoats," *Rochester Daily Advertiser*, reprinted in Stanton, Anthony, and Gage, *History*, 803–04.

11. "The Woman's Rights Convention—The Last Act of the Drama," *New York Herald*, 12 September 1852, 2; "Insurrection Among the Women," *Worcester Telegraph*, reprinted in Stanton, Anthony, and Gage, *History*, 803; "The Women of Philadelphia," *Philadelphia Ledger and Daily Transcript*, reprinted in Stanton, Anthony, and Gage, *History*, 804.

12. *Syracuse Weekly Star*, 11 September 1852, reprinted in Stanton, Anthony, and Gage, *History*, 852–53; "Women's Rights in the Legislature," *Albany Daily State Register*, 6 March 1854, 1.

13. "Women Out of Their Latitude," *Mechanic's Advocate*, reprinted in Stanton, Anthony, and Gage, *History*, 802–03; "The Woman's Rights Convention—The Last Act of the Drama," *New York Herald*, 12 September 1852, 2.

14. "Female Follies and Fourrierism," *New York Herald*, 12 September 1852, 2.

15. "Woman's Rights," *New York Times*, 18 October 1851, 2.

16. *New York Herald:* "Female Follies and Fourrierism," 12 September 1852, 2; "The Woman's Rights Convention—The Last Act of the Drama," 12 September 1852, 2.

17. *New York Sun*, reprinted in Ida Husted Harper, *The Life and Work of Susan B. Anthony* (Indianapolis: Hollenbeck, 1898), vol. 1, 90; "The Last Vagary of the Greeley Clique—The Women, Their Rights, and Their Champions," *New York Herald*, 7 September 1853, 4.

18. *Syracuse Weekly Star*, reprinted in Harper, *Anthony*, vol. 1, 267; "The Last Vagary of the Greeley Clique—The Women, Their Rights, and Their Champions," *New York Herald*, 7 September 1853, 4; "The Woman's Rights

Convention—The Last Act of the Drama," *New York Herald*, 12 September 1852, 2; "Women's Rights in the Legislature," *Albany Daily State Register*, 7 March 1854, 1; "The Last Vagary of the Greeley Clique—The Women, Their Rights, and Their Champions," *New York Herald*, 7 September 1853, 2.

19. Miriam Gurko, *The Ladies of Seneca Falls: The Birth of the Woman's Rights Movement* (New York: Macmillan, 1974), 104.

20. Lucretia Mott, "National Convention at Cincinnati, Ohio," in Elizabeth Cady Stanton, Susan B. Anthony, and Matilda Joslyn Gage, eds., *History of Woman Suffrage* (New York: Fowler & Wells, 1881), 164.

21. Laura Ballard, "What Flag Shall We Fly?" *Revolution*, October 1870, 265.

22. Josephine St. Pierre Ruffin, "Editorial," *Woman's Era*, 24 March 1894, 8.

23. "A Cry from the Females," *New York Tribune*, reprinted in Harper, *Anthony*, vol. 1, 267; *New York World*, reprinted in Harper, *Anthony*, vol. 1, 264.

24. *New York World*, reprinted in Harper, *Anthony*, vol. 1, 264; *Utica Herald*, reprinted in Harper, *Anthony*, vol. 1, 367; *Richmond Herald*, 29 October 1879, reprinted in Harper, *Anthony*, vol. 1, 504.

25. "Manly Women," *Saturday Review*, 22 June 1889, 756–57; "Is Marriage a Failure?" *Cosmopolitan*, November 1888-April 1889, 196–203.

26. E. Lynn Linton, *Nineteenth Century*, "The Wild Women as Social Insurgents," October 1891, 596; "The Partisans of the Wild Women," March 1892, 455.

27. *Life:* "In Days to Come, Churches May Be Fuller," 23 July 1896, 588–89; "In a Twentieth Century Club," 13 June 1895, 395; William H. Walker, "The New Navy, About 1900 A.D.," 16 April 1896, 310–11.

28. "Her Ideal Journal; Miss Anthony Tells How She Would Make a Newspaper," *Chicago Tribune*, 28 May 1893, 33.

Chapter 4

1. Albert B. Paine, *Thomas Nast: His Period and His Pictures* (Gloucester, Mass.: Peter Smith, 1967), 179.

2. "Our Case Plainly Stated," *New York Times*, 27 July 1871, 4.

3. James Jackson Jarves, *The Art-Idea* (New York: Hurd and Houghton, 1864), 242.

4. Paine, *Thomas Nast*, 106; Morton Keller, *The Art and Politics of Thomas Nast* (New York: Oxford University Press, 1968), 13.

5. Thomas Nast, *Harper's Weekly:* "Robinson Crusoe," 4 December 1869, 777; "The Economical Council, Albany, New York," 25 December 1869, 825.

6. "The Democratic Millennium," *New York Times*, 20 September 1870, 4.

7. Thomas Nast, "The 'Brains,'" *Harper's Weekly*, 21 October 1871, 792.

8. Gustavus Myers, *The History of Tammany Hall* (New York: Burt Franklin, 1917), 239; Paine, *Thomas Nast*, 179.

9. Thomas Nast St. Hill, *Thomas Nast Cartoons and Illustrations* (New York: Dover, 1974), 18.

10. Thomas Nast, "The New Board of Education," *Harper's Weekly*, 13 May 1871, 440.

11. Untitled article, *New York Times*, 19 July 1871, 4.

12. "More Ring Villainy," *New York Times*, 8 July 1871, 4.

13. *New York Times:* "Will It 'Blow Over?'" 21 July 1871, 4; "The Tammany Frauds," 24 July 1871, 4; "Our Proofs of Fraud Against the City Government," 23 July 1871, 4; "The Secret Accounts," 22 July 1871, 4; "More Bills Which Are 'Perhaps Exorbitant,'" 26 July 1871, 4.

14. *New York Times:* "The Secret Accounts," 24 July 1871, 1; "The Tammany Frauds," 24 July 1871, 4.

15. *New York Times:* "More Ring Villainy," 8 July 1871, 4; "Two Thieves," 19 July 1871, 4; "The Decoy-Ducks of the Ring," 11 July 1871, 4; "Stampede of the Ring," 29 July 1871, 1; "More Bills Which Are 'Perhaps Exorbitant,'" 26 July 1871, 4; "Proofs of Theft; How the Public Money Is Embezzled by the Tammany Rulers," 20 July 1871, 4; "The Betrayal of Public Liberties," 11 July 1871, 4.

16. "Democratic Economy," *Philadelphia Press*, 21 July 1871, 4; "Exposure of Tammany Corruption," *Boston Daily Advertiser*, 21 July 1871, 2; "Very Plain Talk," *Providence Daily Journal*, 24 July 1871, 2; "Hoffman and Tammany," *Chicago Tribune*, 15 July 1871, 2.

17. "The Times and Our City Administration—The Disease and the Remedy," *New York Herald*, 3 August 1871, 6; "The City Expenditures—Plumbing and Gas-Fitting," *New York Tribune*, 27 July 1871, 4.

18. "A Presbyterian View of Tammany," *New York World*, 10 July 1871, 4.

19. *New York Times*: "Our Case Plainly Stated," 27 July 1871, 4; "Two Thieves," 19 July 1871, 4; "Our Proof of Fraud Against the City Government," 23 July 1871, 4.

20. *New York Times:* A.G.C., "The *Times* and the City Government," 23 July 1871, 8; N. J. Newton, "A Carpet Calculation," 25 July 1871, 2; C. A. Schindler, "A Grateful German," 25 July 1871, 2; A Convert from Tammany, "The *Times* and the City," 25 July 1871, 2.

21. A Taxpayer, "To the Editor of the *New York Times*," *New York Times*, 23 July 1871, 8. The supplement was published on 29 July 1871.

22. "The Tammany Leaders Still Admit Their Guilt," *New York Times*, 1 August 1871, 4; Thomas Nast, "Who Stole the People's Money?" *Harper's Weekly*, 19 August 1871, 764; "Will It 'Blow Over?'" *New York Times*, 21 July 1871, 4; Thomas Nast, "A Group of Vultures Waiting for the Storm to 'Blow Over'—'Let us *Prey*,'" *Harper's Weekly*, 23 September 1871, 889.

23. Thomas Nast, *Harper's Weekly:* "What are you going to do about it?" 14 October 1871, 960; "The Only Thing They Respect or Fear," 21 October 1871, 977.

24. Thomas Nast, "The Tammany Tiger Loose—'What are you going to do about it?'" *Harper's Weekly*, 11 November 1871, 1056–57.

25. "Unto the Breach!" *Harper's Weekly*, 11 November 1871, 1050.

26. Thomas Nast, "What Are You Laughing at?" *Harper's Weekly*, 25 November 1871, 1097.

27. "The Capture of Tweed," *Harper's Weekly*, 7 October 1876, 821.

28. *The Nation*, "Who Killed the Ring," 23 November 1871, 334–35.
29. *Milwaukee Sentinel*, untitled article, 25 July 1871, 2.
30. *Harper's Weekly*, "The Victory of the People," 25 November 1871, 1098.

Chapter 5

1. Untitled editorial, *New York Post*, 17 March 1898, 6; "The *Maine* and the Freak Press," *New York Times*, 18 February 1898, 6.
2. Ireland Alleyne, *Joseph Pulitzer: Reminiscences of a Secretary* (New York: Mitchell Kennerley, 1914), 110.
3. *New York World:* "Baptized in Blood," 31 May 1883, 1; "A Child Flayed Alive: A Brutal Negro Whips His Nephew to Death," 4 March 1884, 1.
4. Ishbel Ross, *Ladies of the Press* (New York: Harper, 1936), 61.
5. W. A. Swanberg, *Citizen Hearst: A Biography of William Randolph Hearst* (New York: Charles Scribner's Sons, 1961), 162.
6. W. R. Hearst, "The Appeal of Cuba," *New York Journal*, 11 October 1895, 4.
7. *New York Evening Journal:* "Spanish Brutality," 15 October 1896, 1; "Cuba," 23 October 1896, 1.
8. Willard G. Bleyer, *Main Currents in the History of American Journalism* (Boston: Houghton Mifflin, 1927), 342.
9. James Creelman, *On the Great Highway: The Wanderings and Adventures of a Special Correspondent* (Boston: Lothrop, 1901), 177–78.
10. Richard Harding Davis, "Does Our Flag Shield Women?" *New York Journal*, 12 February 1897, 1; George Bronson Rea, *Facts and Fakes About Cuba* (New York: G. Munro's Sons, 1897), 230; "Mr. Davis Explains; The Unclothed Woman Searched by Men Was an Invention of a New York Newspaper," *New York World*, 17 February 1897, 2.
11. *New York World:* "Cuba," 10 June 1896, 4; Sylvester Scovel, "Cuba," 29 May 1896, 1; James Creelman, "Cuba," 17 May 1896, 1.
12. "Cubans Again Whip Their Spanish Foes; Feeding Prisoners to Sharks," *New York Journal*, 7 October 1896, 5; "Butchered 300 Cuban Women," *New York Journal*, 30 November 1896, 1; George Eugene Bryson, "Weyler Throws Nuns into Prison," *New York Journal*, 17 January 1897, 1; James Creelman, "Cuban Atrocities," *New York World*, 29 May 1896, 7.
13. *Congressional Record*, 26 January 1897, 1157.
14. "The Spanish-*Journal* War," *New York Journal*, 12 February 1898, 1.
15. *New York Journal*, 17 February 1898, 1: "Destruction of the War Ship *Maine* Was the Work of an Enemy"; "$50,000!"
16. *New York Journal:* "The War Ship *Maine* Was Split in Two by an Enemy's Secret Infernal Machine," 17 February 1898, 1; "War! Sure! *Maine* Destroyed by Spanish," 17 February 1898, 1; "The Whole Country Thrills with War Fever," 18 February 1898, 1; "How the *Maine* Actually Looks as It Lies, Wrecked by Spanish Treachery, in Havana Bay," 20 February 1898, 1.
17. "Game of War with Spain," *New York Journal*, 20 February 1898, 2; "The People's Letters," *New York Journal*, 26 February 1898, 12; Ferdinand

Lundberg, *Imperial Hearst: A Social Biography* (New York: Modern Library, 1937), 81.

18. Swanberg, *Citizen Hearst*, 138.

19. *New York World: "Maine* Explosion Caused by Bomb or Torpedo?" 17 February 1898, 1; "Midnight Opinion from the President," 18 February 1898, 1; "*World's* Latest Discoveries Indicate *Maine* Was Blown Up by Submarine Mine," 20 February 1898, 1; "*World's* News of the Evidence of a Mine Under the *Maine* Changes the Feeling Throughout the Country," 20 February 1898, 1; "Free Cuba the Only Atonement," 26 February 1898, 6.

20. W. R. Hearst, "The Situation," *New York Evening Journal*, 24 February 1898, 10; "Peace—on a 'Cash Basis,'" *New York World*, 16 March 1898, 6.

21. "What the Court of Inquiry Has Found," *New York Evening Journal*, 11 March 1898, 1.

22. "Mob Burned M'Kinley in Effigy in Colorado," *New York Evening Journal*, 30 March 1898, 2; "M'Kinley Burned in Effigy, Jeered and Flouted," *New York Evening Journal*, 30 March 1898, 2; "M'Kinley and Hanna Burned in Effigy," *New York Evening Journal*, 31 March 1898, 2; "Patient Under the Loss of Her First Born," *New York Evening Journal*, 9 April 1898, 7; "A Chilly Message," *New York World*, 29 March 1898, 1.

23. "Now to Avenge the *Maine*!" *New York Journal*, 20 April 1898, 1.

24. "How Do You Like the *Journal*'s War?" *New York Journal*, 9 May 1898, 1.

25. W. R. Hearst, "First American Newspaper Published in the Island," *New York Journal*, 11 July 1898, 1.

26. "Six Killed on the *Reina Merecedes*," *New York Journal*, 8 June 1898, 2; "Cervera Waits for the Blow that Will Crush Spain's Navy," *New York World*, 9 June 1898, 2.

27. Willis J. Abbot, *Watching the World Go By* (New York: Beekman, 1974), 141.

28. Creelman, *On the Great Highway*, 211–12; W. R. Hearst, "Journal's Editor Describes the Capture of El Caney," *New York Journal*, 4 July 1898, 1.

29. On Hearst blowing up the *Maine*, see, for example, Lundberg, *Imperial Hearst*, 81–82; Joyce Milton, *The Yellow Kids: Foreign Correspondents in the Heyday of Yellow Journalism* (New York: Harper & Row, 1989), 232–33. On Creelman's comments, see Creelman, *On the Great Highway*, 186.

30. Creelman, *On the Great Highway*, 160, 187; John K. Winkler, *W. R. Hearst* (New York: Simon and Schuster, 1928), 146; Richard Harding Davis, "Cervera's Fleet Smashed," *New York Journal*, 4 July 1898, 1; Joseph E. Wisan, *The Cuban Crisis as Reflected in the New York Press* (New York, 1934), 458–59.

31. Abbot, *Watching*, 217; W. R. Hearst, "The Importance of Union Among Newspapers," *New York Journal*, 25 September 1898, Editorial Section 1.

Chapter 6

1. David M. Chalmers, *The Social and Political Ideas of the Muckrakers* (New York: Citadel, 1964), 11.

2. Theodore Roosevelt first used the term "muckraker" in April 1906, referring to a passage from John Bunyan's allegorical novel *Pilgrim's Progress*.

3. Lincoln Steffens, "Tweed Days in St. Louis," *McClure's*, October 1902, 577.

4. Arthur M. Schlesinger, *Political and Social History of the United States, 1829–1925* (New York: Macmillan, 1925), 442.

5. Lincoln Steffens, *McClure's:* "The Shame of Minneapolis," January 1903, 227–39; "Pittsburgh: A City Ashamed," May 1903, 24–39; "Philadelphia: Corrupt and Contented," July 1903, 249–64; "Chicago: Half Free and Fighting On," October 1903, 563–77; "New York: Good Government in Danger," November 1903, 84–92; "Enemies of the Republic," April 1904, 587–99; "Enemies of the Republic," August 1904, 395–408; "Rhode Island: A State for Sale," February 1905, 337–53; "New Jersey: A Traitor State," April 1905, 649–64.

6. *McClure's:* "On the Making of McClure's Magazine," November 1904, 108, 110–11; William Allen White, "Editorial," June 1904, 221.

7. Lincoln Steffens, *The Shame of the Cities* (New York: Peter Smith, 1948).

8. Ida M. Tarbell, "The History of the Standard Oil Company," *McClure's*, November 1902, 3–16.

9. Ida M. Tarbell, "The Rise of the Standard Oil Company," *McClure's*, December 1902, 115.

10. Tarbell, *McClure's:* "The History of the Standard Oil Company," March 1903, 505–07; "The History of the Standard Oil Company: Part Two," March 1904, 497–98.

11. "On the Making of McClure's Magazine," *McClure's*, November 1904, 107–08.

12. H.E.G., Bradford, Pa, "From Other Readers," *McClure's*, June 1904, 224.

13. Tarbell, "History, Part Two," *McClure's*, April 1904, 651.

14. Ida M. Tarbell, *The History of the Standard Oil Company* (New York: McClure, Phillips, 1904).

15. "The Mother of Trusts," *Public Opinion*, 5 January 1905, 26; Louis Filler, *Crusaders for American Liberalism* (Yellow Springs, Ohio: Antioch, 1939), 109.

16. Ray Stannard Baker, *McClure's:* "The Railroad Rate," November 1905, 47–59; "Railroad Rebates," December 1905, 179–94; "Railroads on Trial," January 1906, 318–31; "Railroads on Trial," February 1906, 398–411; "Railroads on Trial," March 1906, 535–49; also, Daniel L. Cruice, "The Chicago Election," *Arena*, July 1904, 21–28; "Annual Net Earnings of State-owned Railroads," *Arena*, July 1904, 87; Josiah Flynt, "Telegraph and Telephone Companies as Allies of the Criminal Pool Rooms," *Cosmopolitan*, May 1907, 50–57; Eugene P. Lyle Jr., "The Guggenheims and the Smelter Trust," *Hampton's*, March 1910, 411–22; Judson C. Welliver, "The Mormon Church and the Sugar Trust," *Hampton's*, January 1910, 82–93; Judson C. Welliver, "The Annexation of Cuba by the Sugar Trust," *Hampton's*, March 1910, 375–88; Judson C. Welliver, "The Secret of the Sugar Trust's Power," *Hampton's*, May 1910, 717–22; Will Irwin, "Tainted New Methods of the Liquor Interests," *Collier's*, 13 March 1909, 27–31; Charles Edward Russell, "The Greatest Trust in the World," *Everybody's*, February 1905, 147–56.

17. Ray Stannard Baker, "The Right to Work," *McClure's*, January 1903, 323–36.

18. Baker, "Right," *McClure's*, January 1903, 329.

19. Ray Stannard Baker, "A Corner in Labor," *McClure's*, February 1904, 366.

20. "On the Making of McClure's Magazine," *McClure's*, November 1904, 108.

21. "Making of McClure's," *McClure's*, November 1904, 108.

22. Rheta Childe Dorr: "The Prodigal Daughter," *Hampton's*, April 1910, 534–35; "A Waitress's Story," *New York Evening Post*, 23 August 1905, 7; "The Wreck of the Home," *Hampton's*, November 1908, 546–47; *What Eight Million Women Want* (Boston: Small, Maynard, 1910).

23. Edwin Markham, "The Hoe-Man in the Making," *Cosmopolitan*, October 1906, 567, 569.

24. Markham, "The Hoe-Man in the Making," *Cosmopolitan*, September 1906, 487.

25. Arthur Weinberg and Lila Weinberg, *The Muckrakers* (New York: Simon and Schuster, 1961), 359.

26. Upton Sinclair, "The Jungle," *Appeal to Reason*, 29 April 1905, 2.

27. Upton Sinclair, "What Life Means to Me," *Cosmopolitan*, October 1906, 593; Filler, *Crusaders*, 163.

28. George Brown Tindall, *America: A Narrative History* (New York: W. W. Norton, 1984), 918–19.

29. Edward Bok, *Ladies' Home Journal*, May 1904, 18: "The 'Patent-Medicine' Curse"; "The Alcohol in 'Patent Medicines.'"

30. Mark Sullivan, *Collier's:* "The Patent Medicine Conspiracy Against Freedom of the Press," 4 November 1905, 15; "Will the 'Free' Press Free Itself?" 4 November 1905, 26.

31. "We Are Not So 'Holy,'" *Collier's*, 4 November 1905, 26; Edward Bok, "A Few Words to the W.C.T.U.," *Ladies' Home Journal*, September 1904, 16; "A Bold Paper," *Collier's*, 10 November 1906, 9.

32. Samuel Hopkins Adams, "The Great American Fraud," *Collier's*, 7 October 1905, 14.

33. Adams, "Fraud," *Collier's*, 7 October 1905, 14.

34. E. W. Kemble, "Death's Laboratory," *Collier's*, 3 June 1905, 5.

35. *Ladies' Home Journal:* "For the Safety of Yourself and Your Child," February 1906, 1; Edward Bok, "To You: A Personal Word," February 1906, 20.

36. See, for example, "Samuel Hopkins Adams Is Dead," *New York Times*, 17 November 1958, 31; Weinberg and Weinberg, *Muckrakers*, 206.

37. Tindall, *America*, 907.

38. David Graham Phillips, "Treason of the Senate," *Cosmopolitan*, March 1906, 488.

39. Phillips, "Treason," *Cosmopolitan*, March 1906, 489–90.

40. "Letters," *Cosmopolitan*, April 1906, 567.

41. Phillips, "Treason," *Cosmopolitan:* April 1906, 628–38; May 1906, 3–12; June 1906, 123–32; July 1906, 267–76; August 1906, 368–77; September 1906, 525–35; October 1906, 627–36.

42. *Cosmopolitan*, June 1906, cover.
43. David Graham Phillips, "The Treason of the Senate," *Cosmopolitan*, November 1906, 84.
44. Filler, *Crusaders*, 256–57.
45. Schlesinger, *Political and Social History*, 441.
46. Weinberg and Weinberg, *Muckrakers*, xx; C. C. Regier, *The Era of the Muckrakers* (Chapel Hill: University of North Carolina Press, 1932), 13; Vernon Parrington, *Main Currents in American Thought* (New York: Harcourt Brace, 1939), vol. III, 406; Chalmers, *Social and Political Ideas*, 115.
47. Thomas W. Lawson, "Frenzied Finance: The Story of Amalgamated," *Everybody's*: July 1904, 1–10; August 1904, 154–64; September 1904, 289–301; October 1904, 455–68; November 1904, 599–613; December 1904, 747–60; also, William Allen White, "Roosevelt and the Postal Frauds," *McClure's*, September 1904, 506–20; Mark Sullivan, "The People's One Hour in Two Years," *Collier's*, 13 March 1909, 10–11; Ellery Sedgwick, "The Land of Disasters," *Leslie's*, September 1904, 566–67; Ray Stannard Baker, "Following the Color Line," *American Magazine*, April 1907, 563–79; William English Walling, "The Race War in the North," *The Independent*, 3 September 1908, 529–34; Ida Husted Harper, "Susan B. Anthony," *Independent*, 22 March 1906, 676–82; Thomas Dixon Jr., "Is Christianity on the Decline?" *Hampton's*, May 1908, 149–53; Charles Edward Russell, "Trinity Corporation: A Riddle of Riches," *Hampton's*, May 1908, 187–95.
48. Max Lerner, "Introduction," in Louis Filler, *Randolph Bourne* (Washington, D.C.: American Council on Public Affairs, 1943), vi; Allan Nevins, *John D. Rockefeller* (New York: Scribner's, 1940), vol. II, 520–21.
49. "Do We Care?" *McClure's*, June 1904, 222; "The Literature of Exposure," *Independent*, 22 March 1906, 691; I.L.C., Madison, Wis., "From Business Men," *McClure's*, June 1904, 223.
50. Schlesinger, *Political and Social History*, 442.

Chapter 7

1. "Congressional Committee Told of Outrages by Ku Klux Klan," *New York World*, 12 October 1921, 2; Kenneth T. Jackson, *The Ku Klux Klan in the City: 1915–1930* (New York: Oxford University Press, 1967), 254.
2. "Ku Klux Klan Exposed!" *New York World*, 5 September 1921, 12.
3. Rowland Thomas, "Secrets of the Ku Klux Klan Exposed by the *World*," *New York World*, 6 September 1921, 1.
4. *New York World*: Rowland Thomas, "Holds Simmons Has Avowed Klan Aims to Restore Slavery," 13 October 1921, 2; Rowland Thomas, "The *World* Exposes Klan's Oath-Bound Secret Ritual and Ku Klux Tests of Racial and Religious Hate," 10 September 1921, 1; "Kleagles Peddle Membership; Grand Goblin Their District Boss," 9 September 1921, 1–2.
5. *New York World*: Rowland Thomas, "Ku Klux Questionnaire," 10 September 1921, 1; "Received by the *World* Yesterday," 6 September 1921, 1; "Threat Received by the *World*," 7 September 1921, 2.

6. Rowland Thomas, "Clarke and Mrs. Tyler Arrested While in House of Ill Repute," *New York World*, 19 September 1921, 1.

7. *New York World:* "U. S. Must Get Rid of Ku Klux Klan, Leaders in Nation's Life Insist," 9 September 1921, 2; "Enright Says Klan Won't Be Permitted to Operate in City," 9 September 1921, 1; "Aldermen Call Klan 'Masked Band of Criminal Lawbreakers,'" 12 October 1921, 2.

8. *New York World:* Rowland Thomas, "Ku Klux's Record of Atrocities Grows," 19 September 1921, 1; "152 Valid Objections," 19 September 1921, 1.

9. "U.S. Must Get Rid of Ku Klux, Leaders in Nation's Life Insist," *New York World*, 9 September 1921, 2; Irene Osgood Andrews letter; George Gordon Battle letter; Nathaniel Philips letter.

10. Robert M. Fogelson and Richard E. Rubenstein, eds., *Mass Violence in America: Hearings on the Ku Klux Klan, 1921* (New York: Arno Press, 1969), 4, 6–7.

11. Fogelson and Rubenstein, *Mass Violence*, 9.

12. Fogelson and Rubenstein, *Mass Violence*, 67.

13. Fogelson and Rubenstein, *Mass Violence*, 77.

14. Fogelson and Rubenstein, *Mass Violence*, 75.

15. Jackson, *Ku Klux Klan*, 12; David M. Chalmers, *Hooded Americanism: The History of the Ku Klux Klan* (Durham, N.C.: Duke University Press, 1987), 38.

16. Chalmers, *Hooded Americanism*, 198–99; Jackson, *Ku Klux Klan*, 11; John Hohenberg, ed., *The Pulitzer Prize Story* (New York: Columbia University Press, 1959), 336.

17. C.P.J. Mooney, "The Affair at Mer Rouge," *Commercial Appeal*, 17 March 1923, 4.

18. J. P. Alley, *Commercial Appeal:* "His 'noble work,' done in the dark!" 21 August 1923, 1; "No wonder he puts a sack over that mug!" 18 September 1923, 1; "I'm unworthy—my religion ain't right!" 28 August 1923, 1.

19. J. P. Alley, "The Trials of a Cartoonist," *Commercial Appeal*, 24 August 1923, 1.

20. *Commercial Appeal:* "Wizard Evans Silent While Kamelia Gains," 15 May 1923, 1; "Come Out in the Open, Challenge to Evans," 9 November 1923, 13; "Klan Boodle Campaign Laid to Evans Regime," 30 October 1923, 1.

21. C.P.J. Mooney, "The Illogical Emperor of an Invisible Empire," *Commercial Appeal*, 21 April 1923, 16.

22. "Election," *Tri-State American*, 7 November 1923, 1.

23. *Commercial Appeal:* "Eyes of Nation Turn to Memphis Election," 5 November 1923, 1; "Charge Klan Balked Mer Rouge Inquiry," 31 October 1923, 1; "Gov. Walker's Talk to Kluxes Quoted," 4 November 1923, 1; "Klan's Press Agent Kills Chief Lawyer of Simmons Faction; Bloody Climax in Klan Feud; 'I'm Glad He's Dead,'" 6 November 1923, 1; "Warrants for Arrest of Klan Wizard Evans and Advisors Issued," 7 November 1923, 1; "Victim and Slayer in Klan Blood-Feud," 8 November 1923, 1.

24. *Commercial Appeal*, 8 November 1923: C.P.J. Mooney, "The Off-Year Results," 6; C.P.J. Mooney, "As An Atlantic Monthly Reader Sees the Klan in

Oklahoma," 6; "Claims Klan Leaders Demanded Floggings," 1; "Evans Faces Grilling in Klan Feud Mystery," 1; "Victim and Slayer in Klan Blood-Feud," 1; "Which? The Men Who Wear The Hood or the Men Who Wore the Uniform?" 26.

25. J. P. Alley, "The Sinister Hand," *Commercial Appeal*, 8 November 1923, 1.

26. "Paine Wins Victory in Race for Mayor: Kluck Runs Second," *Commercial Appeal*, 9 November 1923, 1.

27. "100,000 Klansmen Go to Fort Wayne," *New York Times*, 10 November 1923, 15; Hohenberg, *Pulitzer Prize*, 336.

28. Grover Cleveland Hall, "Imperial Jefferson Flogs a Helpless Negro," *Montgomery Advertiser*, 14 July 1927, 4.

29. Grover Cleveland Hall, "Unmask!" *Montgomery Advertiser*, 14 July 1927, 4.

30. Reprinted from *Alabama Christian Advocate* in Grover Cleveland Hall, "The Comic Gyrations of 'Fraid Cat Editors," *Montgomery Advertiser*, 31 July 1927, 4; reprinted from *Monroe Journal* as "The Advertiser and the Weekly Press," *Montgomery Advertiser*, 23 July 1927, 4; reprinted from *Monroe Journal* as "Lawlessness and the Press," *Montgomery Advertiser*, 16 July 1927, 4; reprinted from *Evergreen Courant* in Hall, "Comic Gyrations," *Montgomery Advertiser*, 31 July 1927, 4.

31. Reprinted from *New York Herald Tribune* as "As Ye Sow," *Montgomery Advertiser*, 21 July 1927, 4; reprinted from *Milwaukee Journal* as "'Chivalry' in the South," *Montgomery Advertiser*, 22 July 1927, 4; reprinted from *New York Times* as "Alabama Law Enforcement," *Montgomery Advertiser*, 15 July 1927, 4.

32. *Montgomery Advertiser:* "Fifteen Persons Jailed in Lash Probe," 20 July 1927, 1; Grover Cleveland Hall, "Alabama's Good Name Vindicated," 5 August 1927, 4; "Clayton Gets 8 to 10 Years as Flogger," 7 August 1927, 1; Grover Cleveland Hall, "The Knell of Barbarism in Alabama," 8 August 1927, 4.

33. Grover Cleveland Hall, "A Shameless Speech for a Sinister Measure," *Montgomery Advertiser*, 21 July 1927, 4.

34. Grover Cleveland Hall, *Montgomery Advertiser:* "The State of Silent Treads Threatened with a Silent Press," 21 August 1927, 4; "The Klan Would Strike Down a Free and Untrammeled Press in Alabama!" 20 August 1927, 4.

35. "Press Muzzling Bill Defeated in House," *Montgomery Advertiser*, 24 August 1927, 1.

36. Hohenberg, *Pulitzer Prize*, 348.

37. Henry P. Fry, *The Modern Ku Klux Klan* (New York: Negro Universities Press, 1922), 247; "100,000 Klansmen Go to Fort Wayne," *New York Times*, 10 November 1923, 15; Chalmers, *Hooded Americanism*, 78–82.

38. Chalmers, *Hooded Americanism*, 38; Jackson, *Ku Klux Klan*, 12.

39. Hohenberg, *Pulitzer Prize*, 71; Silas Bent, *Newspaper Crusaders: A Neglected Story* (Freeport, N.Y.: Books for Libraries, 1939), 138, 154.

Chapter 8

1. Martin Ostrow, producer, *America and the Holocaust: Deceit and Indifference* (Alexandria, Va.: Public Broadcasting Service, 1994).

2. "Communism Is Jewish," *American-Ranger*, August 1938, 1; "Jews Defile Our Christmas!" *National American*, 31 October 1935, 1.

3. Charles E. Coughlin, radio broadcast delivered 14 February 1932, excerpts of which were reprinted in David H. Bennett, *Demagogues in the Depression: American Radicals and the Union Party, 1932–1936* (New Brunswick, N.J.: Rutgers University Press, 1969), 34.

4. Sheldon Marcus, *Father Coughlin: The Tumultuous Life of the Priest of the Little Flower* (Boston: Little, Brown, 1973), 34.

5. Alan Brinkley, *Voices of Protest: Huey Long, Father Coughlin, and the Great Depression* (New York: Knopf, 1982), 97; Wallace Stegner, "The Radio Priest and His Flock," in Isabel Leighton, ed., *The Aspirin Age: 1919–1941* (New York: Simon and Schuster), 234; Marcus, *Tumultuous Life*, 37, 222.

6. "Smith Denounces Coughlin's Charge of Link to Morgan," *New York Times*, 29 November 1933, 1.

7. Charles E. Coughlin, "The National Union for Social Justice," radio broadcast delivered 11 November 1934 and reprinted in *A Series of Lectures on Social Justice* (Royal Oak, Mich.: Radio League of the Little Flower, 1935), 7.

8. "Coughlin Asserts America 'Retains Her Sovereignty,'" *New York Times*, 30 January 1935, 2; "Senate Beats World Court, 52–36, 7 Less Than 2/3 Vote; Defeat for the President," *New York Times*, 30 January 1935, 1; Arthur Krock, "Defeat for Court a Roosevelt Upset," *New York Times*, 30 January 1935, 1; Elliott Roosevelt, ed., *F.D.R.: His Personal Letters, 1928–1945* (New York: Duell, Sloan and Pearce, 1950), vol. I, 45.

9. The first issue of *Social Justice* was published in March 1936.

10. T.R.B., "Coughlin Calls the Tune," *New Republic*, 3 June 1936, 100–01.

11. Charles E. Coughlin, "Driving Out the Money Changers," radio broadcast delivered between 1 January and 16 April 1933 and reprinted in *Driving Out the Money Changers* (Royal Oak, Mich.: Radio League of the Little Flower, 1933), 56, 58, 60; "Father Coughlin on the Jewish Question," *Social Justice*, 31 August 1936, 2.

12. "Gentile Silver," *Nation*, 9 May 1934, 522; E. Francis Brown, "Three 'Pied Pipers' of the Depression," 17 March 1935, *New York Times Magazine*, 3, 20.

13. "Coughlin: Thousands Salute Their Leader and Swear Fealty," *Newsweek*, 22 August 1936, 12.

14. "Spellman Warned on Christian Front," *New York Times*, 26 September 1939, 24.

15. Charles E. Coughlin, "From the Tower: 'The Protocols of Zion,'" *Social Justice*, 18 July 1938, 5.

16. Coughlin, "From the Tower: 'The Protocols of Zion,'" *Social Justice*, 18 July 1938, 5.

17. Charles E. Coughlin, *Social Justice:* "From the Tower: 'The Protocols of Zion,'" 18 July 1938, 5; "From the Tower: 'Protocols of the Wise Men of Zion,'" 8 August 1938, 5.

18. Coughlin, *Social Justice:* "From the Tower: 'Protocols of the Wise Men of Zion,'" 8 August 1938, 5; "The Fifth Protocol," 29 August 1938, 5.

19. *Detroit Free Press:* "Dr. Wise Scores Coughlin Charges," 5 December 1938, 2; "Ford Statement Was Authorized," 5 December 1938, 1.

20. Charles E. Coughlin, "Persecution—Jewish and Christian," radio broadcast delivered 20 November 1938 and reprinted in *Am I an Anti-Semite?* (Royal Oak, Mich.: Radio League of the Little Flower, 1939), 37, 39.

21. *New York Times:* "WMCA Contradicts Coughlin on Jews," 21 November 1938, 7; "Priest Won't Meet WMCA Conditions," 27 November 1938, 42.

22. Charles E. Coughlin, "Let Us Consider the Record," radio broadcast delivered 27 November 1938 and reprinted in *Am I an Anti-Semite?* 62; United States Treasury Department Press Release No. 15–45 dated 28 November 1938.

23. "WMCA Contradicts Coughlin on Jews," *New York Times,* 21 November 1938, 7.

24. Charles E. Coughlin, *Social Justice:* "The Birth of a Corporate State," 1 August 1938, 3; "From the Tower," 25 April 1938, 4.

25. "Coughlin Answered by Catholic Layman," *Detroit News,* 12 December 1938, 1.

26. The letter was dated 11 April 1939 and is reproduced in Marcus, *Tumultuous Life,* 171.

27. "Catholic 'Worker' in Smear Campaign," *Social Justice,* 22 May 1939, 15; "Anti-Semitism Is Part of the Coughlin Campaign," *Christian Century,* 24 May 1939, 661.

28. Charles E. Coughlin, "I Know Three Germanies," *Social Justice,* 7 December 1936, 5; "Coughlin Denounces 'Mongerers of War,'" *New York Times,* 27 March 1939, 7.

29. Charles E. Coughlin, radio broadcast delivered 30 July 1939, excerpts of which were reprinted in Donald S. Strong, *Organized Anti-Semitism in America: The Rise of Group Prejudice During the Decade 1930–40* (Washington, D.C.: American Council on Public Affairs, 1941), 66.

30. "Ninfo Son, on Fast, Jailed for 75 Days," *New York Times,* 26 September 1939, 24.

31. Marcus, *Tumultuous Life,* 176.

32. "New Radio Code Hits Coughlin," *Detroit News,* 4 October 1939, 1.

33. "Federal Officials Prepare 'Front' Case," *New York Times,* 18 January 1940, 3.

34. Charles E. Coughlin, "I Take My Stand," *Social Justice,* 29 January 1940, 4. The seventeen men ultimately were not convicted.

35. "Abraham Lincoln and Rothschilds," *Social Justice,* 12 February 1940, 8.

36. "Comment: No Coughlin Broadcast," *Social Justice,* 23 September 1940, 4.

37. M. G., "Avoid Fights," *Social Justice*, 22 May 1939, 2; John Roy Carlson, *Undercover* (New York: Dutton, 1943), 251.

38. "Comment: Who Started the 'Sacred' War?—and When? Mr. Untermeyer Answers the Question," *Social Justice*, 16 March 1942, 3.

39. "Text of the Dep't of Justice Coughlin Document," *In Fact*, 11 February 1946, 2.

40. "Coughlin Weekly Ends Publication," *New York Times*, 5 May 1942, 23.

41. "Coughlin Weekly Ends Publication," *New York Times*, 5 May 1942, 23.

42. "Calm for a Stormy Priest," *Life*, 14 November 1955, 119.

43. "Father Coughlin," *Fortune*, February 1934, 34; "Catholic 'Worker' in Smear Campaign," *Social Justice*, 22 May 1939, 15.

44. Bennett, *Demagogues*, 79.

45. Marcus, *Tumultuous Life*, 37.

Chapter 9

1. *Saturday Evening Post*, 29 May 1943, cover; U.S. Department of Labor, Bureau of Labor Statistics, *Handbook of Labor Statistics*, bulletin 916 (Washington, D.C.: Government Printing Office, 1947).

2. Among the works that argue World War II did not have permanent impact on women's rate of employment is Leila J. Rupp, *Mobilizing Women for War: German and American Propaganda, 1939–1945* (Princeton: Princeton University Press, 1978), especially 176. Dorothy Thompson, "Women and the Coming World," *Ladies' Home Journal*, October 1943, 6.

3. "Cherchez la Femme," *Business Week*, 25 September 1943, 108.

4. "Recruiting by Air," *Business Week*, 10 July 1943, 115.

5. Elizabeth Gordon, "Needed: 50,000 Nurses," *New York Times Magazine*, 12 April 1942, 10; Nona Baldwin, "Woman Mans the Machine," *New York Times Magazine*, 23 August 1942, 8; Mary Kelly, "Calling All Women," *Christian Science Monitor*, 27 May 1944, 3; Josephine Ripley, "It's Woman's Day Right Now," *Christian Science Monitor*, 23 October 1943, 7; "Output: Ladies Welcome," *Newsweek*, 30 November 1942, 56; "More Women Must Go to Work as 3,200,000 New Jobs Beckon," *Newsweek*, 6 September 1943, 74; "Nightingales Needed," *Time*, 28 December 1942, 55; "The Ladies!" *Time*, 26 January 1942, 61; "The Margin Now Is Womanpower," *Fortune*, February 1943, 99; Paul V. McNutt, "Why You Must Take a War Job," *American Magazine*, December 1943, 100.

6. Maxwell S. Stewart, "Shall We Draft Women?" *Nation*, 25 April 1942, 484.

7. "The Margin Now Is Womanpower," *Fortune*, February 1943, 99.

8. Frank S. Adams, "Women in Democracy's Arsenal," *New York Times Magazine*, 19 October 1941, 10.

9. Gordon, "Needed: 50,000 Nurses," *New York Times Magazine*, 12 April 1942, 10.

10. Mary Hornaday, "From French Heels to Slacks," *Christian Science Monitor Weekly Magazine*, 27 June 1942, 5; Ripley, "It's Woman's Day Right Now," *Christian Science Monitor*, 23 October 1943, 7.

11. Elinore M. Herrick, "With Women at Work, the Factory Changes," *New York Times Magazine*, 24 January 1943, 4; Adams, "Women in Democracy's Arsenal," *New York Times Magazine*, 19 October 1941, 29; Sally Reston, "Girls' Town—Washington," *New York Times Magazine*, 23 November 1941, 8–9.

12. "Civilian Defense," *Time*, 26 January 1942, 61; "Girls in Uniform," *Life*, 6 July 1942, 41; "Glory Girls," *American Magazine*, March 1942, 83.

13. "Ladies of Washington's Working Press," *Newsweek*, 1 March 1943, 64.

14. "Ladies of Washington's Working Press," *Newsweek*, 1 March 1943, 64; "Skirted," *Time*, 13 March 1944, 83.

15. "Output: Ladies Welcome," *Newsweek*, 30 November 1942, 56; "Females in Factories," *Time*, 17 July 1944, 60; Elizabeth Hawes, "Do Women Workers Get an Even Break?" *New York Times Magazine*, 19 November 1944, 13.

16. Herrick, "With Women at Work, the Factory Changes," *New York Times Magazine*, 24 January 1943, 34.

17. William H. Chafe, *The American Woman: Her Changing Social, Economic, and Political Roles, 1920–1970* (New York: Oxford University Press, 1972), 146–47.

18. *Business Week:* "Women—Now!" 9 January 1943, 72–73; "Manless Industry," 10 March 1945, 41.

19. "Woman's Place," *Business Week*, May 1942, 20; Herrick, "With Women at Work, the Factory Changes," *New York Times Magazine*, 24 January 1943, 34.

20. Elizabeth Hawes, "Woman War Worker: A Case History," *New York Times Magazine*, 21 December 1943, 9.

21. Hawes, "War Worker," *New York Times Magazine*, 21 December 1943, 9.

22. Hawes, "War Worker," *New York Times Magazine*, 21 December 1943, 9.

23. *Christian Science Monitor:* Hornaday, "From French Heels to Slacks," 27 June 1942, 4; Ripley, "It's Woman's Day Right Now," 23 October 1943, 7.

24. *American Magazine:* Steve King, "Danger! Women at Work," September 1942, 117; "Amazons of Aberdeen," January 1943, 98–99.

25. "Women in Forestry," *New York Times Magazine*, 4 October 1942, 31; Mary Chute, "They Wear Wings of Paratroopers," *Christian Science Monitor*, 20 January 1945, 8; "Daughters for Harvard," *Time*, 9 October 1944, 90.

26. "Output: Ladies Welcome," *Newsweek*, 30 November 1942, 54.

27. *Opportunity:* George E. DeMar, "Negro Women Are American Workers, Too," April 1943, 41; Mabel Keaton Staupers, "The Negro Nurse," November 1942, 332; "Negro Women Employed for First Time by Washington Navy Yard," April 1943, 79; Mary Anderson, "Negro Women on the Production Front," April 1943, 37.

28. Margaret Bourke-White, "Women in Lifeboats," *Life*, 22 February 1943, 49.

29. Bourke-White, "Women in Lifeboats," *Life*, 22 February 1943, 48.

30. Margaret Bourke-White, "Women in Steel," *Life*, 9 August 1943, 76, 79.

31. "Girls in Uniform," *Life*, 6 July 1942, 41–43.

32. "Females in Factories," *Time*, 17 July 1944, 60; "Women at Work," *Newsweek*, 5 January 1942, 36; Anderson, "Negro Women on the Production Front," *Opportunity*, April 1943, 37, 38; Amy Lyon Schaeffer, "She Works in an Arms Plant," *New York Times Magazine*, 12 April 1942, 9; Baldwin, "Woman Mans the Machine," *New York Times Magazine*, 23 August 1942, 8; Herrick, "With Women at Work, the Factory Changes," *New York Times Magazine*, 24 January 1943, 4.

33. On scholars seeing the American media's influence as central to changing women's role in society, see, for example, Karen Anderson, *Wartime Women: Sex Roles, Family Relations, and the Status of Women During World War II* (Westport, Conn.: Greenwood, 1981), especially 27–28, 60–61; Carol Berkin and Mary Beth Norton, *Women of America: A History* (Boston: Houghton Mifflin, 1979), 344; Chafe, *American Woman*, 146–47; Sherna Berger Gluck, *Rosie the Riveter Revisited: Women, the War and Social Change* (Boston: Twayne, 1987), especially pages 15–16; Susan M. Hartmann, *The Home Front and Beyond: American Women in the 1940s* (Boston: Twayne, 1982), especially 189, 210–11; Maureen Honey, *Creating Rosie the Riveter: Class, Gender, and Propaganda During World War II* (Amherst: University of Massachusetts Press, 1984), especially 12–14; Susan Mathis, "Propaganda to Mobilize Women for World War II," *Social Education*, February 1994, 94–96; Rupp, *Mobilizing Women*, especially 137–65; Mary Martha Thomas, *Riveting and Rationing in Dixie: Alabama Women and the Second World War* (Tuscaloosa: University of Alabama Press, 1987), 23–24; Doris Weatherford, *American Women and World War II* (New York: Facts on File, 1990), especially 116–17. For the specific quotations, see Chafe, *American Woman*, 146–47; Rupp, *Mobilizing Women*, 165; Hartmann, *Home Front*, 189.

Chapter 10

1. Frank Desmond, "M'Carthy Charges Reds Hold U.S. Jobs," *Wheeling Intelligencer*, 10 February 1950, 1. McCarthy based the 205 figure on a letter that Secretary of State James Byrnes had written to a congressman in 1946. In the letter, Byrnes stated that after the war, 3,000 workers had been transferred to the State Department. After being subjected to preliminary examination, 284 of them were recommended for dismissal for various reasons such as frequent absences from work and lack of dependability. Of this number, seventy-nine were fired, although no comment was made about them being communists or even security risks. Nevertheless, McCarthy subtracted the seventy-nine fired workers from the 284 identified and came up with the idea that 205 communists were still working in the State Department.

2. Edwin R. Bayley, *Joe McCarthy and the Press* (New York: Pantheon, 1981), 8, 67, 69–70.

3. Bayley, *McCarthy and the Press*, 70.

4. Bayley, *McCarthy and the Press*, 71.

5. Bayley, *McCarthy and the Press*, 67, 68.

6. Bayley, *McCarthy and the Press*, 68–69.

7. Hugh Greene in "Good Night and Good Luck" (1975 British Broadcasting Corporation production), distributed by Instructional Media Services, Washington State University; Gary Paul Gates, *Air Time: The Inside Story of CBS News* (New York: Harper & Row, 1978), 13; Archibald MacLeish, "To Ed Murrow, Reporter," *Journal of Home Economics* 34 (1942), 361.

8. Alexander Kendrick, *Prime Time: The Life of Edward R. Murrow* (Boston: Little, Brown, 1969), 4; A. William Bluem, *Documentary in American Television* (New York: Hastings House, 1970), 99–100; Christopher H. Sterling and John M. Kitross, *Stay Tuned: A Concise History of American Broadcasting*, 2nd ed., (Belmont, Calif.: Wadsworth, 1990), 657–58.

9. *New York Times*, 20 October 1953, B-21.

10. "The Case of Milo Radulovich, A0589839," *See It Now*, 20 October 1953. Transcripts of the *See It Now* programs are held in the Edward R. Murrow Papers, Edwin Ginn Library, Fletcher School of Law and Diplomacy, Tufts University, Medford, Massachusetts.

11. "Radulovich," *See It Now*, 20 October 1953.

12. "Radulovich," *See It Now*, 20 October 1953.

13. "Eyes of Conscience: 'See It Now,'" *Newsweek*, 7 December 1953, 65–66; "Edward R. Murrow, or the 'See' Around Us," *Variety*, 6 January 1954, 196; Jack Gould, "Video Journalism: Treatment of Radulovich Case History by 'See It Now' Is Fine Reporting," *New York Times*, 25 October 1953, B-13.

14. Fred W. Friendly, *Due To Circumstances Beyond Our Control . . .* (New York: Random House, 1967), 18.

15. Laurence Bergreen, *Look Now, Pay Later: The Rise of Network Broadcasting* (Garden City, N.Y.: Doubleday, 1980), 186.

16. *New York Times*, 9 March 1954, A-34.

17. "A Report on Senator Joseph R. McCarthy," *See It Now*, 9 March 1954.

18. "McCarthy," *See It Now*, 9 March 1954.

19. "McCarthy," *See It Now*, 9 March 1954.

20. Bergreen, *Look Now*, 187; Gilbert Seldes, "Murrow, McCarthy and the Empty Formula," *Saturday Review*, 24 April 1954, 26; "Salute to a Brave Man," *New York Herald Tribune*, 12 March 1954, 19.

21. Val Adams, "Praise Pours in on Murrow Show," *New York Times*, 11 March 1954, A-12.

22. Philip Hamburger, "Man from Wisconsin," *New Yorker*, 20 March 1954, 71; "TV in Controversy," *Newsweek*, 22 March 1954, 50; "Tele Review," *Variety*, 17 March 1954, 14; "Murrow Wins the Nation's Applause," *Broadcasting* 46 (15 March 1954), 7.

23. John Crosby, "McCarthy and the Networks," *New York Herald Tribune*, 11 March 1954, A-18; "When Television Came of Age," *St. Louis Post-Dispatch*, 21 March 1954, E-2.

24. Jack Gould, "TV and McCarthy: Network's Decision and Murrow Show Represent Advance for Medium," *New York Times*, 14 March 1954, X-13; Jack Gould, "Murrow Versus McCarthy," *New York Times*, 11 March 1954, B-38; "The Scorched Air: Murrow Versus Senator McCarthy," *Newsweek*, 22 March 1954, 89.

25. On scholars identifying the broadcast as the most important news program in history, see, for example, Fred J. Cook, *The Nightmare Decade: The Life and Times of Senator Joe McCarthy* (New York: Random House, 1971), 497; Kendrick, *Prime Time*, 4; Daniel J. Leab, "'See It Now': A Legend Reassessed," in John E. O'Connor, ed., *American History/American Television: Interpreting the Video Past* (New York: Frederick Ungar, 1983), 26; Thomas Rosteck, *See It Now Confronts McCarthyism* (Tuscaloosa: University of Alabama Press, 1994), 113; Gilbert Seldes, *The Public Arts* (New York: Simon and Schuster, 1956), 226. On historians extolling the program's impact on McCarthy, see, for example, George N. Gordon, *The Communications Revolution: A History of Mass Media in the United States* (New York: Hastings House, 1977), 270–71; Kendrick, *Prime Time*, 53–54; Michael D. Murray, "The Persuasive Dimensions of See It Now's 'Report on Senator Joseph R. McCarthy,'" *Today's Speech* 22 (1975), 18; Rosteck, *See It Now*, 134–35; Seldes, *Public Arts*, 226. For the specific quotations, see Rosteck, *See It Now*, 134–35; Seldes, *Public Arts*, 226; Murray, "Persuasive Dimensions," 18; Gordon, *Communications Revolution*, 270–71.

26. Jack Gould, "Public Service," *New York Times*, 13 June 1954, X-11.

27. Gould, "Public Service," *New York Times*, 13 June 1954, X-11.

28. Michael Straight, *Trial by Television* (Boston: Beacon, 1954), 249.

29. Straight, *Trial by Television*, 251.

30. Straight, *Trial by Television*, 251.

31. Straight, *Trial by Television*, 252.

32. Straight, *Trial by Television*, 253.

33. James Reston, "On McCarthy," *New York Times*, 30 May 1954, X-9.

34. Bayley, *McCarthy and the Press*, 209; Erik Barnouw, *Tube of Plenty: The Evolution of American Television* (New York: Oxford University Press, 1975), 182; Richard M. Fried, *Nightmare in Red: The McCarthy Era in Perspective* (New York: Oxford University Press, 1990), 138; Roy L. Cohn, *McCarthy* (New York: New American Library, 1968), 204.

35. Fried, *Nightmare in Red*, 138.

36. Barnouw, *Tube of Plenty*, 183; Bayley, *McCarthy and the Press*, 209.

37. On television playing a central role in destroying McCarthy, see, for example, Barnouw, *Tube of Plenty*, 182; Bayley, *McCarthy and the Press*, x; Raymond L. Carroll, "Factual Television in America: An Analysis of Network Television Documentary Programs, 1948–1975," Ph.D. dissertation, University of Wisconsin (Madison), 1978, 101; Michael D. Murray, *The Political Performers: CBS Broadcasts in the Public Interest* (Westport, Conn.: Praeger, 1994), 73. For the specific quotations, see Murray, *Political Performers*, 73; Barnouw, *Tube of Plenty*, 182; Carroll, "Factual Television," 101.

Chapter 11

1. The Supreme Court announced its *Brown vs. Board of Education of Topeka* decision on 17 May 1963.

2. On journalists discussing the vital role that television played in the Civil Rights Movement, see, for example, Joseph L. Brechner, "Were Broadcasters Color Blind?" in Paul L. Fisher and Ralph L. Lowenstein, eds., *Race and the News Media* (New York: Praeger, 1967), 100–01; William J. Drummond, "About Face: Blacks and the News Media," *American Enterprise*, July/August 1990, 24–26; Edward Jay Epstein, *News From Nowhere* (New York: Random House, 1973), 219, 225; David Halberstam, "Live from Little Rock," *Washington Post*, 16 May 1993, C-1; Robert E. Kintner, "Televising the Real World," *Harper's*, June 1965, 95; Robert MacNeil, *The People Machine: The Influence of Television on American Politics* (New York: Harper & Row, 1968), 71; Jack Lyle, ed., *The Black American and the Press* (Los Angeles: Ward Ritchie, 1968), 41–42; William B. Monroe Jr., "Television: The Chosen Instrument of Revolution," in Paul L. Fisher and Ralph L. Lowenstein, eds., *Race and the News Media* (New York: Praeger, 1967), 84, 89; William Peters, "The Visible and Invisible Images," in Paul L. Fisher and Ralph L. Lowenstein, eds., *Race and the News Media* (New York: Praeger, 1967), 81–82, 89, 97; James Reston, "Washington: The Rising Spirit of Protest," *New York Times*, 19 March 1965, 34; William Small, *To Kill a Messenger* (New York: Hastings House, 1970), 3, 43–44; *Television*, Public Broadcasting System, aired on Washington, D.C., station WETA, 15 February 1988; Mary Ann Watson, *The Expanding Vista: American Television in the Kennedy Years* (New York: Oxford University Press, 1990), 94; William A. Wood, *Electronic Journalism* (New York: Columbia University Press, 1967), 106. On scholars praising the role that broadcast journalism played in the Civil Rights Movement, see, for example, Ben H. Bagdikian, *The Information Machines* (New York: Harper & Row, 1971), 16; Epstein, *News From Nowhere*, 9; Amitai Etzioni, *Demonstration Democracy* (New York: Gordon and Breach, 1970), 12–13; David J. Garrow, *Protest at Selma* (New Haven, Conn.: Yale University Press, 1978), 163; Todd Gitlin, *The Whole World Is Watching* (Berkeley: University of California Press, 1980), 243; Samuel Huntington, *American Politics: The Promise of Disharmony* (Cambridge, Mass.: Harvard University Press, 1981), 205; Benjamin Muse, *The American Negro Revolution* (Bloomington: Indiana University Press, 1968), 102; Gary Orfield, *The Reconstruction of Southern Education* (New York: Wiley-Interscience, 1969), 33, 265, 309; Michael J. Robinson, "Television and American Politics: 1956–1976," *Public Interest* 48 (Summer 1977), 12–13; Bayard Rustin, *Strategies For Freedom* (New York: Columbia University Press, 1976), 44–45; *Television*, Public Broadcasting System, aired on Washington, D.C., station WETA, 15 February 1988; Wood, *Electronic Journalism*, 89, 101–06. For specific quotations, see Wood, *Electronic Journalism*, 105, 106; Peters, "Visible and Invisible," 81; Rustin, *Strategies*, 44–45.

3. Because the television networks did not record the film shown on their newscasts during the late 1950s and early 1960s, it is impossible to identify the specific date or network on which particular images were shown. All footage referred to in this chapter appeared on ABC, CBS, or NBC between 1957 and 1965. That footage can be viewed on one or more of three sources: *Dateline Freedom: Civil Rights and the Press*, Public Broadcasting System,

aired on Washington, D.C., station WETA, 18 January 1989; *Television*, Public Broadcasting System, aired on Washington, D.C., station WETA, 15 February 1988; *A Time For Justice* (video) (Washington, D.C.: Guggenheim Productions, 1992).

4. Monroe, "Television," 84.

5. *Dateline Freedom*, Public Broadcasting System.

6. Watson, *Expanding Vista*, 95; *Dateline Freedom*, Public Broadcasting System.

7. *Dateline Freedom*, Public Broadcasting System.

8. *Dateline Freedom*, Public Broadcasting System.

9. Interview with Ethel L. Payne by Kathleen Currie, Women in Journalism oral history project of the Washington Press Club Foundation, 25 August 1987 through 17 November 1987, Oral History Collection, Columbia University, 127.

10. *Dateline Freedom*, Public Broadcasting System.

11. The first day of classes was 4 September 1957. On Little Rock coverage, see Brechner, "Were Broadcasters," 99; Garrow, *Protest at Selma*, 166; Halberstam, "Live from Little Rock," C-1; Kintner, "Televising," 95; MacNeil, *People Machine*, 8; Orfield, *Reconstruction*, 1; Watson, *Expanding Vista*, 90–91; Wood, *Electronic Journalism*, 18.

12. *A Time For Justice*, Guggenheim.

13. *Dateline Freedom*, Public Broadcasting System. The black students entered the school for the first time 25 September 1957.

14. *A Time For Justice*, Guggenheim.

15. On television coverage of university desegregation crises, see Garrow, *Protest at Selma*, 144; Gary Paul Gates, *Air Time: The Inside Story of CBS News* (New York: Harper & Row, 1978), 292; MacNeil, *People Machine*, 306; Muse, *Negro Revolution*, 6–7; Watson, *Expanding Vista*, 57, 95–98, 103, 145; Wood, *Electronic Journalism*, 99.

16. Charlayne Hunter-Gault, "We Overcame Too," *TV Guide*, 17 January 1987, 34.

17. Claude Sitton, "Georgia Students Riot on Campus; Two Negroes Out," *New York Times*, 12 January 1961, 1.

18. On coverage of the Freedom Riders, see Small, *To Kill*, 43; Arthur I. Waskow, *From Race Riot to Sit-In* (Garden City, N.Y.: Doubleday, 1966), 231–32; Watson, *Expanding Vista*, 92–93; Wood, *Electronic Journalism*, 99.

19. *A Time For Justice*, Guggenheim. The first two buses left Washington, D.C., on 4 May 1961.

20. *A Time For Justice*, Guggenheim.

21. *A Time For Justice*, Guggenheim.

22. On television coverage of the Birmingham crisis, see Erik Barnouw, *The Image Empire: Broadcasting in the United States* (New York: Oxford University Press, 1970), 220; Michael Dorman, *We Shall Overcome* (New York: Delacorte, 1964), 150; Garrow, *Protest at Selma*, 2–3, 136–44, 167; Gitlin, *Whole World*, 243; MacNeil, *People Machine*, 70–71; Muse, *Negro Revolution*, 5–6, 26–27; Small, *To Kill*, 45; Waskow, *From Race Riot*, 233–36, 238; Watson, *Expanding Vista*, 101–02.

23. The pickets and sit-ins began on 3 April 1963.

24. The protest began including children on 2 May 1963.

25. Garrow, *Protest at Selma*, 139.

26. Orfield, *Reconstruction*, 33; Garrow, *Protest at Selma*, 141; *A Time For Justice*, Guggenheim.

27. Garrow, *Protest at Selma*, 167–68; Waskow, *From Race Riot*, 234.

28. "Outrage in Alabama," *New York Times*, 5 May 1963, E-10.

29. The agreement was announced on 10 May 1963.

30. Watson, *Expanding Vista*, 105.

31. On television coverage of the March on Washington, see Erik Barnouw, *Tube of Plenty: The Evolution of American Television* (New York: Oxford University Press, 1990), 324–25; Bill Gold, "March Provided Unequaled TV Show," *Washington Post*, 29 August 1963, D-16; Bill Greeley, "TV's 'Great Coverage of Great Event' Citation on D.C. March," *Variety*, 4 September 1963, 25; Paul L. Fisher and Ralph L. Lowenstein, eds., *Race and the News Media* (New York: Praeger, 1967), 157; Small, *To Kill*, 45; Watson, *Expanding Vista*, 106–09.

32. Gold, "March Provided Unequaled TV Show," D-16; Greeley, "TV's 'Great Coverage of Great Event,'" 25.

33. Muse, *Negro Revolution*, 16.

34. Wood, *Electronic Journalism*, 100; Jack Gould, "N.B.C. Devotes Three Hours to Civil Rights," *New York Times*, 3 September 1963, 67. *The American Revolution of '63* aired on 2 September 1963.

35. Wood, *Electronic Journalism*, 100.

36. Watson, *Expanding Vista*, 110.

37. Kintner, "Televising," 94.

38. Watson, *Expanding Vista*, 110.

39. Val Adams, "Reaction to a Cancellation," *New York Times*, 14 November 1963, 71; "Stanton Raps House Probe into Web Coverage of Civil Rights Issue," *Variety*, 3 July 1963, 20.

40. The bomb exploded on 15 September 1963.

41. *A Time For Justice*, Guggenheim.

42. On television coverage of the voter registration campaign, see Brechner, "Were Broadcasters," 99; Garrow, *Protest at Selma*, 163; MacNeil, *People Machine*, 70–71; Muse, *Negro Revolution*, 163–73; Orfield, *Reconstruction*, 265; Reston, "Washington," 34; Edwin Newman, *Television*, Public Broadcasting System, 15 February 1988.

43. *Television*, Public Broadcasting System.

44. Muse, *Negro Revolution*, 166.

45. *Television*, Public Broadcasting System.

46. *Television*, Public Broadcasting System.

47. *Television*, Public Broadcasting System.

48. Muse, *Negro Revolution*, 168.

49. Muse, *Negro Revolution*, 169.

50. *Television*, Public Broadcasting System; Monroe, "Television," 89; Lyle, *Black American*, 42.

51. Orfield, *Reconstruction*, 33; *Television*, Public Broadcasting System.

Chapter 12

1. See, for example, Erik Barnouw, *Tube of Plenty: The Evolution of American Television* (New York: Oxford University Press, 1975), 401; Sam Brown, "The Defeat of the Antiwar Movement," in Anthony Lake, ed., *The Vietnam Legacy: The War, American Society and the Future of American Foreign Policy* (New York: New York University Press, 1976), 122; Robert Elegant, "How to Lose a War," *Encounter*, August 1981, 78; Edward Jay Epstein, *Between Fact and Fiction* (New York: Vintage, 1975), 232; Edward Jay Epstein, *News from Nowhere: Television and the News* (New York: Random House, 1973), 9; Martin Esslin, *The Age of Television* (San Francisco: W. H. Freeman, 1982), 74; David J. Garrow, *Protest at Selma* (New Haven, Conn.: Yale University Press, 1978), 294; Philip Geyelin, "Vietnam and the Press: Limited War and an Open Society," in Anthony Lake, ed., *The Vietnam Legacy: The War, American Society and the Future of American Foreign Policy* (New York: New York University Press, 1976), 178; George N. Gordon, *The Communications Revolution: A History of Mass Media in the United States* (New York: Hastings House, 1977), 226, 315–16; Bob Greene, "How Do You Fight a War with TV Looking On?" *Los Angeles Times*, 13 April 1982, B–5; David Halberstam, *The Powers That Be* (New York: Knopf, 1979), 429; Daniel C. Hallin, *The "Uncensored War": The Media and Vietnam* (New York: Oxford University Press, 1986), 147; Samuel Huntington, *American Politics: The Promise of Disharmony* (Cambridge, Mass.: Harvard University Press, 1981), 205; Lyndon B. Johnson, speech to the National Association of Broadcasters, 1 April 1968; Robert E. Kintner, "Televising the Real World," *Harper's*, June 1965, 95; Guenter Lewy, *America in Vietnam* (New York: Oxford University Press, 1978), 433; Timothy P. Meyer, "Some Effects of Real Newsfilm Violence on the Behavior of Viewers," *Journal of Broadcasting* 15 (Summer 1971), 275–85; Richard Nixon, *The Memoirs* (New York: Grosset & Dunlap, 1978), 350; Don Oberdorfer, *Tet!* (Garden City, N.Y.: Doubleday, 1971), 239, 241; Don Oberdorfer, "Tet: The Turning Point," *Washington Post Magazine*, 29 January 1978, 17; Austin Ranney, *Channels of Power: The Impact of Television on American Politics* (New York: Basic, 1983), 4–5, 133–34; James Reston, "The End of the Tunnel," *New York Times*, 30 April 1975, A–41; Edward Shils, "American Society and the War in Indochina," in Anthony Lake, ed., *The Vietnam Legacy: The War, American Society and the Future of American Foreign Policy* (New York: New York University Press, 1976), 49; Jerome H. Skolnick, ed., *The Politics of Protest* (New York: Simon and Schuster, 1969), 42; William Small, *To Kill a Messenger: Television News and the Real World* (New York: Hastings House, 1970), 3; *Television*, Public Broadcasting System, aired on Washington, D.C., station WETA, 15 February 1988; Kathleen J. Turner, *Lyndon Johnson's Dual War: Vietnam and the Press* (Chicago: University of Chicago Press, 1985), 4; "Vietnam Reappraised," *International Security*, vol. 6, no. 1 (Summer 1981), 8, 22. For specific quotations, see Shils, "American Society," 49; Greene, "How Do You Fight," B–5; *Television*, Public Broadcasting System.

2. Ranney, *Channels of Power*, 13–14; United States Senate, Committee on Governmental Operations, *Confidence and Concern: Citizens View American Government* (Washington, D.C.: Government Printing Office, 1973), 79. In the Roper survey, which allowed multiple responses, 58 percent of the respondents said television; 56 percent newspapers, 26 percent radio, and 8 percent magazines. According to the Louis Harris poll commissioned by the United States Senate, 64 percent of respondents said they relied on television as their major news source.

3. Epstein, *News from Nowhere*, 183.

4. *NBC Huntley-Brinkley Report*, 27 October 1967.

5. *NBC Huntley-Brinkley Report*, 11 January 1966.

6. Epstein, *News from Nowhere*, 250.

7. *NBC Huntley-Brinkley Report*, 11 August 1967.

8. *CBS Evening News with Walter Cronkite*, 5 August 1965.

9. Halberstam, *Powers That Be*, 490.

10. *NBC Huntley-Brinkley Report*, 30 January 1968.

11. *CBS Evening News with Walter Cronkite*, 1 February 1968; *NBC Huntley-Brinkley Report*, 1 February 1968; *ABC Evening News*, 1 February 1968.

12. *CBS Evening News with Walter Cronkite*, 2 February 1968; *ABC Evening News*, 1 February 1968.

13. Edward Jay Epstein, *Between Fact and Fiction* (New York: Vintage, 1975), 225.

14. George A. Bailey and Lawrence W. Lichty, "Rough Justice on a Saigon Street: A Gatekeeper Study of NBC's Tet Execution Film," *Journalism Quarterly*, vol. 49, no. 2 (Summer 1972), 222–23.

15. Bailey and Lichty, "Rough Justice," 224.

16. Epstein, *Between Fact*, 221.

17. Bailey and Lichty, "Rough Justice," 227.

18. Bailey and Lichty, "Rough Justice," 229, 238.

19. Oberdorfer, *Tet!* caption with photographs 25 and 26, pages inserted between 248 and 249; Oberdorfer, *Tet!* 170; "Viet Prisoners," Associated Press dispatch, 4 February 1968; "By Book and Bullet," *Time*, 23 February 1968, 32; *Television*, Public Broadcasting System.

20. Oberdorfer, *Tet!* 158.

21. *Report from Vietnam by Walter Cronkite*, 27 February 1968.

22. *Report from Vietnam by Walter Cronkite*, 27 February 1968.

23. *Report from Vietnam by Walter Cronkite*, 27 February 1968.

24. For the Johnson quotation see presidential aide Tom Johnson on *Cronkite Remembered*, CBS, 23 May 1996; Hallin, *Uncensored War*, 170; Ranney, *Channels of Power*, 5; Small, *To Kill*, 123; Turner, *Johnson's Dual War*, 232. On the shift in public opinion see John E. Mueller, *War, Presidents, and Public Opinion* (New York: Wiley, 1973), 201.

25. Hallin, *Uncensored War*, 170;

26. Halberstam, *Powers That Be*, 514; *Television*, Public Broadcasting System.

27. Hallin, *Uncensored War*, 161.

28. *Vietnam: A New Year, A New War*, 10 March 1968.
29. *NBC Huntley-Brinkley Report*, 26 June 1969.
30. *ABC Evening News*, 13 April 1972.
31. *ABC Evening News*, 27 October 1965.
32. *CBS Evening News with Walter Cronkite*, 14 October 1967.
33. *CBS Evening News with Walter Cronkite*, 15 October 1969.
34. Greene, "How Do You Fight," B-5; *Television*, Public Broadcasting System.

Chapter 13

1. Alfred E. Lewis, "5 Held in Plot to Bug Democrats' Office Here," *Washington Post*, 18 June 1972, A-1.
2. *Washington Post*, Bob Woodward and E. J. Bachinski: "White House Consultant Tied to Bugging Figure," 20 June 1972, A-1; "Mission Incredible," 21 June 1972, A-22.
3. Carl Bernstein, "Watergate: Tracking It Down," *Quill*, June 1973, 46; James McCartney, "The Washington 'Post' and Watergate: How Two Davids Slew Goliath," *Columbia Journalism Review*, July/August 1973, 14.
4. Woodward and Bachinski, "White House Consultant Tied to Bugging Figure," A-1.
5. Carl Bernstein and Bob Woodward, "Bug Suspect Got Campaign Funds," *Washington Post*, 1 August 1972, A-1.
6. Carl Bernstein and Bob Woodward, "Spy Funds Linked to GOP Aides," *Washington Post*, 17 September 1972, A-1.
7. Carl Bernstein and Bob Woodward, "FBI Finds Nixon Aides Sabotaged Democrats," *Washington Post*, 10 October 1972, A-1.
8. Carl Bernstein and Bob Woodward, "Key Nixon Aide Named As 'Sabotage' Contact," *Washington Post*, 15 October 1972, A-1.
9. Carl Bernstein and Bob Woodward, "Testimony Ties Top Nixon Aide To Secret Fund," *Washington Post*, 25 October 1972, A-1.
10. Sanford J. Ungar, "Calif. Court Enjoined Nixon's Tactics in '62," *Washington Post*, 27 October 1972, A-1.
11. *Watergate: The Secret Story*, CBS, 17 June 1992.
12. Bernstein, "Watergate: Tracking It Down," 45; Dave Griffiths, "The Watergate Pair: Bernstein & Woodward," *Editor & Publisher*, 28 April 1973, 12; McCartney, "'Post' and Watergate," 14.
13. "'All the President's Men'—And Two of Journalism's Finest," *Senior Scholastic*, 13 January 1976, 14; McCartney, "'Post' and Watergate," 14.
14. Griffiths, "Watergate Pair," 12.
15. John J. Sirica, *To Set the Record Straight* (New York: W. W. Norton, 1979), 54.
16. *Watergate: The Secret Story*, CBS.
17. McCartney, "'Post' and Watergate," *Columbia Journalism Review*, 9.

18. Charles Peters, "Why the Press Didn't Get the Watergate Story," *Washington Monthly*, July/August 1973, 8.
19. "Dynamic Duo," *Newsweek*, 30 October 1972, 77.
20. *CBS Evening News with Walter Cronkite:* 27 October 1972; 3 October 1972.
21. McCartney, "'Post' and Watergate," *Columbia Journalism Review*, 11, 19.
22. McCartney, "'Post' and Watergate," *Columbia Journalism Review*, 18; *Watergate: The Secret Story*, CBS.
23. Carl Bernstein and Bob Woodward, "GOP Hits Post for 'Hearsay,'" *Washington Post*, 17 October 1972, A-1.
24. Carl Bernstein and Bob Woodward, "Magazine Says Nixon Aide Admits Disruption Effort," *Washington Post*, 30 October 1972, A-6.
25. Bernstein and Woodward, "Testimony Ties Top Nixon Aide To Secret Fund," A-1.
26. McCartney, "'Post' and Watergate," *Columbia Journalism Review*, 21; Bernstein and Woodward, "Magazine Says Nixon Aide Admits Disruption Effort," A-1.
27. Walter Rugaber, "House Report Raises Questions on Nixon Campaign Financing; The Watergate Mystery," *New York Times*, 1 November 1972, A-28.
28. *Watergate: The Secret Story*, CBS.
29. "'Woodstein' Meets 'Deep Throat,'" *Time*, 22 April 1974, 56.
30. "An 'Awfully Rough' Game," *Newsweek*, 27 May 1974, 29. The taped conversation took place 15 September 1972.
31. "'Awfully Rough,'" *Newsweek*, 29.
32. "'Awfully Rough,'" *Newsweek*, 29; "'Woodstein,'" *Time*, 56; Robert Parry, "The Rise of the Right-Wing Media Machine," *Extra!* March/April 1995, 6. Haldeman's diary entry was dated 29 May 1971.
33. McCartney, "'Post' and Watergate," *Columbia Journalism Review*, 19.
34. Lou Cannon, "The Confrontation: Nixon Proclaims His Coolness in Hostile Session with Press," *Washington Post*, 27 October 1973, A-1.
35. "Dynamic Duo," *Newsweek*, 76–77; "'Woodstein,'" *Time*, 55–56; McCartney, "'Post' and Watergate," *Columbia Journalism Review*, 8–22; Murray Levin, "Investigative Reporting as a Research Method: An Analysis of Bernstein and Woodward's 'All the President's Men,'" *American Psychologist*, July 1980, 626–38; "'All the President's Men,'" *Senior Scholastic*, 13–14; Allene Talmey, "Who Broke the Watergate Story, and How?" *Vogue*, August 1973, 96–97.
36. "'Woodstein,'" *Time*, 56; Carl Bernstein and Bob Woodward, *All the President's Men* (New York: Simon and Schuster, 1974); Margaret Ronan, "A Rap With . . . ," *Senior Scholastic*, 13 January 1976, 12.
37. William B. Dickinson, *Watergate: Chronology of a Crisis* (Washington, D.C.: Congressional Quarterly, 1973), 6.
38. Katharine Graham, "The Activism of the Press," *Nieman Reports*, Spring/Summer 1974, 22.

Chapter 14

1. Reprinted in James Bowman, "The Leader of the Opposition," *National Review*, 6 September 1993, 44.

2. Clinton's accusation that Limbaugh is a racist came during remarks delivered at the May 1993 White House Correspondents' Dinner. Clinton told the 2,400 guests that Limbaugh had come to the defense of Attorney General Janet Reno after the disastrous climax of the fifty-one-day standoff against cult members in Waco, Texas, only "because she was attacked by a black guy." The reference was to criticism of Reno by Michigan Representative John Conyers, who is African American. Douglas Jehl, "Clinton Calls Show to Assail Press, Falwell and Limbaugh," *New York Times*, 25 June 1994, A-1; William Raspberry, "Rush to Judgment," *Washington Post*, 1 February 1993, A-19; David Remnick, "Day of the Dittohead," *Washington Post*, 20 February 1994, C-4; Peter J. Boyer, "Bull Rush," *Vanity Fair*, May 1992, 159; Howard Rosenberg, "The Devastating Truth About Rush Limbaugh on TV," *Los Angeles Times*, 21 September 1992, F-1; Kurt Anderson, "Big Mouths," *Time*, 1 November 1993, 63; Anthony Lewis, "Where Power Lies," *New York Times*, 18 July 1994, A-15; Remnick, "Day of the Dittohead," *Washington Post*, C-1; Tom Lewis, "Triumph of the Idol—Rush Limbaugh and a Hot Medium," *Media Studies Journal*, vol. 7, no. 3 (Summer 1993), 55–58; Tom McNichol, "Rush Is Always Right," *USA Today Weekend*, 24–26 January 1992, 7.

3. The radio station was KGMO-AM, which later became KAPE-AM.

4. The station was WIXZ-AM.

5. The stations where Limbaugh worked, in addition to WIXZ-AM in McKeesport, were KQV in Pittsburgh and KUDL-AM, KUDL-FM, and KFIX in Kansas City.

6. The station was KMBZ-AM.

7. Rush Limbaugh, *The Way Things Ought To Be* (New York: Pocket Books, 1992), 146.

8. Richard Gehr, "Mouth at Work," *Newsday*, 8 October 1990, Part II, 5; McNichol, "Rush Is Always Right," *USA Today Weekend*, 6.

9. Limbaugh, *The Way Things Ought To Be*, 162; Rush Limbaugh, "The Rush Limbaugh Show" national radio broadcast, 2 February 1994.

10. Steven V. Roberts, "What a RUSH!" *U.S. News & World Report*, 16 August 1993, 35.

11. Richard Carliss, "Conservative Provocateur or Big Blowhard?" *Time*, 26 October 1992, 78.

12. Tom Lewis, "Triumph of the Idol," 51.

13. Limbaugh, *The Way Things Ought To Be*; Rush Limbaugh, *See, I Told You So* (New York: Pocket Books, 1993).

14. Richard Carliss, "A Man, a Legend, a What?" *Time*, 23 September 1991, 65.

15. Howard King and Geoffrey Morris, *Rush to Us* (New York: Windsor, 1994), 280.

16. Dan Kening, "Motormouth," *Chicago Tribune*, 28 August 1990, E-2; Remnick, "Day of the Dittohead," *Washington Post*, C-1.

17. James W. Michaels, "Filling a Need," *Forbes*, 11 April 1994, 61.

18. Joshua Shenk, "Limbaugh's Lies," *The New Republic*, 23 May 1994, 12; Rush Limbaugh, radio broadcasts, 20 July 1995, 30 August 1993; Gehr, "Mouth at Work," *Newsday*, 4.

19. Rush Limbaugh, *Rush Limbaugh: The Television Show* national television broadcast, 19 January 1994, 17 February 1994; Rush Limbaugh, radio broadcast, 1 August 1995; Jeff Gerth, "Clintons Joined S. & L. Operator in an Ozark Real-Estate Venture," *New York Times*, 8 March 1992, A-1.

20. Limbaugh, *The Way Things Ought To Be*, 58, 242–43.

21. Howard Rosenberg, "Truthman Slips Up in His Rush to Judgment," *Los Angeles Times*, 29 June 1994, F-10. Limbaugh's low regard for accuracy has spawned two books: Steven Rendall, Jim Naureckas, and Jeff Cohen, *The Way Things Aren't: Rush Limbaugh's Reign of Error* (New York: New Press, 1995); and Brian Keliher, *Flush Rush* (Berkeley: Ten Speed, 1994).

22. Richard Corliss, "Look Who's Talking," *Time*, 23 January 1995, 22; Robert LaFranco, "Radio Redux," *Forbes*, 11 April 1994, 60.

23. Boyer, "Bull Rush," *Vanity Fair*, 205.

24. Rendall, Naureckas, and Cohen, *The Way Things Aren't*, 42; King and Morris, *Rush to Us*, 223, 227; Roberts, "What a RUSH!" *U.S. News & World Report*, 27–28; Todd Diamond, "Fairness Doctrine Battle Brews over Regulating Airwaves," *Christian Science Monitor*, 12 October 1993, 9.

25. Rendall, Naureckas, and Cohen, *The Way Things Aren't*, 42; King and Morris, *Rush to Us*, 235.

26. Rush Limbaugh, radio broadcast, 10 March 1994; Shenk, "Limbaugh's Lies," *The New Republic*, 12.

27. Bowman, "Leader of the Opposition," *National Review*, 44; Boyer, "Bull Rush," *Vanity Fair*, 205.

28. Reprinted in Bowman, "Leader of the Opposition," 44.

29. "Inside Politics," CNN national broadcast, 24 June 1994; Rush Limbaugh, television broadcast, 7 November 1994.

30. Remnick, "Day of the Dittohead," *Washington Post*, C-4.

31. Howard Kurtz, "Talk Radio Hosts, Waking Up on the Right Side of the Bed," *Washington Post*, 10 November 1994, D-4.

32. Edward Epstein, "The Mouths That Roared," *San Francisco Chronicle*, 25 December 1994, S-1; "The Rush of the Year," *Detroit News*, 30 December 1994, A-10.

33. Katharine Q. Seelye, "Republicans Get a Pep Talk from Rush Limbaugh," *New York Times*, 12 December 1994, A-16.

34. Kevin Merida, "Rush Limbaugh Saluted as a 'Majority Maker,'" *Washington Post*, 11 December 1994, A-30.

35. Seelye, "Republicans Get a Pep Talk," *New York Times*, A-16; Thomas B. Rosenstiel, "It's Rush Night for GOP's Lawmakers-in-Waiting," *Los Angeles Times*, 11 December 1994, A-41; Merida, "'Majority Maker,'" *Washington Post*, A-30.

36. Seelye, "Republicans Get a Pep Talk," *New York Times*, A-16; Rosenstiel, "It's Rush Night," *Los Angeles Times*, A-41.
37. Remnick, "Day of the Dittohead," *Washington Post*, C-4.
38. Corliss, "Look Who's Talking," *Time*, 23.

Chapter 15

1. William F. Woo, "Even in the Bad Old Days of Newspapers, the Readers Believed," *Chicago Tribune*, 29 April 1993, N-29. The 68 percent figure was from a 1972 poll by the Gallup Organization. Arianna Huffington, "The People vs. the Press," *Atlanta Constitution*, 1 October 1995, B-1. The 21 percent figure was from a 1995 *Wall Street Journal*/NBC poll.

Bibliography

This brief listing contains some of the principal writings that may be of interest to readers of this volume, arranged by chapter.

Chapter 1: Sowing the Seeds of Revolution

Bailyn, Bernard, *The Ideological Origins of the American Revolution,* Cambridge, Mass.: Harvard University Press, 1967.
Conway, Moncure D., *The Writings of Thomas Paine,* New York: AMS, 1967.
Davidson, Philip, *Propaganda and the American Revolution,* Chapel Hill: University of North Carolina Press, 1941.
Dickerson, Oliver M., comp., *Boston Under Military Rule, 1768–1769,* Boston: Chapman & Grimes, 1936.
Foner, Eric, *Tom Paine and Revolutionary America,* New York: Oxford University Press, 1976.
Miller, John C., *Sam Adams: Pioneer in Propaganda,* Stanford, Calif.: Stanford University Press, 1936.

Chapter 2: Abolition

Dillon, Merton L., *Elijah P. Lovejoy, Abolitionist Editor,* Urbana: University of Illinois Press, 1961.
Garrison, W. P., and F. J. Garrison, *William Lloyd Garrison: The Story of His Life as Told by His Children,* 4 volumes, New York, 1885–1889.
Merrill, Walter M., *Against Wind and Tide: A Biography of Wm. Lloyd Garrison,* Cambridge, Mass.: Harvard University Press, 1963.
Tripp, Bernell E., *Origins of the Black Press: New York, 1827–1847,* Northport, Ala.: Vision, 1992.

Chapter 3: Slowing the Momentum for Women's Rights

List, Karen K., "The Post-Revolutionary Woman Idealized: Philadelphia Media's 'Republican Mother,'" *Journalism Quarterly* 66 (Spring 1989): 65–75.
Harper, Ida Husted, *The Life and Work of Susan B. Anthony,* Indianapolis, Ind.: Hollenbeck, 1898.

Solomon, Martha M., ed., *A Voice of Their Own: The Woman Suffrage Press, 1840–1910,* Tuscaloosa: University of Alabama Press, 1991.
Stanton, Elizabeth Cady, Susan B. Anthony, and Matilda Joslyn Gage, eds., *History of Woman Suffrage,* New York: Fowler & Wells, 1881.

Chapter 4: Attacking Municipal Corruption

Keller, Morton, *The Art and Politics of Thomas Nast,* New York: Oxford University Press, 1968.
Paine, Albert B., *Thomas Nast: His Period and His Pictures,* Gloucester, Mass.: Peter Smith, 1967.

Chapter 5: Journalism as Warmonger

Milton, Joyce, *The Yellow Kids: Foreign Correspondents in the Heyday of Yellow Journalism,* New York: Harper & Row, 1989.
Swanberg, W. A., *Citizen Hearst: A Biography of William Randolph Hearst,* New York: Charles Scribner's Sons, 1961.
Wisan, Joseph E., *The Cuban Crisis as Reflected in the New York Press (1895–1898),* New York: Columbia University Press, 1934.

Chapter 6: Muckraking

Filler, Louis, *Crusaders for American Liberalism,* Yellow Springs, Ohio: Antioch, 1939.
McGlashan, Zena Beth, "Club 'Ladies' and Working 'Girls': Rheta Childe Dorr and the *New York Evening Post,*" *Journalism History* 8 (1981): 7–13.
Weinberg, Arthur, and Lila Weinberg, *The Muckrakers,* New York: Simon and Schuster, 1961.

Chapter 7: Defying the Ku Klux Klan

Although the topic of how American newspapers defied the Ku Klux Klan during the 1920s has not previously attracted a significant quantity of scholarship, several secondary sources were used to provide background on the Ku Klux Klan and on the newspapers that received Pulitzer Prizes for their crusades against the Ku Klux Klan. Those sources include David M. Chalmers, *Hooded Americanism: The History of the Ku Klux Klan* (Durham, N.C.: Duke University Press, 1987); John Hohenberg, ed., *The Pulitzer Prize Story* (New York: Columbia University Press, 1959); Kenneth T. Jackson, *The Ku Klux Klan in the City: 1915–1930* (New York: Oxford University Press, 1967); and Silas Bent, *Newspaper Crusaders: A Neglected Story* (Freeport, N.Y.: Books for Libraries, 1939).

Chapter 8: Father Coughlin

Brinkley, Alan, *Voices of Protest: Huey Long, Father Coughlin, and the Great Depression,* New York: Knopf, 1982.

Marcus, Sheldon, *Father Coughlin: The Tumultuous Life of the Priest of the Little Flower,* Boston: Little, Brown, 1973.

Strong, Donald S., *Organized Anti-Semitism in America: The Rise of Group Prejudice During the Decade 1930–40,* Washington, D.C.: American Council on Public Affairs, 1941.

Chapter 9: Creating "Rosie the Riveter"

Although the topic of how the American news media helped propel American women into the workforce during World War II has not previously attracted a significant quantity of scholarship, several secondary sources were used to provide background on the more general topic of how the *mass* media contributed to that effort. Those sources include Karen Anderson, *Wartime Women: Sex Roles, Family Relations, and the Status of Women During World War II* (Westport, Conn.: Greenwood, 1981); William H. Chafe, *The American Woman: Her Changing Social, Economic, and Political Roles, 1920–1970* (New York: Oxford University Press, 1972); Maureen Honey, *Creating Rosie the Riveter: Class, Gender, and Propaganda During World War II* (Amherst: University of Massachusetts Press, 1984); Leila J. Rupp, *Mobilizing Women for War: German and American Propaganda, 1939–1945* (Princeton: Princeton University Press, 1978); and Doris Weatherford, *American Women and World War II* (New York: Facts on File, 1990).

Chapter 10: Exposing Joe McCarthy

Barnouw, Erik, *The Image Empire: A History of Broadcasting in the United States from 1953,* New York: Oxford University Press, 1970.

Barnouw, Erik, *Tube of Plenty: The Evolution of American Television,* New York: Oxford University Press, 1975.

Bayley, Edwin R., *Joe McCarthy and the Press,* New York: Pantheon, 1981.

Bergreen, Laurence, *Look Now, Pay Later: The Rise of Network Broadcasting,* Garden City, N.Y.: Doubleday, 1980.

Gordon, George N., *The Communications Revolution: A History of Mass Media in the United States,* New York: Hastings House, 1977.

Halberstam, David, *The Powers That Be,* New York: Knopf, 1979.

Kendrick, Alexander, *Prime Time: The Life of Edward R. Murrow,* Boston: Little, Brown, 1969.

Leab, Daniel J., "'See It Now': A Legend Reassessed," in John E. O'Connor, ed., *American History/American Television: Interpreting the Video Past,* New York: Frederick Ungar, 1983.

Rosteck, Thomas, *See It Now Confronts McCarthyism,* Tuscaloosa: University of Alabama Press, 1994.
Straight, Michael, *Trial by Television,* Boston: Beacon, 1954.

Chapter 11: Pushing the Civil Rights Movement onto the National Agenda

Bagdikian, Ben H., *The Information Machines,* New York: Harper & Row, 1971.
Barnouw, Erik, *The Image Empire: A History of Broadcasting in the United States,* New York: Oxford University Press, 1970.
Epstein, Edward Jay, *News From Nowhere,* New York: Random House, 1973.
Fisher, Paul L., and Ralph L. Lowenstein, eds., *Race and the News Media,* New York: Praeger, 1967.
Garrow, David J., *Protest at Selma,* New Haven, Conn.: Yale University Press, 1978.
Gates, Gary Paul, *Air Time: The Inside Story of CBS News,* New York: Harper & Row, 1978.
Gitlin, Todd, *The Whole World Is Watching,* Berkeley: University of California Press, 1980.
MacNeil, Robert, *The People Machine: The Influence of Television on American Politics,* New York: Harper & Row, 1968.
Muse, Benjamin, *The American Negro Revolution,* Bloomington: Indiana University Press, 1968.
Orfield, Gary, *The Reconstruction of Southern Education,* New York: Wiley-Interscience, 1969.
Small, William, *To Kill a Messenger,* New York: Hastings House, 1970.
Television, Public Broadcasting System, aired on Washington, D.C., station WETA, 15 February 1988.
Watson, Mary Ann, *The Expanding Vista: American Television in the Kennedy Years,* New York: Oxford University Press, 1990.
Wood, William A., *Electronic Journalism,* New York: Columbia University Press, 1967.

Chapter 12: Vietnam War

Braestrup, Peter, *Big Story: How the American Press and Television Reported and Interpreted the Crisis of Tet 1968 in Vietnam and Washington,* Boulder, Colo.: Westview, 1977.
Hallin, Daniel C., *The "Uncensored War": The Media and Vietnam,* New York: Oxford University Press, 1986, 147.
Oberdorfer, Don, *Tet!* Garden City, N.Y.: Doubleday, 1971.

Chapter 13: Watergate Forces the President to His Knees

McCartney, James, "The Washington 'Post' and Watergate: How Two Davids Slew Goliath," *Columbia Journalism Review,* July/August 1973, 8–22.

Chapter 14: Rush Limbaugh

Arkush, Michael, *Rush!* New York: Avon, 1993.
Colford, Paul D., *The Rush Limbaugh Story: Talent on Loan from God: The Unauthorized Biography,* New York: St. Martin's, 1993.
King, Howard, and Geoffrey Morris, *Rush to Us,* New York: Windsor, 1994.
Rendall, Steven, Jim Naureckas, and Jeff Cohen, *The Way Things Aren't: Rush Limbaugh's Reign of Error,* New York: New Press, 1995.

About the Book and Author

IN THIS PATHBREAKING BOOK, Rodger Streitmatter takes the reader on a sightseeing tour of American history as influenced by the public press, visiting fourteen landmark events in U.S. history—including the abolitionist movement, the struggle for women's rights, the civil rights movement, and Watergate. These are events that stir the political imagination; but, as Streitmatter shows, they also demonstrate how American journalism, since the 1760s, has not merely *recorded* this nation's history but has played a role in *shaping* it.

This book is the first of its kind. Streitmatter avoids the mind-numbing lists of names, dates, and newspaper headlines that bog down the standard journalism history textbook. Instead, *Mightier than the Sword* focuses on a limited number of episodes, identifying common characteristics within the news media. In his final chapter, Streitmatter looks at *how* the news media have shaped our understanding of events.

The book's engaging narrative style, manageable length, and affordable price make it particularly attractive for introductory mass media courses as well as courses focusing specifically on the history of American journalism or American politics.

Rodger Streitmatter teaches at the School of Communication at American University in Washington, D.C. He is the author of *Raising Her Voice: African-American Women Journalists Who Changed History* and *Unspeakable: The Rise of the Gay and Lesbian Press in America.*

Index

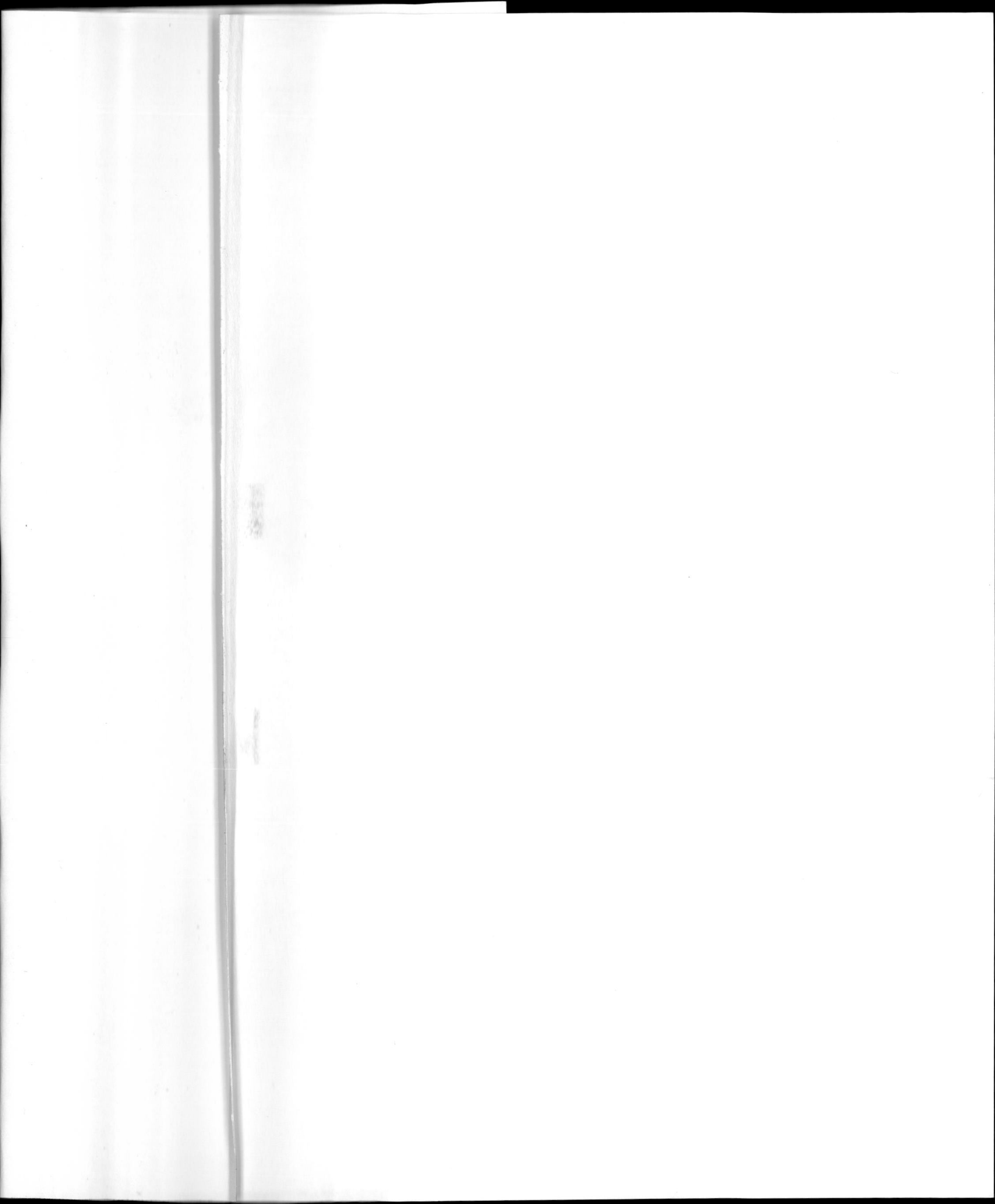